For Singing Teachers

How To

Sing&See

Singing Pedagogy in the Digital Era

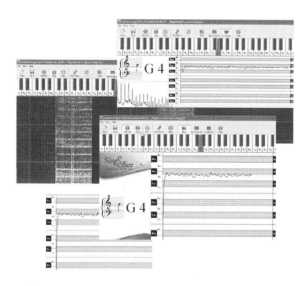

By Jean Callaghan and Pat Wilson

A Cantare Systems Publication

Cantare Systems

Sing&See™ is a trademark of Cantare Systems Pty Ltd.
Windows is a registered trademark of Microsoft Corporation
in the United State and other countries.

First published in 2004 by:

Cantare Systems Pty Ltd
PO Box 496
Surry Hills NSW 2010
Australia

pedagogy@singandsee.com
www.singandsee.com

National Library of Australia CIP data

Callaghan, Jean.
How to sing and see : singing pedagogy in the digital era.

Bibliography.
ISBN 0 646 42925 6.

1. Singing - Instruction and study. 2. Music - Data processing. I. Wilson, Pat, 1943- . II. Title.

783

Cover and Page Design by Media One

CONTENTS

Foreword   vii

Introduction to Sing&See™   1

Musical and Vocal Questions   12

Getting Started with Sing&See™   19

List of Intervals   25

List of Scales and Modes   31

The Exercises

     Single notes   38

     Intervals   40

     Arpeggios   88

     Scales and Modes   126

     Pentachords   145

     Tetrachords   149

Appendices

     1. International Phonetic Alphabet (IPA)   275

     2. International Pitch Labelling   275

Glossary   278

Select Bibliography   282

ACKNOWLEDGEMENTS

During development of the text we were most grateful to Dr Robert Mitchell and Dr Edward McDonald for their informed reading, questions and suggestions.

We also thank Media One for the creative cover and page design; in addition, Carmen Watts' contribution in setting text and graphics has been invaluable.

In addition, thanks are due to all the singing teachers and their students who tested the software and offered ideas and criticisms.

FOREWORD

Singing is a natural, creative, musical act. It is also a set of highly skilled neuromuscular co-ordinations which must work in service of the musical imagination. In the past, when teacher and student together approached the learning of these musical/vocal skills there were few tools available to help them. Traditionally, teachers used modelling and feedback and historically there have always been limits on the ways in which learner singers made sense of their lessons.

In modelling, the teacher demonstrates the desired end-product and hopes that the student can emulate it. In the 21st century, however, we are surrounded by musics from many centuries, and from around the world, covering a vast range of genres and styles; it is unlikely, then, that the teacher can provide an expert model in a sufficient number of them to meet the needs of the students in today's studio.

Teachers can give feedback in a number of ways—visual, aural, kinaesthetic and verbal. Most common is verbal feedback based on the success of the just-completed vocal task, followed by advice on strategies for the student to adopt in order to bring about improvements. Unfortunately, for the student there is a delay between executing the task and receiving the feedback. And there is always the risk of misinterpretation: the student may take the assessment of their success at the task as a judgment of their personal worth, or may have difficulty understanding the advice on strategies offered by the teacher.

When Thorpe, Callaghan and van Doorn turned their attention to the these difficulties in the training of singers, they envisaged computer software which would become the singing teacher's ally and the singing student's friend. A long period of research, practical experimentation and consultation on the needs of singers and singing teachers followed at the University of Sydney with the support of an Australian Research Council grant.

Since some 60% of today's students are predominantly visually oriented in their learning style, we have developed **Sing&See**™ as a computer-assisted visual feedback system that provides accurate acoustic analysis of the voice. The feedback is presented on-screen in real time and in an intuitively accessible form, while being completely objective.

We trust all singing students and teachers will enjoy and benefit from using **Sing&See**™.

Jean Callaghan   **Pat Wilson**

Sydney, Australia,
January, 2004

Introduction to Sing&See™

Welcome

Congratulations on your purchase of Sing&See™, the integrated system designed by musicians, for musicians. In your initial exploration of Sing&See™ on your computer you will have observed that it allows target sounds to be played on the inbuilt keyboard, enabling a singer to match these sounds, to hear the recorded sound played back, and simultaneously see displayed the different acoustic features of the vocal sound. We have written this manual for singing teachers. It gives you detailed information on Sing&See™ and many vocal and musical applications of the software in your teaching studio.

What Sing&See™ Can do for You:

- Sing&See™ is designed to complement your individual teaching style
- Sing&See™ displays acoustic features of the voice in a way that is musically meaningful
- Sing&See™ allows you to tailor programs unique to each student
- Sing&See™ enables you to hear the sound while seeing the acoustic analysis
- Sing&See™ helps you to focus training on the areas of voice which need most attention
- Sing&See™ makes sense to visually-oriented students in a world of computers, television, and film
- Sing&See™ facilitates immediate review of the work just finished

Sing&See™ developed out of a research project at the University of Sydney examining the use of visual feedback in singing training. Since no available software provided the combination of features and flexibility we judged important for singing training, we decided to design our own system. The key requirements were that the system should provide clear feedback, be relevant to singers, and should be very easy to operate. Sing&See™ converts vocal sound into visual displays showing different aspects of the voice (including pitch, timbre and loudness). Sing&See™ offers immediate, varied, appropriate feedback to meet the individual needs of each student.

Singing is a creative, musical act. It is also a psychomotor skill, requiring good hearing (to perceive pitch and timbre), good mental hearing (audiation) in order to be able to conceptualise the vocal sound, and neuromuscular co-ordination to allow what is conceptualised to be produced by the vocal mechanism. Many studies have shown that feedback is an essential part of learning psychomotor skills and, since more than 60 percent of the population are visual learners, visual feedback is particularly effective.

Incorporating Sing&See™ into the structure of your teaching allows students to see their vocal progress. No matter how carefully the teacher phrases verbal feedback, there are times when the student may misunderstand, and times when the feedback will be perceived as negative and judgmental. The on-screen feedback is impartial; vocal changes are reflected in changes in the visual display. This impersonal information gives realistic encouragement and helps present technical work as an engaging challenge.

Because Sing&See™ is designed to complement your individual teaching style, this manual has been written to assist you to use the software with your students in ways which will foster both vocal and musical development. While the complete set of exercises is comprehensive, it is unlikely that you will work through all the exercises with any one student. They are there so that you can choose elements appropriate to the needs of each individual student and combine them to make a unique structured pedagogical program. Sing&See™ provides a variety of feedback displays that you can use to focus on particular aspects of your students' voices. The software can be used as part of your normal lesson, in a special session working on a specific task, or as a practice aid.

In addition to the pedagogical guidelines in the this manual, the built-in Help files on the software provide specific instructions on using the system. Support on technical issues relating to the software is also available through the website www.singandsee.com. We also run workshops to introduce teachers and singers to optimal use of Sing&See™; check the website for workshops near you, or email us at pedagogy@singingandsee.com if you would like to set up a Sing&See™ workshop in your area. We may also be able to answer specific questions relating to the use of the software in pedagogical practice.

To help you make best use of this manual, this introduction should be read first, as it contains important background material relating to:
- ❱ minimum technical requirements for your computer;
- ❱ explanation of the on-screen visual displays;
- ❱ information about how we've laid out the exercises;
- ❱ the musical thinking behind the structure of this pedagogy;
- ❱ vocal questions that need to be considered in the individual application of the software;
- ❱ information on how you can use Sing&See™ with your students; and
- ❱ some preliminary exercises using the screen displays.

Technical Requirements

To use Sing&See™ effectively we recommend that your computer should be a PC with at least a Pentium 3 processor, or equivalent, running at 450 MHz, 128 MB of RAM, Windows 98, 2000, XP, or later, a good quality sound card and a good quality microphone.

Sing&See •

Operating Sing&See™

When you start the Sing&See™ program, it opens to the following display layout, for both Student Version and Professional Version. This layout contains four individual displays, the Piano Keyboard, the Stave, the Pitch Trace, and the Level Meter (see below for descriptions of these displays.)

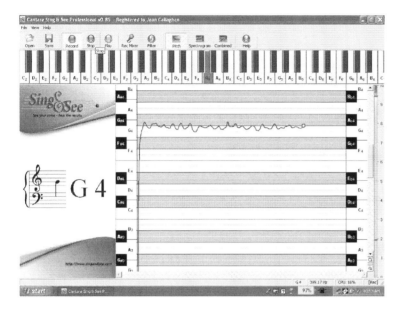

The Professional Version also has two additional display layouts, which can be selected by means of the tool bar across the top of the screen.

1. The Spectrogram layout (below) shows a large spectrogram display, together with the Level Meter and Piano Keyboard display.

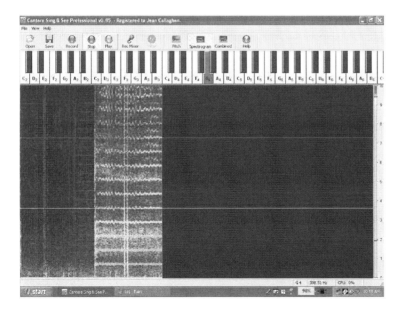

2. The Combination Layout (below) contains both pitch and spectrographic displays for a multi-factor representation of the singing voice.

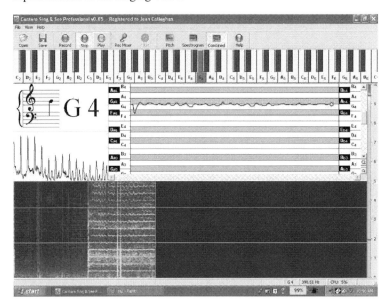

Sing&See™ Controls

Sing&See™ is controlled primarily by means of the menu bar and tool bar commands, as described below. There are also scroll bars for changing the pitch range shown, and keyboard shortcuts can be used for some common commands.

Menu bar

The menu bar contains several menu entries for controlling aspects of the software.
These include the ability to Open and Save sound files, situated under the 'File' menu entry.

Under the 'View' menu are commands to open the Audio Properties control panel and to adjust the spectrogram colours (Professional Version only)

Tool bar

Along the top of the screen underneath the menu bar is a row of buttons called the tool bar. These buttons allow you to quickly control the operation of the Sing&See™ software simply by pressing the buttons with the mouse pointer. A single click with the left mouse button is all that is required to activate them.

The Professional Version has the following tool bar buttons:

The Student Version has the following tool bar buttons:

The buttons are as follows:
- **Open** - Open a sound file (WAV format only) for replay
- **Save** - Save the recorded sound into a WAV file for later replay
- **Record** - Start recording and displaying sound from the microphone
- **Stop** - Stop recording or playback
- **Play** - Start playback of recorded sound or sound loaded from file
- **Rec Level** - Open the Windows Recording Mixer panel to adjust the recording level.
- **Help** - Open Help file

Professional Version only:
- **Filter** - Turn Noise Reduction on or off
- **Pitch** - Switch to the Pitch Display Layout
- **Spectrogram** - Switch to the Spectrogram Display Layout
- **Combined** - Switch to the Combined Pitch and Spectrogram Display Layout

Scrolling

The Scroll Bar and Zoom buttons on the right-hand side of the Pitch Trace display allow you to change the range of pitch displayed.

Scroll: ▲ ▼ Click on the scroll bar with the mouse pointer and slide it up or down, or click on the arrows at each end. This will change the range of pitch displayed, but will not alter the number of notes shown in the display.

Zoom: 🔍 🔍 Click on the magnifying icons—the large one to zoom in (enlarge), and the small one to zoom out (reduce). An enlarged display will show fewer notes, while a reduced display will show more notes.

You can also click on the separator bar ▌ on the right-hand margin of the display, and hold the (left) mouse button down. By moving the pointer up or down, you then have a continuous adjustment in the range of notes displayed, ranging from a single note to the entire range.

Keyboard Shortcuts

Several of the commands in Sing&See™ are linked to specific keys on the computer keyboard, so that they can be easily activated by simply pressing on the key rather than by having to move the mouse pointer around on the screen:

▶ The space bar starts or stops PLAY.

▶ The Enter key starts or stops RECORD.

▶ The piano can be 'played' on the computer keyboard, in the range from C_3 to E_5. In the first octave, the keys along the bottom row of the keyboard (Z,X,...M) control the white notes from C_3 to E_4, and in the second octave the top line of letters (Q,W,...P) control the white notes from C_4 to G_5. The black notes are controlled by the appropriate keys in the second (A,S,...J) and fourth rows (1,2,...0) of the keyboard. The diagram below shows how it works:

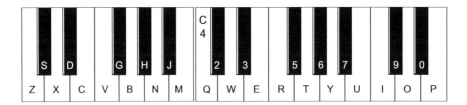

Screen Displays

Sing&See™ has a variety of displays which show aspects of the singing voice. The displays are presented in different groupings, depending on the configuration of the software. For instance, the Student Version has only the pitch-related displays, while the Professional Version has a wider range of display options including spectrographic analysis.

Pitch displays show the pitch of your voice as you sing. In pitch display mode, the following displays are available:

▶ Pitch trace
▶ Piano keyboard
▶ Musical stave

Spectrum displays show the pattern of harmonics in the voice. These can be displayed in a two-dimensional picture called a spectrogram or as a single line showing the spectrum at one instant.

The level meter display shows the loudness of the voice.

The Professional Version of Sing & See™ contains all the displays. The simplified Student Version contains Pitch Displays only.

Pitch Trace Display

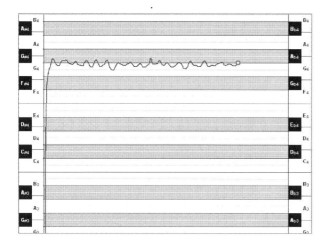

The **Pitch Trace** display shows your pitch as a continuous blue line on a graduated scale.

The vertical direction indicates pitch, whereas time goes from left to right. The red dot shows the latest pitch detected, and the blue line trailing behind it indicates the changes in pitch over the last few seconds.

As you sing, the red dot indicates the pitch of what you are singing as soon as you sing it. During replay mode, the red dot indicates the pitch of the sound as it is being played.

The dark and white bands represent the black and white keys on the piano. These are labelled on the left and right of the display for easy reference, with flats indicated on the left and sharps on the right.

The range of pitch that is shown at any one time can be changed by scrolling and zooming with the bar along the right side of the display.

To move the range up or down, point the mouse pointer to the scroll bar on the right, click and hold down the left button, and drag the mouse pointer up or down.

Piano Keyboard Display

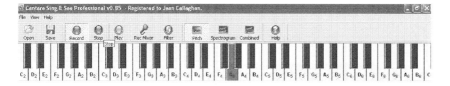

In the **Piano Keyboard** display, the sung pitch is shown highlighted in red on the piano keyboard. The keyboard can also be played, to provide target pitches to sing.

The piano keyboard allows you to play a note by clicking on it with the left mouse button. When you sing any note, the corresponding piano key lights up in red.

You can also 'play' the piano by pointing to and clicking on any of the keys with the (left) mouse button. Keyboard shortcuts are also available for most notes.

Stave Display

The **Stave** display shows the note that is currently detected, and also displays the name of the note.

Level Meter Display

In the **Level Meter** display, the loudness of the sound is shown by the height of the green bar. The level meter can be used in teaching such skills as *messa di voce* and maintaining consistent volume throughout register changes.

The level meter shows how loud you are singing. The higher the green bar, the more total energy is in the sound.

The pitch algorithm which captures and displays vocal sound works best when the volume level is between 2 and 9.5 (red lines are marked on the level meter at these points).

If the background noise (when you are not singing) is much greater than 2 on the meter, the pitch algorithm may have difficulty. If this excess noise is not due to something outside your computer, it could be coming from a low quality sound-card device or microphone. See p. 9 for instructions on setting the noise reduction function.

The scale is marked off in 10 steps. Each step is 6 dB, which is a doubling of the sound pressure amplitude.

The actual loudness of the voice will depend on your microphone, how far it is from your mouth, and how much amplification is given by your audio recording device. See your computer set-up instructions for details of altering the sound control panel and recording mixer on your computer.

Spectrogram Display
(Professional version only)

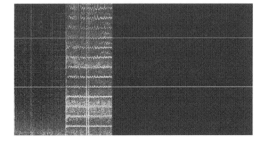

The **Spectrogram** display shows the power within the range of frequencies in the vocal sound, from low frequencies at the bottom to high frequencies at the top. As the sung sound commences the image scrolls from left to right, so that the timbre of the voice and the time elapsed are graphically displayed.

The intensity of the vocal sound is shown by the intensity of shading in the spectrogram. The brightness of each harmonic represents its strength. The yellow vertical line indicates the time. When it reaches the right-hand end of the display, it scrolls right around to the left edge and starts moving across the display again. The frequency range of the display is from 0 (at the bottom) to 5 kHz (5000 cycles per second) at the top. The horizontal lines drawn on the display show 2 kHz and 4 kHz. You can change the colours of the display by means of the options in the View Menu.

Two thin yellow horizontal lines divide the spectrogram display. The lower third of the spectrogram (below approx. 2,000 Hz) should display the singer's fundamental frequency (F_0) and first and second formants (F_1 and F_2), the frequencies that distinguish one vowel from the other. The presence of the third formant (F_3) and above signals a desirable brightness of resonance and carrying power (the singer's formant). This should appear in the upper two-thirds of the spectrogram (at around 3,000 Hz), above the lower of the two yellow horizontal lines. The exact frequency of the singer's formant will depend on voice type.

Real-time Spectrum Display
(Professional version only)

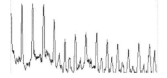

This display shows the **Spectrum** of the sound as it is sung. The spectrum is a single slice of the spectrogram showing the energy in the vocal sound at different frequencies. In this display, the frequencies are arranged horizontally. The frequency axis extends from 0 on the left to 5 kHz on the right. Vertical lines indicate 2 kHz and 4 kHz. The higher the peak, the more energy at that particular frequency. Some smoothing has been incorporated so that when a sound suddenly stops, the displayed spectrum takes about a second to decay.

Noise Reduction

There is a noise reduction feature in the Professional Version of Sing & See™. This provides a smoothed spectral subtraction algorithm, which can reduce the effects of steady-state low-frequency noise such as from air conditioning or computer noise. The accuracy of displays may be adversely affected, so this feature should be used with care.

Activating Noise Reduction
Click on the 'Filter' button in the toolbar.

Wait for the noise filter to reset itself. During this time it is important to be silent so that the filter records only the background noise that you wish to remove.

How This Manual is Designed

This manual not only gives instruction on using the software, but also offers a graded vocal and musical developmental program. It begins with the most basic singing task and builds from there, combining vocal and musical elements with feedback from the visual displays. For a structured program of vocal and musical development, you can follow the sequence of the manual. Alternatively, you can choose particular exercises to meet the needs of individual students. To further the work done in lessons, you can construct individual practice regimes for your students to do using the Student Version of Sing&See™ at home. You can choose elements appropriate to the needs of each individual student and combine them to make a unique graded pedagogical program.

The manual gives a series of exercises which combine a vocal task with a musical task. With a beginner, you might choose to follow the whole program in sequence; more advanced students can be directed to specific exercises that meet their needs at particular stages of their development. We begin with a focus on accurate pitch, then add musical articulation (legato and staccato), timbre and dynamics. The first exercise is the basic (though not necessarily easy!) task of singing a single sustained note. We then move on to singing a *messa di voce* on that note with consistent resonance andvibrato. Thus each task is stripped down to its basic elements, with succeeding exercises building on that by adding elements. This pattern is followed for singing intervals and arpeggios, singing pentachords and tetrachords, and then combining these elements into many different scales to answer the demands of different musical genres and styles.

The page layout for each exercise follows a similar format:

▶ **Exercise #**
In this first box, the exercise is notated on the stave, a suggested vowel written in phonetic script (see Appendix 1 for the International Phonetic Alphabet), and the exercise briefly labelled in words.

▶ **Screen Shot**
The screen shot to the right of the description of the exercise gives a view of the exercise as displayed on the Pitch Grid.

▶ **Aim:**
The focus of the exercise – both immediate and longer term – is spelled out.

▶ **Objectives:**
The overall objective which the exercise is designed to address is explained.

▶ **Physical involvement:**
The body demands of the vocal tasks are specified: this is a list of what needs to be done and in what order.

▶ **Instructions**
In this box the sequence of actions required to achieve the aim is listed.

▶ **Screen display**
Here the aim of the exercise is related to what visual feedback to expect from the various displays on screen and how to interpret this.

Assessment Pages and Lists of Intervals and Exercises

To help you keep track of the progress of individual students you can download assessment pages and the lists of intervals and exercises from our website: www.singandsee.com. On each assessment page you will find:

❱ The Name of the Exercise

❱ Assigned
A box where you can note the name of the student to whom the exercise was assigned, when, and for how long it was worked on. It can provide a record of progress towards a goal.

❱ Evaluation
The two evaluation panels allow you to assess the success of this attempt against the stated aim and objectives. You can also pinpoint particular difficulties for students to focus on in their own practice sessions. Using this in conjunction with the **For next time** box sets planned outcomes and engages the student in the learning process.

❱ For next time:
Under this heading is a list of suggestions for extending the exercise.

Musical and Vocal Questions

Musical Rationale for the Exercises

Musical and Vocal Skills

The teaching of technique for any musical instrument aims to provide the student with control of the instrument in order to meet musical demands. In singing, the fact that the performer is the instrument means that control over the basic musical requirements of pitch, loudness, duration, and timbre rests on a complex of neuromuscular skills. Musical skills come from audiation, allied with control of the vocal instrument. The on-screen feedback is designed to help in the development of those skills, while the exercises are designed to employ them in a range of musical tasks. Beginning with one note, proceeding to intervals, then to pentachords, tetrachords, scales and modes, the exercises are designed to build integrated musical/vocal skills.

Acoustics of the Vocal Sound

For singers, the acoustic characteristics of the voice are the raw material of music, and different musics may attach different values to the same acoustic phenomena: what is great vocal sound for Country may not be great vocal sound for opera; what is great vocal sound for Monteverdi opera may not be great vocal sound for Verdi opera. Sing&See™ is intended for use in a wide range of musics: classical, pop, rock, Broadway, Country, and the ethnic styles of many different regions, and the many stylistic differences within those musics. For this reason, while we have identified the body demands of the vocal task (what needs to be done and in what order), we have not been prescriptive about the specifics of those bodily skills. For example, the direction might be 'position the larynx'; we do not say at what height or in what plane, since this will vary according to the kind of vocal sound appropriate to a particular genre and style. Similarly, with breath management we have identified muscle groups that need to be activated, but have not stipulated exactly how; we have drawn attention to how the feedback can be used to develop vibrato, but have not talked about when it should be used, or what the rate and extent should be. These considerations of the appropriate vocal sound for the genre and style are within the expert judgment of the teacher.

Signs and Abbreviations

In the lists of exercises we have used the following signs and abbreviations.

⇨	sustained on one note
⇧	rising
⇩	falling
M3	major third
P5	perfect fifth
P4	perfect fourth
m3	minor third
M6	major sixth
M7	major seventh
8ve	octave
S	semitone
T	tone
T+	augmented 2nd

1	tonic (I)
3	mediant (III)
5	dominant (V)
8	upper tonic (I)

Thus a spread triad is notated as 1-3-5.

Order of the Exercises

Intervals and Triads

We begin with thirds and fifths—the most common intervals in Western tonal music—and use these as the building blocks of common melodic patterns of spread triads and arpeggios. We then go back to fill in the intervals of the major scale. Other intervals are addressed in pentachords and tetrachords.

Scales and Modes

Scales and modes are ways of organising pitch, usually within the octave. In Western music, most scales and modes consist of a sequence of semitones and/or tones. It is these intervals and their order that define the type of scale or mode. Many of the scales used in Western music are largely modifications of major or minor scales, the music using that kind of pitch organisation being essentially tonal. Familiar non-tonal scales are the pentatonic scale and the whole-tone scale.

The modes now in common use are those built on the white keys of the keyboard. They are:

Beginning on C—Ionian (the same as a major scale)

Beginning on D—Dorian

Beginning on E—Phrygian

Beginning on F—Lydian

Beginning on G—Mixolydian

Beginning on A—Aeolian (the same as a natural minor scale)

Beginning on B—Locrian

However, in contemporary usage, a mode can begin on any note, with the relationship of tones and semitones defining the particular mode.

Scales are often analysed as two tetrachords (four pitches) separated by a tone. Or they may be regarded as one pentachord (five pitches) plus one tetrachord. We have adopted the latter approach, since it is a consistent way of learning a range of scales and modes, and is a good basis for singing in a very wide range of genres and styles. We begin with the chromatic scale, an exercise in the accurate singing of semitones, then move to the whole-tone scale, an exercise in the accurate singing of tones. Then follows a range of exercises on pentachords and tetrachords from which scales and modes are built.

Blues/Jazz Scales

In the blues and jazz, African melody is superimposed on European harmony. This has given rise to scales in which the 3rd, 5th and 7th degrees may be raised or lowered. Different forms of 3rd, 5th and 7th are alternatives which may exist in the same piece, so while we have notated scales using one or other form of 3rd, 5th or 7th, the singer needs the flexibility to move between them. We have notated a number of scales in terms of semitones, tones and augmented seconds, but the extent of 'bending' of blue notes by accomplished singers varies considerably, with a subtlety that defies conventional notation.

Voice Classification

Unlike some packages, Sing&See™ can be used for all voice types (male and female; adult and child). However, best use relies on first defining the voice classification, in order to establish the singer's usable range, where the register transitions occur, and the appropriate tessitura for the exercises.

Range and Starting Notes

Teachers will probably want to decide for themselves what are the best starting notes for the exercises in *How to Sing and See* and also what range is appropriate for individual students. Obviously the starting note of an exercise will depend on the range covered by the exercise, whether it is intended to be in one register only or to cover a register transition, whether it is intended to be in an easy middle range or to expand limits of range, and so on. The following tables may help.

Child and Adolescent Voice

Voice Type	Approximate Range*	Major Register Transition Point*	Comfortable Tessitura*
MALE			
Unchanged (treble)	Bb_3-F_5	C_4 (middle C)	D_4-D_5
Changing:			
Level I (beginning approx. 12-13 years of age)	A_3-F_5	C_4	$C\#_4$-$A\#_4$
Level II (beginning approx. 13 years of age)	G_3-D_5	C_4-E_4	B_3-G_4
Level III (beginning approx. 13-14 years of age)	F_3-A_5 (including falsetto)	F_4-C_5	$G\#_3$-D_4
Level IV (beginning approx. 14 years of age)	D_3-$F\#_5$ (including falsetto)	E_4-G_4	$F\#_3$-C_4
FEMALE			
Level 1 Unchanged (treble)	Bb_3-F_5	C_4	D_4-D_5
Changing:			
Level IIA (beginning approx. 11-12 years of age)	A_3-G_5	G_4-B_4; D_5-$F\#_5$	D_4-D_5
Level IIB (beginning approx. 13-14 years of age)	A_3-F_5	G_4-B_4; D_5-$F\#_5$	B_3-C_5
Level III (beginning approx. 14-15 years of age)	A_3-A_5	D_5-$F\#_5$	A_3-G_5

* See Appendix 2 for an explanation of pitch labelling.

Adult Voice

Voice Type	Approximate Range*	Major Register Transition Point*	Comfortable Tessitura*
MALE			
Bass/bass-baritone	Eb_2-G_4	Ab_3-A_3	A_2-C_4
Baritone	G_2-A_4	Ab_3-B_3	D_3-E_4
Tenor	A_2-C_5	C_4-F_4	F_3-G_4
Countertenor	G_3-A_5	D_4-F_4	C_4-E_5
FEMALE			
Contralto	E_3-G_5	G_4-Ab_4	C_4-E_5
Mezzo Soprano	G_3-B_5	Eb_4-F_4	D_4-F_5
Soprano	B_3-E_6	Eb_4	F_4-G_5

* See Appendix 2 for an explanation of pitch labelling.

Sing&See

Vowels and Vocal Registers

In order to interpret the spectrogram display and help the student to make modifications in response to this feedback, the teacher needs to know how vowels are produced and the ways in which physical manoeuvres affect the acoustic output.

The acoustic energy in voiced sounds such as vowels is generated by vibration of the vocal folds. The **frequency** at which the folds vibrate determines the pitch of the resulting sound, and the **manner** in which the folds vibrate largely determines the acoustic power that is produced and the frequencies across which that power is distributed. The acoustic energy is then modified by passage through the vocal tract so that the character of the final output sound is affected by a combination of laryngeal and vocal tract effects.

Vocal resonance and word articulation are interdependent in singing, both depending on movements of the articulators (pharynx, jaw, soft palate, tongue, lips). Vowel production for speech involves the shape of the lips, the opening between the jaws, the position of the soft palate, and the shape of the tongue. Linguistic classification of vowels, however, has usually been done by reference only to the position of the main body of the tongue in the oral cavity: high-low and front-back (see, for example, Denes & Pinson, 1993). This results in the classic vowel chart, which relates vowels to the configuration of the tongue position and jaw opening. In this chart, /i/ is at the high front corner, /u/ at the high back corner, and /ɑ/ at the low back corner. Other vowels, such as the neutral /ə/ vowel, are classified as central. [See Appendix 1 for the International Phonetic Alphabet.] Vowels may also be classified as 'closed' (the tongue near the palate) or 'open' (the tongue low, at the bottom of the mouth). In moving from speaking to singing, vowels are modified to produce a wider dynamic range, to maintain a balance in loudness across phonemes, and in order to produce particular vocal timbres.

Vocal register change is regulated mainly by the ratio of vocalis and cricothyroid activities in the larynx. If the ratio is changed abruptly, the register change is also abrupt and a sudden change in timbre can be clearly heard; in some circumstances, in some musics, this may be desirable. However, if a less perceptible register change is required, then the ratio (and therefore the timbre) needs to be changed gradually over some significant range. To achieve this consistent timbre through the register change, vowel modification is linked to changes in laryngeal adjustment and subglottic pressure .

Systematic vowel modification requires a knowledge of the phonetic categorisation of vowels on the front-back/open-closed dimensions. Modification to an adjacent vowel (from back vowels to more central, from closed vowels to more open) is employed at the *passaggio* as the pitch rises. [See Miller's 'Systematic Vowel Modification Chart', 1986, p. 157.]

Vocal Efficiency and Vocal Health

In singing, as in other fields, elegant solutions are economical solutions. The exercises are structured with a view to addressing a range of basic co-ordinations as simply as possible. We are relying on teachers to ensure that their students show due respect for economy of effort and the efficient functioning of the mechanism. The singer needs the maximum return for the minimum investment.

Allied to concerns of efficiency are those of vocal health and vocal longevity. No doubt you have advised your students of the need for hydration, of the adverse effects on the voice of many prescription and non-prescription drugs, smoking and alcohol, of the need for general physical health and fitness; and of the importance of using the speaking voice well. Since the body is the vocal instrument, good body alignment is crucial, and may need particular attention when a student is using a microphone and looking at a computer screen. It is equally important to make safe voice use an integral part of vocal technique, training the singer's 'ear' and 'feel' to be able to discriminate what is safe from what is dangerous. We expect that teachers will, as a matter of course, ensure that their students achieve the appropriate on-screen results in a safe, efficient way.

Getting Started with Sing&See™

Sing&See™ and Your Students

You can use the software and the manual to set goals for your students, co-ordinating lessons with practice. It is important to discuss with students how to structure their home practice. Psychomotor skills are best learnt through many short practice sessions with specific goals. You can use assessment pages to keep a record of the exercises set for each student, what they have achieved on those exercises and what still needs work. Using the **Evaluation** boxes in conjunction with the **For next time** and **Practised** boxes provides a structured learning plan in which the student is actively involved.

To further the work done in lessons, you can structure individual practice regimes for your students to do using the Student Edition of Sing&See™ at home.

What Sing&See™ Can do for Your Students:

▶ Sing&See gives immediate feedback on pitch accuracy
▶ Sing&See helps students maintain an even tone when changing pitch
▶ Sing&See gives information on the accuracy of sung intervals, whether in exercises or songs
▶ Sing&See gives a visual image of the specifics of vocal timbre, assisting you to teach appropriate tonal qualities
▶ Sing&See enables student to cultivate the singer's formant ('ring', 'ping', 'resonance' or 'carrying power') on every vowel and at every pitch
▶ Sing&See facilitates work on vibrato
▶ Sing&See facilitates glissandi throughout the range
▶ Sing&See assists students to produce a consistent legato tone
▶ Sing&See enables trill practice with great accuracy
▶ Sing&See reinforces musicianship with music stave and piano keyboard reminders which instantly display the sung pitch
▶ Sing&See encourages students to play with their voice while learning from the resultant visual displays
▶ Sing&See complements your verbal feedback helping to clarify explanations of voice features
▶ Sing&See is a visual style of learning which better suits many students than oral and aural feed back

Some Preliminary Exercises Using the Screen Displays

Before embarking on the very specific exercises that follow, you might find it helpful to try some of these preliminary exercises with your students.

Pitch

▶ If your student has trouble identifying pitch
When the student hears the note on which the vocal exercise starts, sings the wrong one, then turns to you and says, 'How was that? Did I get it?', you know that their pitch perception is under-developed.

Set the **Pitch Grid** to show roughly an octave, with the targeted note (well within the student's comfortable vocal range) in the middle of the display of notes. Play the targeted note on the inbuilt keyboard and direct your student's attention to how that target note is coloured red. Now ask the student to sing, commencing below that pitch and sliding up to and past that pitch, watching for the target note to show red. This should avoid the vocal tensions that sometimes result from a student trying really hard to hit a single note with accuracy. If the student can slide the tone up to the targeted pitch, and stop when they get there, then they are already setting up a biofeedback programme for that particular pitch within their body.

Once the student can confidently achieve the target pitch through sliding up to it, they can practice singing it directly, using the inbuilt keyboard to hear the target note and using the feedback to help build the aural and bodily knowledge of the pitch.

▶ If your student can hear pitch but is slow to match it

These are the students who hear the note on your piano, sing their response to it, and immediately wince. They know they are wrong, but have difficulty in modifying their laryngeal equipment quickly and accurately.

Use the scrolling symbol on the side of the **Pitch Grid** to make the note areas fewer and larger. Ask your student to sing a tonic-mediant-tonic pattern (which in this manual we abbreviate to 1-3-1) on one breath, using a vowel (perhaps /u/ or /ɑ/) into the microphone at a pitch that is easily within their voice range. Direct their attention to the pattern the blue line makes as they pass from one pitch to the other. Get them to check for themselves whether they hit the centre of each pitch – when the pitch field is sufficiently enlarged, it displays a thin yellow line at the centre of each note. Once they can successfully, even if slowly, attain the centres of both notes in a 1-3-1 pattern, ask them to try a 1-3-1-3-1 on the same notes, still on one breath, and see if they can maintain the same degree of accuracy. This will test their breath stamina as well as their focus and neuromuscular development.

Carrying Power

▶ If your student sings accurately and clearly, but lacks resonance

Direct your student's attention to the **Spectrogram** section of the display. (You may choose the display colours which work best for you by clicking the pull-down menu 'View', then selecting 'Spectrogram Colours'.)

The horizontal axis of the Spectrogram shows the time elapsed. The left-hand side (vertical axis) of the Spectrogram shows the frequency of the sound waves that the voice produces. This frequency is measured in Hertz (Hz), which is the number of cycles per second of the sound. The spectrogram display is divided into three sections by two thin, horizontal yellow lines. These are approximate indicators of the formants (resonance regions) in the voice.

As a rule of thumb, the line that appears lowest on the Spectrogram when it displays sung sound will be the fundamental frequency of the note, i.e. what we recognise as the pitch of the note. Lines above this but below the first yellow horizontal dividing line will be first and second formants—the resonance regions devoted to the production of vowel sounds. If you ask your student to sing a continuous /i/-/e/-/ɑ/-/o/-/u/ while watching that region of the spectrogram, you will notice the different patterns formed by the vowel changes. [See Miller, 1996a and 1996b.]

When the voice starts to show activity above the lower of the two yellow dividing lines (approx. 3,000 Hz +), this indicates the presence of third and fourth formants in the sung tone. This region of resonance, often dubbed 'the Singer's Formant', enhances the timbre of the sung sound and enables it to 'carry' better. Activity above the higher of the two horizontal dividing lines indicates rarer fifth formant qualities in the voice.

Ask the student to sing the /i/-/e/-/ɑ/-/o/-/u/ sequence maintaining the Singer's Formant across all vowels.

Legato

▶ **If your student has difficulty in producing a clean and continuous legato tone:**
Set the **Pitch Grid** to show a little over an octave's worth of notes, in a range that best suits the student. Invite the student to sing a smooth, unhurried sliding tone (portamento) on one breath and with a single vowel from the lowest note of the octave you have selected to the highest note. This will, if done correctly, produce a bright blue diagonal line going from the bottom left-hand side of the screen to the top right-hand side of the screen. It is clear to the student when there are drop-outs in the smoothly continuous line. Barring pathologies, faulty breath management and register discontinuities are the usual culprits here.

Breath Management

▶ **If your student's singing tone is breathy, poorly or erratically supported, and lacks tonal clarity:**
Ask your student to sing a short exercise on a vowel—perhaps a traditional 1-3-5-3-1 on /i/ or /ɑ/, into the microphone and observe the **Pitch Trace**.

Encourage them to watch the smoothness with which the blue wiggly line moves from pitch to pitch, and ask them to try and stop the line from dropping out because of faulty breath support. Students need little coaching on this; the difference between supported and unsupported tone are clearly evident; their improved tone is instantly rewarded with smoothly-drawn pitch transitions instead of ragged lines.

▶ **If your student is plagued by clumsy pitch changing, evidencing dynamic changes and breath mismanagement:**
Direct your student's attention to the **Level Meter** directly to the right of the Pitch Grid. Louder singing makes the gauge rise, and softer singing causes it to fall. The red lines appearing at levels 2 and 9-1/2 indicate the outer limits of effectiveness for this meter. Now invite your student to sing a pattern of notes on a single vowel and with one breath. Adjust the Pitch Display so that you will be able to view all the notes in the exercise pattern chosen. Next, instruct the student that during the whole exercise you would like them to keep the green Level Meter at approximately the same level—say, between 3 and 4. This challenge will focus the student's attention on the smoothness with which they transition from one pitch to another, and encourage them to work economically with breath through these changes.

Onset

▶ If your student has a weak, breathy onset:

Direct your student's attention to the **Spectrogram**, and then ask them to start singing whatever exercise or repertoire is currently being worked on, vowels only or sung words. Watch the commencement of the Spectrogram display when the student starts to sing. If the onset is breathy, the pattern of lines at all levels will be staggered, with the usual response being frequencies in the lowest third of the Spectrogram (fundamental frequency, and first and second formants) being in a straight line, and frequencies above them coming in afterwards, forming a jagged, diagonal commencement line. A 'flow phonation' onset with free and simultaneous breath and voice will display as a vertically-aligned straight line.

▶ If your student has a hard, glottal (pressed) onset:

Direct your student's attention to the **Spectrogram**, and then ask them to start singing whatever exercise or repertoire is currently being worked on, vowels only or sung words. Watch the commencement of the Spectrogram display when the student starts to sing. If the onset is pressed, the pattern of lines at all levels will be compressed, with the usual response being frequencies in a straight line spread throughout the spectrum. A 'flow phonation' onset with free and simultaneous breath and voice will display as a vertically-aligned straight line.

Flexibility

▶ If your student has difficulty executing trills:

Use the scrolling symbol to the right of the **Pitch Grid** to show fewer notes with larger areas. Preferably start with a simple two-note trill, and ensure that the display is sufficiently large to show the yellow line at the centre of each note field. Invite your student to begin by singing the two separate notes slowly and alternately as if they were a legato exercise, ensuring that each time they hit the yellow line in the centre of the note field. When you judge that the singing is able to be shifted into trill mode, ask the student to slowly accelerate the rate at which they alternate the notes. In a good trill the moving blue pitch line will undulate evenly between the two notes and reach the yellow centre line of each note.

Vibrato

▶ If your student has difficulty controlling vibrato

Use the scrolling symbol to the right of the Pitch Grid to show fewer notes with larger areas. Have the student sing a single, sustained note, moving the blue line evenly both above and below the yellow central pitch line. The regularity and width of the vibrato also shows on the Spectrogram as a continuous wavy line in all the harmonics of the spectrum.

Split Screen

During lessons, teachers may find the split screen option a useful application, especially when the work being undertaken involves the teacher modelling a preferred vocal quality. the teacher can press the Record button, sing the note or phrase onto either the pitch grid or the spectrogram, and then press the Stop button. What the teacher has sung will be displayed on the screen. Now, if the teacher reduces the size of the Sing&See™ screen (so that it only occupies the upper half of the whole screen) by click-and-dragging- its bottom right-hand corner there will be sufficient space to start up another Sing&See™ screen (either from the Start menu or from the desktop icon). When this arrives on the screen, re-size this new one so it takes up the lower half of the whole screen. Ask the student to sing the note or phrase that the teacher sang, record it, and stop it when completed. The two performance displays will sit side-by-side on the one screen, providing invaluable visual comparisons which will aid the student's perception of their vocal progress.

LIST OF INTERVALS

No.	Exercise	QuickReference	Page
I-1	Single sustained note	⇨ 1	38
I-2	*Messa di voce* on a single sustained note	⇧ 2	39
I-3	Ascending major third	⇧ M3	40
I-4	Ascending major third, legato	⇧ M3	41
I-5	Ascending perfect fifth	⇧ P5	42
I-6	Ascending perfect fifth, portamento, with consistent resonance and volume	⇧ P5	43
I-7	Ascending perfect fifth, legato	⇧ P5	44
I-8	Ascending minor third	⇧ m3	45
I-9	Ascending minor third, legato	⇧ m3	46
I-10	Descending major third	⇩ M3	47
I-11	Descending major third, legato	⇩ M3	48
I-12	Descending perfect fifth	⇩ P5	49
I-13	Descending perfect fifth, portamento, with consistent resonance and volume	⇩ P5	50
I-14	Descending perfect fifth, legato	⇩ P5	51
I-15	Descending minor third	⇩ m3	52
I-16	Descending minor third, legato	⇩ m3	53
I-17	Ascending and descending major third	⇗⇘ M3	54
I-18	Ascending and descending major third, legato	⇗⇘ M3	55
I-19	Ascending and descending perfect fifth	⇗⇘ P5	56
I-20	Ascending and descending perfect fifth, portamento, with consistent resonance and volume	⇗⇘ P5	57
I-21	Ascending and descending perfect fifth, legato	⇗⇘ P5	58
I-22	Ascending and descending minor third	⇗⇘ m3	59
I-23	Ascending and descending minor third, legato	⇗⇘ m3	60
I-24	Ascending major triad (I-III-V)	⇧ 1M35	61
I-25	Ascending major triad (I-III-V), portamento, with consistent resonance and volume	⇧ 1M35	62
I-26	Ascending major triad (I-III-V), legato	⇧ 1M35	63
I-27	Descending major triad (V-III-I)	⇩ 5M31	64
I-28	Descending major triad (V-III-I), portamento, with consistent resonance and volume	⇩ 5M31	65
I-29	Descending major triad (V-III-I), legato	⇩ 5M31	66
I-30	Ascending and descending major triad	⇗⇘ 1M3531M	67
I-31	Ascending and descending major triad, portamento, with consistent resonance and volume	⇗⇘ 1M3531M	68

No.	Exercise	QuickReference	Page
I- 32	Ascending and descending major triad, legato	⬀⬂ 1M3531M	69
I- 33	Ascending minor triad	⬆ 1m35	70
I- 34	Ascending minor triad, portamento, with consistent resonance and volume	⬆ 1m35	71
I- 35	Ascending minor triad, legato	⬆ 1m35	72
I- 36	Descending minor triad	⬇ 5m31	73
I- 37	Descending minor triad, portamento, with consistent resonance and volume	⬇ 5m31	74
I- 38	Descending minor triad, legato	⬇ 5m31	75
I- 39	Ascending and descending minor triad	⬀⬂ 1m3531m	76
I- 40	Ascending and descending minor triad, portamento, with consistent resonance and volume	⬀⬂ 1m3531m	77
I- 41	Ascending and descending minor triad, legato	⬀⬂ 1m3531m	78
I- 42	Ascending octave	⬆ 8ve	79
I- 43	Ascending octave, portamento, with consistent resonance and volume	⬆ 8ve	80
I- 44	Ascending octave, legato	⬆ 8ve	81
I- 45	Descending octave	⬇ 8ve	82
I- 46	Descending octave, portamento, with consistent resonance and volume	⬇ 8ve	83
I- 47	Descending octave, legato	⬇ 8ve	84
I- 48	Ascending and descending octave	⬀⬂ 8ve	85
I- 49	Ascending and descending octave, portamento, with consistent resonance and volume	⬀⬂ 8ve	86
I- 50	Ascending and descending octave, legato	⬀⬂ 8ve	87
I- 51	Arpeggio - I-III-V-VIII sequence	⬆ 1358	88
I- 52	Arpeggio - I-III-V-VIII sequence, portamento, with consistent resonance and volume	⬆ 1358	89
I- 53	Arpeggio - I-III-V-VIII sequence, legato	⬆ 1358	90
I- 54	Arpeggio - VIII-V-III-I sequence	⬇ 8531	91
I- 55	Arpeggio - VIII-V-III-I sequence, portamento, with consistent resonance and volume	⬆ 8531	92
I- 56	Arpeggio - VIII-V-III-I sequence, legato	⬆ 8531	93
I- 57	Arpeggio - I-III-V-VIII-V-III-I sequence	⬀⬂ 1358531	94
I- 58	Arpeggio - I-III-V-VIII-V-III-I sequence, portamento, with consistent resonance and volume	⬀⬂ 1358531	95

No.	Exercise	QuickReference	Page
I- 59	Arpeggio - I-III-V-VIII-V-III-I sequence, staccato	⬈⬊ 1358531	96
I- 60	Arpeggio - I-III-V-VIII-V-III-I sequence, legato	⬈⬊ 1358531	97
I- 61	Arpeggio - I-III-V-VIII-V-III-I sequence, staccato and then legato	⬈⬊ 1358531	98
I- 62	Ascending major second	⬈⬊ M2	99
I- 63	Ascending major second, legato	⇧ M2	100
I- 64	Descending major second	⇩ M2	101
I- 65	Descending major second, legato	⇩ M2	102
I- 66	Ascending minor second (semitone)	⇧ m2	103
I- 67	Ascending minor second (semitone), legato	⇧ m2	104
I- 68	Descending minor second (semitone)	⇩ m2	105
I- 69	Descending minor second (semitone), legato	⇩ m2	106
I- 70	Ascending perfect fourth	⇧ P4	107
I- 71	Ascending perfect fourth, portamento, with consistent resonance and volume	⇧ P4	108
I- 72	Ascending perfect fourth, legato	⇧ P4	109
I- 73	Ascending major sixth	⇧ M6	110
I- 74	Ascending major sixth, portamento, with consistent resonance and volume	⇧ M6	111
I- 75	Ascending major sixth, legato	⇧ M6	112
I- 76	Ascending major seventh	⇧ M7	113
I- 77	Ascending major seventh, portamento, with consistent resonance and volume	⇧ M7	114
I- 78	Ascending major seventh, legato	⇧ M7	115
I- 79	Descending perfect fourth	⇩ P4	116
I- 80	Descending perfect fourth, portamento, with consistent resonance and volume	⇩ P4	117
I- 81	Descending perfect fourth, legato	⇩ P4	118
I- 82	Descending major sixth	⇩ M6	119
I- 83	Descending major sixth, portamento, with consistent resonance and volume	⇩ M6	120
I- 84	Descending major sixth, legato	⇩ M6	121
I- 85	Descending major seventh	⇩ M7	122
I- 86	Descending major seventh, portamento, with consistent resonance and volume	⇩ M7	123
I- 87	Descending major seventh, legato	⇩ M7	124

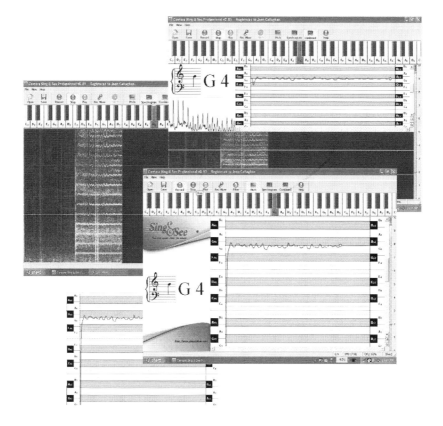

See your Voice -
Hear the Results

LIST OF SCALES and MODES

No.	Exercise	Page
S-1	Ascending chromatic scale	126
S-2	Ascending chromatic scale, legato	127
S-3	Descending chromatic scale	128
S-4	Descending chromatic scale, legato	129
S-5	Ascending and descending chromatic scale	130
S-6	Ascending and descending chromatic scale, staccato	131
S-7	Ascending and descending chromatic scale, legato	132
S-8	Ascending and descending chromatic scale, staccato, and then legato	133
S-9	Ascending whole-tone scale	134
S-10	Ascending whole-tone scale, legato	135
S-11	Descending whole-tone scale	136
S-12	Descending whole-tone scale, legato	137
S-13	Ascending and descending whole-tone scale	138
S-14	Ascending and descending whole-tone scale, staccato	139
S-15	Ascending and descending whole-tone scale, legato	140
S-16	Ascending and descending whole-tone scale, staccato, and then legato	141
S-17	Ascending and descending pentatonic (TTmin.3T) scale	142
S-18	Ascending and descending pentatonic (maj.3 ST maj.3) scale	143
S-19	Ascending and descending pentatonic (maj.3 S maj.3T) scale	144
S-20	Ascending and descending pentachord (TTST)	145
S-21	Ascending and descending pentachord (TSTT)	146
S-22	Ascending and descending pentachord (STTT)	147
S-23	Ascending and descending pentachord (TTST+)	148
S-24	Ascending and descending tetrachord (TTS)	149
S-25	Ascending and descending tetrachord (TST)	150
S-26	Ascending and descending tetrachord (TTT)	151
S-27	Ascending and descending tetrachord (STT)	152
S-28	Ascending major scale (Ionian mode)	153
S-29	Ascending major scale, legato	154
S-30	Descending major scale	155
S-31	Descending major scale, legato	156
S-32	Ascending and descending major scale	157
S-33	Ascending and descending major scale, staccato	158
S-34	Ascending and descending major scale, legato	159

No.	Exercise	Page
S-35	Ascending and descending major scale, staccato and then legato	160
S-36	Ascending Mixolydian mode (TTST TST)	161
S-37	Ascending Mixolydian mode, legato	162
S-38	Descending Mixolydian mode	163
S-39	Descending Mixolydian mode, legato	164
S-40	Ascending and descending Mixolydian mode	165
S-41	Ascending and descending Mixolydian mode, staccato	166
S-42	Ascending and descending Mixolydian mode, legato	167
S-43	Ascending and descending Mixolydian mode, staccato, and then legato	168
S-44	Ascending natural minor scale (Aeolian mode) (TSTT STT)	169
S-45	Ascending natural minor scale, legato	170
S-46	Descending natural minor scale	171
S-47	Descending natural minor scale, legato	172
S-48	Ascending and descending natural minor scale	173
S-49	Ascending and descending natural minor scale, staccato	174
S-50	Ascending and descending natural minor scale, legato	175
S-51	Ascending and descending natural minor scale, staccato, and then legato	176
S-52	Ascending melodic minor scale (TSTT TTS)	177
S-53	Ascending melodic minor scale, legato	178
S-54	Descending melodic minor scale (TTS TTST)	179
S-55	Descending melodic minor scale, legato	180
S-56	Ascending and descending melodic minor scale	181
S-57	Ascending and descending melodic minor scale, staccato	182
S-58	Ascending and descending melodic minor scale, legato	183
S-59	Ascending and descending melodic minor scale, staccato, and then legato	184
S-60	Ascending harmonic minor scale (TSTT ST+S)	185
S-61	Ascending harmonic minor scale, legato	186
S-62	Descending harmonic minor scale	187
S-63	Descending harmonic minor scale, legato	188
S-64	Ascending and descending harmonic minor scale	189
S-65	Ascending and descending harmonic minor scale, staccato	190
S-66	Ascending and descending harmonic minor scale, legato	191
S-67	Ascending and descending harmonic minor scale, staccato, and then legato	192
S-68	Ascending Dorian mode (TSTT TST)	193

No.	Exercise	Page
S-69	Ascending Dorian mode, legato	194
S-70	Descending Dorian mode	195
S-71	Descending Dorian mode, legato	196
S-72	Ascending and descending Dorian mode	197
S-73	Ascending and descending Dorian mode, staccato	198
S-74	Ascending and descending Dorian mode, legato	199
S-75	Ascending and descending Dorian mode, staccato, and then legato	200
S-76	Ascending Phrygian mode (STTT STT)	201
S-77	Ascending Phrygian mode, legato	202
S-78	Descending Phrygian mode	203
S-79	Descending Phrygian mode, legato	204
S-80	Ascending and descending Phrygian mode	205
S-81	Ascending and descending Phrygian mode, staccato	206
S-82	Ascending and descending Phrygian mode, legato	207
S-83	Ascending and descending Phrygian mode, staccato, and then legato	208
S-84	Ascending Locrian mode (STTS TTT)	209
S-85	Ascending Locrian mode, legato	210
S-86	Descending Locrian mode	211
S-87	Descending Locrian mode, legato	212
S-88	Ascending and descending Locrian mode	213
S-89	Ascending and descending Locrian mode, staccato	214
S-90	Ascending and descending Locrian mode, legato	215
S-91	Ascending and descending Locrian mode, staccato, and then legato	216
S-92	Ascending Lydian mode (TTTS TTS)	217
S-93	Ascending Lydian mode, legato	218
S-94	Descending Lydian mode	219
S-95	Descending Lydian mode, legato	220
S-96	Ascending and descending Lydian mode	221
S-97	Ascending and descending Lydian mode, staccato	222
S-98	Ascending and descending Lydian mode, legato	223
S-99	Ascending and descending Lydian mode, staccato, and then legato	224
S-100	Ascending blues scale - Major scale with lowered 3rd (TST+T TTS)	225
S-101	Ascending blues scale - Major scale with lowered 3rd, legato	226
S-102	Descending blues scale - Major scale with lowered 3rd	227

No.	Exercise	Page
S-103	Descending blues scale - Major scale with lowered 3rd, legato	228
S-104	Ascending and descending blues scale - Major scale with lowered 3rd	229
S-105	Ascending and descending blues scale - Major scale with lowered 3rd staccato	230
S-106	Ascending and descending blues scale - Major scale with lowered 3rd, legato	231
S-107	Ascending and descending blues scale - Major scale with lowered 3rd, staccato, and then legato	232
S-108	Ascending blues scale - Natural minor with raised 3rd (TTST STT)	233
S-109	Ascending blues scale - Natural minor with raised 3rd, legato	234
S-110	Descending blues scale - Natural minor with raised 3rd	235
S-111	Descending blues scale - Natural minor with raised 3rd, legato	236
S-112	Ascending and descending blues scale - Natural minor with raised 3rd	237
S-113	Ascending and descending blues scale - Natural minor with raised 3rd, staccato	238
S-114	Ascending and descending blues scale - Natural minor with raised 3rd, legato	239
S-115	Ascending and descending blues scale - Natural minor with raised 3rd, staccato, and then legato	240
S-116	Ascending blues scale - Major scale with raised 5th (TTST+ STT)	241
S-117	Ascending blues scale - Major scale with raised 5th, legato	242
S-118	Descending blues scale - Major scale with raised 5th	243
S-119	Descending blues scale - Major scale with raised 5th, legato	244
S-120	Ascending and descending blues scale - Major scale with raised 5th	245
S-121	Ascending and descending blues scale - Major scale with raised 5th, staccato	246
S-122	Ascending and descending blues scale - Major scale with raised 5th, legato	247
S-123	Ascending and descending blues scale - Major scale with raised 5th, staccato, and then legato	248
S-124	Ascending blues scale - Major scale with lowered 5th (TTSS T+TS)	249
S-125	Ascending blues scale - Major scale with lowered 5th, legato	250
S-126	Descending blues scale - Major scale with lowered 5th	251
S-127	Descending blues scale - Major scale with lowered 5th, legato	252
S-128	Ascending and descending blues scale - Major scale with lowered 5th	253
S-129	Ascending and descending blues scale - Major scale with lowered 5th, staccato	254

No.	Exercise	Page
S-130	Ascending and descending blues scale - Major scale with lowered 5th, legato	255
S-131	Ascending and descending blues scale - Major scale with lowered 5th, staccato, and then legato	256
S-132	Ascending blues scale - Locrian mode with raised 5th (STTT STT)	257
S-133	Ascending blues scale - Locrian mode with raised 5th, legato	258
S-134	Descending blues scale - Locrian mode with raised 5th	259
S-135	Descending blues scale - Locrian mode with raised 5th, legato	260
S-136	Ascending and descending blues scale - Locrian mode with raised 5th	261
S-137	Ascending and descending blues scale - Locrian mode with raised 5th, staccato	262
S-138	Ascending and descending blues scale - Locrian mode with raised 5th, legato	263
S-139	Ascending and descending blues scale - Locrian mode with raised 5th, staccato, and then legato	264
S-140	Ascending blues scale - Major scale with lowered 7th (TTST TST)	265
S-141	Ascending blues scale - Major scale with lowered 7th, legato	266
S-142	Descending blues scale - Major scale with lowered 7th	267
S-143	Descending blues scale - Major scale with lowered 7th, legato	268
S-144	Ascending and descending blues scale - Major scale with lowered 7th	269
S-145	Ascending and descending blues scale - Major scale with lowered 7th, staccato	270
S-146	Ascending and descending blues scale - Major scale with lowered 7th, legato	271
S-147	Ascending and descending blues scale - Major scale with lowered 7th, staccato, and then legato	272

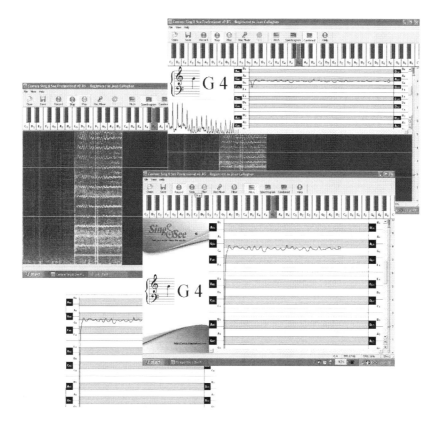

The Exercises

Exercise I-1: Single sustained note

/a/

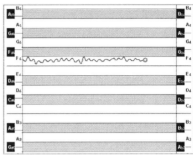

AIM	To sustain a single note on a given vowel for a specified time, maintaining consistent pitch through breath management. To build stamina through increasing the duration of the sustained note.
OBJECTIVES	▶ To develop management of pitch and duration when singing sustained notes. ▶ To build the aural and kinaesthetic memory necessary for this task.
PHYSICAL INVOLVEMENT	▶ Abdominal and thoracic muscle groups to achieve breath management ▶ Larynx height and posture ▶ Articulators, including pharynx, velum (soft palate), tongue, lips and jaw, for appropriate vowel formation
INSTRUCTIONS 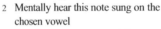	1 Play the target note 2 Mentally hear this note sung on the chosen vowel 3 Breathe the correct vowel shape 4 Position the larynx 5 Activate breath support 6 Start to sing
PITCH DISPLAY	Sing the target pitch, keeping the undulations of the blue line as regular as possible, within the pitch area and as close to the central yellow line as possible.
SPECTROGRAM	
LEVEL METER	

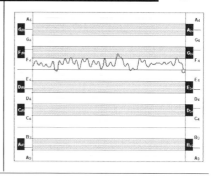

AIM	To sing a *messa di voce* on a single sustained note, mid voice, at correct pitch, maintaining consistent resonance and vibrato while evenly increasing and then decreasing volume throughout the note. To build stamina through increasing the duration of the sustained note.
OBJECTIVES	▶ To develop management of pitch, duration and resonance (including vibrato) while singing a *messa di voce* on a single note. ▶ To manage the balance of intensities over a crescendo and diminuendo of equal duration. ▶ To build the aural and kinaesthetic memory necessary for this task.
PHYSICAL INVOLVEMENT	▶ Abdominal and thoracic muscle groups to achieve breath management ▶ Larynx height and posture ▶ Articulators, including pharynx, velum (soft palate), tongue, lips and jaw, for appropriate vowel formation
INSTRUCTIONS	1 Play the target note 2 Mentally hear this note sung on the chosen vowel 3 Breathe the correct vowel shape 4 Position the larynx 5 Activate breath support 6 Start to sing	7 Increase breath pressure in order to increase pitch, while maintaining the vowel shape 8 Ensure that breath pressure and vowel quality are maintained to the end of the exercise
PITCH DISPLAY	Sing the target pitch, keeping the undulations of the blue line as regular as possible, within the pitch area, and with regular deviations around the central yellow line in order to maintain the timbral richness
SPECTROGRAM	A well-executed *messa di voce* exhibits consistently undulating bands of spectral energy, and clean onset and offset. While the resonance pattern remains the same, the bands of spectral energy become darker and closer together with increasing intensity.
LEVEL METER	The skill integral to this exercise is to gradually raise the volume level to maximum half-way through the note and gradually decrease the volume level to minimum by the end of the note. The volume level should be the same at the beginning and end of the note.

Exercise I-3: Ascending major third

/a/

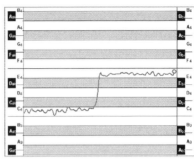

AIM	To sing an ascending major third, in mid-voice, on a specified vowel, with pitch accuracy.
OBJECTIVES	▶ To develop management of pitch when singing intervals. ▶ To build the aural and kinaesthetic memory necessary for this task.
PHYSICAL INVOLVEMENT	▶ Abdominal and thoracic muscle groups to achieve breath management ▶ Larynx height and posture ▶ Articulators, including pharynx, velum (soft palate), tongue, lips and jaw, for appropriate vowel formation and vocal resonance
INSTRUCTIONS	1 Play the target notes 2 Mentally hear this interval sung on the chosen vowel 3 Breathe the correct vowel shape 4 Position the larynx 5 Activate breath support 6 Start to sing 7 Increase breath pressure in order to increase pitch, while keeping the vowel shape
PITCH DISPLAY	Sing the interval by directing the blue pitch line from the centre of the lower note to the centre of the higher note, with minimal deviation.
SPECTROGRAM	
LEVEL METER	

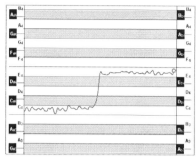

AIM	To sing an ascending major third, legato, in mid-voice, on a specified vowel, with pitch accuracy, consistent resonance and consistent volume.
OBJECTIVES	▶ To develop management of pitch, vowel articulation and volume when singing intervals. ▶ To build the aural and kinaesthetic memory necessary for this task.
PHYSICAL INVOLVEMENT	▶ Abdominal and thoracic muscle groups to achieve breath management ▶ Larynx height and posture ▶ Articulators, including pharynx, velum (soft palate), tongue, lips and jaw, for appropriate vowel formation and vocal resonance
INSTRUCTIONS	1 Play the target notes 2 Mentally hear this interval sung on the chosen vowel 3 Breathe the correct vowel shape 4 Position the larynx 5 Activate breath support 6 Start to sing 7 Gradually increase breath pressure in order to increase pitch, while keeping connected tone and vowel shape
PITCH DISPLAY	Sing the interval by directing the blue pitch line from the centre of the lower note to the centre of the higher note, with minimal deviation.
SPECTROGRAM	The Spectrogram should exhibit the same pattern of resonances throughout the exercise. *Note: This is an essential skill for classical singing styles; for other styles, variations in resonance may be desirable.*
LEVEL METER	The volume should remain consistent throughout the exercise. *Note: Where intervals traverse register changes, this is an especially useful skill to encourage.*

Exercise I-5: Ascending perfect fifth

/a/

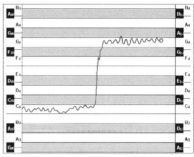

AIM	To sing an ascending perfect fifth, in mid-voice, on a specified vowel, with pitch accuracy.
OBJECTIVES	▶ To develop management of pitch when singing intervals. ▶ To build the aural and kinaesthetic memory necessary for this task.
PHYSICAL INVOLVEMENT	▶ Abdominal and thoracic muscle groups to achieve breath management ▶ Larynx height and posture ▶ Articulators, including pharynx, velum (soft palate), tongue, lips and jaw, for appropriate vowel formation and vocal resonance
INSTRUCTIONS	1 Play the target notes 2 Mentally hear this interval sung on the chosen vowel 3 Breathe the correct vowel shape 4 Position the larynx 5 Activate breath support 6 Start to sing 7 Increase breath pressure in order to increase pitch, while keeping the vowel shape
PITCH DISPLAY	Sing the interval by directing the blue pitch line from the centre of the lower note to the centre of the higher note, with minimal deviation.
SPECTROGRAM	
LEVEL METER	

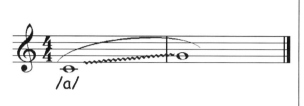

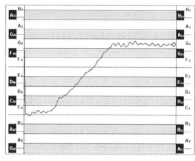

AIM	To sing an ascending perfect fifth, portamento, in mid-voice, on a specified vowel, with pitch accuracy, consistent resonance and consistent volume.
OBJECTIVES	▶ To develop management of pitch, vowel articulation and volume when singing intervals. ▶ To enhance legato capability. ▶ To build the aural and kinaesthetic memory necessary for this task.
PHYSICAL INVOLVEMENT	▶ Abdominal and thoracic muscle groups to achieve breath management ▶ Larynx height and posture ▶ Articulators, including pharynx, velum (soft palate), tongue, lips and jaw, for appropriate vowel formation and vocal resonance
INSTRUCTIONS	1 Play the target notes 2 Mentally hear the continuous series of notes contained between the target pitches, and sung on the chosen vowel 3 Breathe the correct vowel shape 4 Position the larynx 5 Activate breath support 6 Start to sing 7 Gradually increase breath pressure in order to increase pitch, while keeping the vowel shape
PITCH DISPLAY	Sing the interval through the range of notes to the centre of the higher note, with minimal deviation. The optimal display is a steadily ascending diagonal line.
SPECTROGRAM	The Spectrogram should exhibit the same pattern of resonances throughout the exercise.
LEVEL METER	The volume should remain consistent throughout the exercise. *Note: Where intervals traverse register changes, this is an especially useful skill to encourage.*

Exercise I-7: Ascending perfect fifth, legato

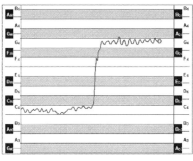

/a/

AIM	To sing an ascending perfect fifth, legato, in mid-voice, on a specified vowel, with pitch accuracy, consistent resonance and consistent volume.
OBJECTIVES	▶ To develop management of pitch, vowel articulation and volume when singing intervals. ▶ To build the aural and kinaesthetic memory necessary for this task.
PHYSICAL INVOLVEMENT	▶ Abdominal and thoracic muscle groups to achieve breath management ▶ Larynx height and posture ▶ Articulators, including pharynx, velum (soft palate), tongue, lips and jaw, for appropriate vowel formation
INSTRUCTIONS	1 Play the target notes 2 Mentally hear this interval sung on the chosen vowel 3 Breathe the correct vowel shape 4 Position the larynx 5 Activate breath support 6 Start to sing 7 Gradually increase breath pressure in order to increase pitch, while keeping connected tone and vowel shape
PITCH DISPLAY	Sing the interval by directing the blue pitch line from the centre of the first note to the centre of each following note, with minimal deviation.
SPECTROGRAM	The Spectrogram should exhibit the same pattern of resonances throughout the exercise.
LEVEL METER	The volume should remain consistent throughout the exercise. *Note: Where intervals traverse register changes, this is an especially useful skill to encourage.*

Exercise I-8: Ascending minor third

I-8

/a/

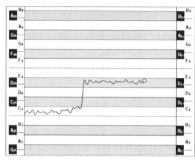

AIM	To sing an ascending minor third in mid-voice, on a specified vowel, with pitch accuracy.

OBJECTIVES

▶ To develop management of pitch when singing intervals.
▶ To build the aural and kinaesthetic memory necessary for this task.

PHYSICAL INVOLVEMENT

▶ Abdominal and thoracic muscle groups to achieve breath management
▶ Larynx height and posture
▶ Articulators, including pharynx, velum (soft palate), tongue, lips and jaw, for appropriate vowel formation and vocal resonance

INSTRUCTIONS

1 Play the target notes
2 Mentally hear this interval sung on the chosen vowel
3 Breathe the correct vowel shape
4 Position the larynx
5 Activate breath support
6 Start to sing

7 Increase breath pressure in order to increase pitch, while keeping the vowel shape

PITCH DISPLAY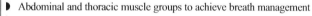

Sing the interval by directing the blue pitch line from the centre of the lower note to the centre of the higher note, with minimal deviation.

SPECTROGRAM

LEVEL METER

Exercise I-9: Ascending minor third, legato

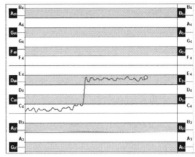

/a/

AIM	To sing an ascending minor third, legato, in mid-voice, on a specified vowel, with pitch accuracy, consistent resonance and consistent volume.
OBJECTIVES	▶ To develop management of pitch, vowel articulation and volume when singing intervals. ▶ To build the aural and kinaesthetic memory necessary for this task.
PHYSICAL INVOLVEMENT	▶ Abdominal and thoracic muscle groups to achieve breath management ▶ Larynx height and posture ▶ Articulators, including pharynx, velum (soft palate), tongue, lips and jaw, for appropriate vowel formation and vocal resonance
INSTRUCTIONS	1 Play the target notes 2 Mentally hear this interval sung on the chosen vowel 3 Breathe the correct vowel shape 4 Position the larynx 5 Activate breath support 6 Start to sing 7 Gradually increase breath pressure in order to increase pitch, while keeping connected tone and vowel shape.
PITCH DISPLAY	Sing the interval by directing the blue pitch line from the centre of the lower note to the centre of the higher note, with minimal deviation.
SPECTROGRAM	The Spectrogram should exhibit the same pattern of resonances throughout the exercise. *Note: This is an essential skill for classical singing styles; for other styles, variations in resonance may be desirable.*
LEVEL METER	The volume should remain consistent throughout the exercise. *Note: Where intervals traverse register changes, this is an especially useful skill to encourage.*

/a/

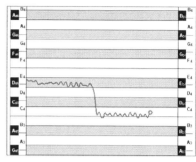

AIM	To sing a descending major third in mid-voice, on a specified vowel, with pitch accuracy.
OBJECTIVES	▶ To develop management of pitch, vowel articulation and volume, when singing intervals. ▶ To build the aural and kinaesthetic memory necessary for this task.
PHYSICAL INVOLVEMENT	▶ Abdominal and thoracic muscle groups to achieve breath management for both pitch and loudness ▶ Larynx height and posture ▶ Articulators, including pharynx, velum (soft palate), tongue, lips and jaw, for appropriate vowel formation and vocal resonance
INSTRUCTIONS	1 Play the target notes 2 Mentally hear this interval sung on the chosen vowel 3 Breathe the correct vowel shape 4 Position the larynx 5 Activate breath support 6 Start to sing 7 Maintain appropriate breath pressure for the descending pitch, while keeping the vowel shape
PITCH DISPLAY	Sing the interval by directing the blue pitch line from the centre of the higher note to the centre of the lower note, with minimal deviation.
SPECTROGRAM	
LEVEL METER	

Exercise I-11: Descending major third, legato

/a/

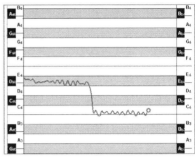

AIM	To sing a descending major third, legato, in mid-voice, on a specified vowel, with pitch accuracy, consistent resonance and consistent volume.
OBJECTIVES	▶ To develop management of pitch, vowel articulation and volume when singing intervals. ▶ To build the aural and kinaesthetic memory necessary for this task.
PHYSICAL INVOLVEMENT	▶ Abdominal and thoracic muscle groups to achieve breath management ▶ Larynx height and posture ▶ Articulators, including pharynx, velum (soft palate), tongue, lips and jaw, for appropriate vowel formation and vocal resonance
INSTRUCTIONS	1 Play the target notes 2 Mentally hear this interval sung on the chosen vowel 3 Breathe the correct vowel shape 4 Position the larynx 5 Activate breath support 6 Start to sing	7 Maintain appropriate breath pressure for the descending pitch, while keeping connected tone and vowel shape
PITCH DISPLAY	Sing the interval by directing the blue pitch line from the centre of the higher note to the centre of the lower note, with minimal deviation.
SPECTROGRAM	The Spectrogram should exhibit the same pattern of resonances throughout the exercise. *Note: This is an essential skill for classical singing styles; for other styles, variations in resonance may be desirable.*
LEVEL METER	The volume should remain consistent throughout the exercise. *Note: Where intervals traverse register changes, this is an especially useful skill to encourage.*

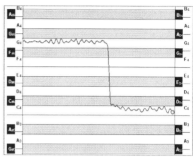

AIM	To sing a descending perfect fifth in mid-voice, on a specified vowel, with pitch accuracy.
OBJECTIVES	▶ To develop management of pitch when singing intervals. ▶ To build the aural and kinaesthetic memory necessary for this task.
PHYSICAL INVOLVEMENT	▶ Abdominal and thoracic muscle groups to achieve breath management ▶ Larynx height and posture ▶ Articulators, including pharynx, velum (soft palate), tongue, lips and jaw, for appropriate vowel formation and vocal resonance
INSTRUCTIONS	1 Play the target notes 2 Mentally hear this interval sung on the chosen vowel 3 Breathe the correct vowel shape 4 Position the larynx 5 Activate breath support 6 Start to sing 7 Maintain appropriate breath pressure for the descending pitch, while keeping the vowel shape
PITCH DISPLAY	Sing the interval by directing the blue pitch line from the centre of the higher note to the centre of the lower note, with minimal deviation.
SPECTROGRAM	
LEVEL METER	

Exercise I-13: Descending perfect fifth, portamento, with consistent resonance and volume

I-13

/a/

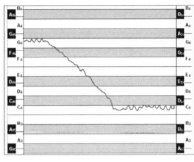

AIM	To sing a descending perfect fifth, portamento, in mid-voice, on a specified vowel, with pitch accuracy, consistent resonance and consistent volume.
OBJECTIVES 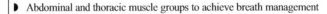	▶ To develop management of pitch, vowel articulation and volume when singing intervals. ▶ To enhance legato capability. ▶ To build the aural and kinaesthetic memory necessary for this task.
PHYSICAL INVOLVEMENT	▶ Abdominal and thoracic muscle groups to achieve breath management ▶ Larynx height and posture ▶ Articulators, including pharynx, velum (soft palate), tongue, lips and jaw, for appropriate vowel formation and vocal resonance
INSTRUCTIONS	1 Play the target notes 2 Mentally hear the continuous series of notes contained between the target pitches, and sung on the chosen vowel 3 Breathe the correct vowel shape 4 Position the larynx	5 Activate breath support 6 Start to sing 7 Maintain appropriate breath pressure for the descending pitch, while keeping the vowel shape
PITCH DISPLAY	Sing the interval through the range of notes to the centre of the lower note, with minimal deviation. The optimal display is a steadily descending diagonal line.
SPECTROGRAM	The Spectrogram should exhibit the same pattern of resonances throughout the exercise.
LEVEL METER	The volume should remain consistent throughout the exercise. *Note: Where intervals traverse register changes, this is an especially useful skill to encourage.*

/a/

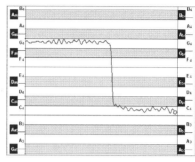

AIM	To sing a descending perfect fifth, legato, in mid-voice, on a specified vowel, with pitch accuracy, consistent resonance and consistent volume.
OBJECTIVES	▶ To develop management of pitch, vowel articulation and volume when singing intervals. ▶ To build the aural and kinaesthetic memory necessary for this task.
PHYSICAL INVOLVEMENT	▶ Abdominal and thoracic muscle groups to achieve breath management ▶ Larynx height and posture ▶ Articulators, including pharynx, velum (soft palate), tongue, lips and jaw, for appropriate vowel formation and vocal resonance

INSTRUCTIONS	1 Play the target notes 2 Mentally hear this interval sung on the chosen vowel 3 Breathe the correct vowel shape 4 Position the larynx 5 Activate breath support 6 Start to sing	7 Maintain appropriate breath pressure for the descending pitch, while keeping connected tone and vowel shape

PITCH DISPLAY	Sing the interval by directing the blue pitch line from the centre of the higher note to the centre of the lower note, with minimal deviation.
SPECTROGRAM	The Spectrogram should exhibit the same pattern of resonances throughout the exercise. *Note: This is an essential skill for classical singing styles; for other styles, variations in resonance may be desirable.*
LEVEL METER	The volume should remain consistent throughout the exercise. *Note: Where intervals traverse register changes, this is an especially useful skill to encourage.*

Exercise I-15: Descending minor third

I-15

/a/

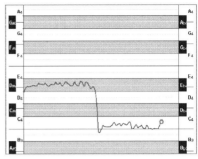

AIM	To sing a descending minor third, in mid-voice, on a specified vowel, with pitch accuracy.
OBJECTIVES	▶ To develop management of pitch when singing intervals. ▶ To build the aural and kinaesthetic memory necessary for this task.
PHYSICAL INVOLVEMENT	▶ Abdominal and thoracic muscle groups to achieve breath management ▶ Larynx height and posture ▶ Articulators, including pharynx, velum (soft palate), tongue, lips and jaw, for appropriate vowel formation and vocal resonance
INSTRUCTIONS	1 Play the target notes 2 Mentally hear this interval sung on the chosen vowel 3 Breathe the correct vowel shape 4 Position the larynx 5 Activate breath support 6 Start to sing	7 Maintain appropriate breath pressure for the descending pitch, while keeping the vowel shape
PITCH DISPLAY	Sing the interval by directing the blue pitch line from the centre of the higher note to the centre of the lower note, with minimal deviation.
SPECTROGRAM	
LEVEL METER	

/a/

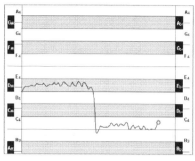

AIM	To sing a descending minor third, legato, in mid-voice, on a specified vowel, with pitch accuracy, consistent resonance and consistent volume.
OBJECTIVES	▶ To develop management of pitch, vowel articulation and volume when singing intervals. ▶ To build the aural and kinaesthetic memory necessary for this task.
PHYSICAL INVOLVEMENT	▶ Abdominal and thoracic muscle groups to achieve breath management ▶ Larynx height and posture ▶ Articulators, including pharynx, velum (soft palate), tongue, lips and jaw, for appropriate vowel formation and vocal resonance
INSTRUCTIONS	1 Play the target notes 2 Mentally hear this interval sung on the chosen vowel 3 Breathe the correct vowel shape 4 Position the larynx 5 Activate breath support 6 Start to sing 7 Maintain appropriate breath pressure for the descending pitch, while keeping connected tone and vowel shape 8 Ensure that breath pressure and vowel quality are maintained to the end of the exercise
PITCH DISPLAY	Sing the interval by directing the blue pitch line from the centre of the higher note to the centre of the lower note, with minimal deviation.
SPECTROGRAM	The Spectrogram should exhibit the same pattern of resonances throughout the exercise. *Note: This is an essential skill for classical singing styles; for other styles, variations in resonance may be desirable.*
LEVEL METER	The volume should remain consistent throughout the exercise. *Note: Where intervals traverse register changes, this is an especially useful skill to encourage.*

Exercise I-17: Ascending and descending major third

/a/

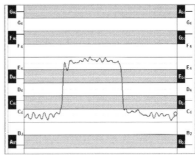

AIM	To sing an ascending and descending major third, in mid-voice, on a specified vowel, with pitch accuracy.
OBJECTIVES	▶ To develop management of pitch when singing intervals. ▶ To build the aural and kinaesthetic memory necessary for this task.
PHYSICAL INVOLVEMENT	▶ Abdominal and thoracic muscle groups to achieve breath management ▶ Larynx height and posture ▶ Articulators, including pharynx, velum (soft palate), tongue, lips and jaw, for appropriate vowel formation and vocal resonance
INSTRUCTIONS	1 Play the target notes 2 Mentally hear this interval sung on the chosen vowel 3 Breathe the correct vowel shape 4 Position the larynx 5 Activate breath support 6 Start to sing 7 Increase breath pressure in order to increase pitch, while maintaining the vowel shape 8 Maintain appropriate breath pressure for the descending pitch, while keeping the vowel shape 9 Ensure that breath pressure and vowel quality are maintained to the end of the exercise
PITCH DISPLAY	Sing the interval by directing the blue pitch line from the centre of the lower note to the centre of the higher note, and back again, with minimal deviation.
SPECTROGRAM	
LEVEL METER	

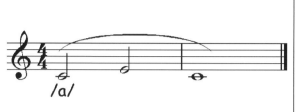

/a/

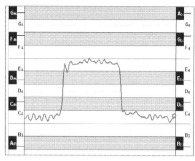

AIM	To sing an ascending and descending major third, legato, in mid-voice, on a specified vowel, with pitch accuracy, consistent resonance and consistent volume.
OBJECTIVES	▶ To develop management of pitch, vowel articulation and volume when singing intervals. ▶ To build the aural and kinaesthetic memory necessary for this task.
PHYSICAL INVOLVEMENT	▶ Abdominal and thoracic muscle groups to achieve breath management ▶ Larynx height and posture ▶ Articulators, including pharynx, velum (soft palate), tongue, lips and jaw, for appropriate vowel formation and vocal resonance

INSTRUCTIONS	1 Play the target notes 2 Mentally hear this interval sung on the chosen vowel 3 Breathe the correct vowel shape 4 Position the larynx 5 Activate breath support 6 Start to sing 7 Gradually increase breath pressure in	order to increase pitch, while keeping connected tone and vowel shape 8 Maintain appropriate breath pressure for the descending pitch, while keeping the vowel shape 9 Ensure that breath pressure and vowel quality are maintained to the end of the exercise

PITCH DISPLAY	Sing the interval by directing the blue pitch line from the centre of the lower note to the centre of the higher note, and back again, with minimal deviation.
SPECTROGRAM	The Spectrogram should exhibit the same pattern of resonances throughout the exercise. *Note: This is an essential skill for classical singing styles; for other styles, variations in resonance may be desirable.*
LEVEL METER	The volume should remain consistent throughout the exercise. *Note: Where intervals traverse register changes, this is an especially useful skill to encourage.*

Exercise I-19: Ascending and descending perfect fifth

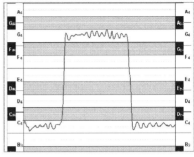

/a/

AIM	To sing an ascending and descending perfect fifth, in mid-voice, on a specified vowel, with pitch accuracy.
OBJECTIVES	▶ To develop management of pitch when singing intervals. ▶ To build the aural and kinaesthetic memory necessary for this task.
PHYSICAL INVOLVEMENT	▶ Abdominal and thoracic muscle groups to achieve breath management ▶ Larynx height and posture ▶ Articulators, including pharynx, velum (soft palate), tongue, lips and jaw, for appropriate vowel formation and vocal resonance
INSTRUCTIONS	1 Play the target notes 2 Mentally hear this interval sung on the chosen vowel 3 Breathe the correct vowel shape 4 Position the larynx 5 Activate breath support 6 Start to sing 7 Increase breath pressure in order to increase pitch, while maintaining the vowel shape 8 Maintain appropriate breath pressure for the descending pitch, while keeping the vowel shape 9 Ensure that breath pressure and vowel quality are maintained to the end of the exercise
PITCH DISPLAY	Sing the interval by directing the blue pitch line from the centre of the lower note to the centre of the higher note, and back again, with minimal deviation.
SPECTROGRAM	
LEVEL METER	

Exercise I-20: Ascending and descending perfect fifth, portamento, with consistent resonance and volume

/a/

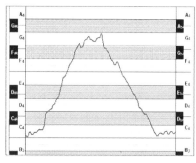

AIM	To sing an ascending and descending perfect fifth, portamento, in mid-voice, on a specified vowel, with pitch accuracy, consistent resonance and consistent volume.
OBJECTIVES	▶ To develop management of pitch, vowel articulation and volume when singing intervals. ▶ To enhance legato capability. ▶ To build the aural and kinaesthetic memory necessary for this task.
PHYSICAL INVOLVEMENT	▶ Abdominal and thoracic muscle groups to achieve breath management ▶ Larynx height and posture ▶ Articulators, including pharynx, velum (soft palate), tongue, lips and jaw, for appropriate vowel formation and vocal resonance

INSTRUCTIONS	1 Play the target notes 2 Mentally hear the continuous series of notes contained between the target pitches, and sung on the chosen vowel 3 Breathe the correct vowel shape 4 Position the larynx 5 Activate breath support	6 Start to sing 7 Gradually increase breath pressure in order to increase pitch, while maintaining the vowel shape 8 Maintain appropriate breath pressure for the descending pitch, while keeping the vowel shape 9 Ensure that breath pressure and vowel quality are maintained to the end of the exercise

PITCH DISPLAY	Sing the interval through the range of notes by directing the blue pitch line from the centre of the lower note to the centre of the higher note, and back again, with minimal deviation. The optimal display is a smoothly ascending diagonal line connected to a smoothly descending diagonal line of equal length and angle.
SPECTROGRAM	The Spectrogram should exhibit the same pattern of resonances throughout the exercise.
LEVEL METER	The volume should remain consistent throughout the exercise. *Note: Where intervals traverse register changes, this is an especially useful skill to encourage.*

Exercise I-21: Ascending and descending perfect fifth, legato

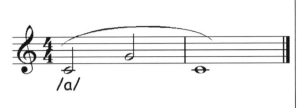

/a/

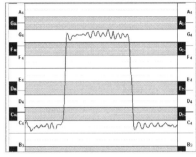

AIM	To sing an ascending and descending perfect fifth, legato, in mid-voice, on a specified vowel, with pitch accuracy, consistent resonance and consistent volume.
OBJECTIVES	▶ To develop management of pitch, vowel articulation and volume when singing intervals. ▶ To build the aural and kinaesthetic memory necessary for this task.
PHYSICAL INVOLVEMENT	▶ Abdominal and thoracic muscle groups to achieve breath management ▶ Larynx height and posture ▶ Articulators, including pharynx, velum (soft palate), tongue, lips and jaw, for appropriate vowel formation and vocal resonance
INSTRUCTIONS	1 Play the target notes 2 Mentally hear this interval sung on the chosen vowel 3 Breathe the correct vowel shape 4 Position the larynx 5 Activate breath support 6 Start to sing 7 Gradually increase breath pressure in order to increase pitch, while keeping connected tone and vowel shape 8 Ensure that breath pressure and vowel quality are maintained to the end of the exercise
PITCH DISPLAY	Sing the interval by directing the blue pitch line from the centre of the lower note to the centre of the higher note, and back again, with minimal deviation.
SPECTROGRAM	The Spectrogram should exhibit the same pattern of resonances throughout the exercise. *Note: This is an essential skill for classical singing styles; for other styles, variations in resonance may be desirable.*
LEVEL METER	The volume should remain consistent throughout the exercise. *Note: Where intervals traverse register changes, this is an especially useful skill to encourage.*

Exercise I-22: Ascending and descending minor third

/a/

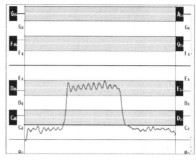

AIM	To sing an ascending and descending minor third, in mid-voice, on a specified vowel, with pitch accuracy, consistent resonance and consistent volume.
OBJECTIVES	▶ To develop management of pitch when singing intervals. ▶ To build the aural and kinaesthetic memory necessary for this task.
PHYSICAL INVOLVEMENT	▶ Abdominal and thoracic muscle groups to achieve breath management ▶ Larynx height and posture ▶ Articulators, including pharynx, velum (soft palate), tongue, lips and jaw, for appropriate vowel formation and vocal resonance
INSTRUCTIONS	1 Play the target notes 2 Mentally hear this interval sung on the chosen vowel 3 Breathe the correct vowel shape 4 Position the larynx 5 Activate breath support 6 Start to sing 7 Increase breath pressure in order to increase pitch, while keeping the vowel shape 8 Maintain appropriate breath pressure for the descending pitch, while keeping the vowel shape 9 Ensure that breath pressure and vowel quality are maintained to the end of the exercise
PITCH DISPLAY	Sing the interval by directing the blue pitch line from the centre of the lower note to the centre of the higher note, and back again, with minimal deviation.
SPECTROGRAM	
LEVEL METER	

Exercise I-23: Ascending and descending minor third, legato

/a/

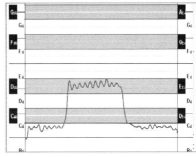

AIM	To sing an ascending and descending minor third, legato, in mid-voice, on a specified vowel, with pitch accuracy, consistent resonance and consistent volume.
OBJECTIVES	▶ To develop management of pitch, vowel articulation and volume when singing intervals. ▶ To build the aural and kinaesthetic memory necessary for this task.
PHYSICAL INVOLVEMENT	▶ Abdominal and thoracic muscle groups to achieve breath management ▶ Larynx height and posture ▶ Articulators, including pharynx, velum (soft palate), tongue, lips and jaw, for appropriate vowel formation and vocal resonance
INSTRUCTIONS	1 Play the target notes 2 Mentally hear this interval sung on the chosen vowel 3 Breathe the correct vowel shape 4 Position the larynx 5 Activate breath support 6 Start to sing 7 Gradually increase breath pressure in order to increase pitch, while keeping connected tone and vowel shape 8 Maintain appropriate breath pressure for the descending pitch, while keeping connected tone and vowel shape
PITCH DISPLAY	Sing the interval by directing the blue pitch line from the centre of the lower note to the centre of the higher note, and back again, with minimal deviation.
SPECTROGRAM	The Spectrogram should exhibit the same pattern of resonances throughout the exercise. *Note: This is an essential skill for classical singing styles; for other styles, variations in resonance may be desirable.*
LEVEL METER	The volume should remain consistent throughout the exercise. *Note: Where intervals traverse register changes, this is an especially useful skill to encourage.*

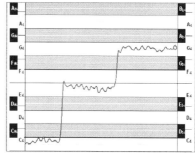

AIM	To sing an ascending major triad in mid-voice, on a specified vowel, with pitch accuracy.
OBJECTIVES	▶ To develop management of pitch when singing a sequence of intervals. Of importance is learning the aural and kinaesthetic skills necessary to make the distinction between major and minor thirds. ▶ To build the aural and kinaesthetic memory necessary for this task.
PHYSICAL INVOLVEMENT	▶ Abdominal and thoracic muscle groups to achieve breath management ▶ Larynx height and posture ▶ Articulators, including pharynx, velum (soft palate), tongue, lips and jaw, for appropriate vowel formation.
INSTRUCTIONS	1 Play the target notes in sequence from the lowest note 2 Mentally hear this interval sung on the chosen vowel 3 Breathe the correct vowel shape 4 Position the larynx 5 Activate breath support 6 Start to sing 7 Increase breath pressure in order to increase pitch, while keeping the vowel shape
PITCH DISPLAY	Sing each interval by directing the blue pitch line from the centre of the lowest note to the centre of the middle note, and then to the centre of the highest note, with minimal deviation. Check that each interval is accurate. [Sometimes there is a tendency to modify rising intervals.]
SPECTROGRAM	
LEVEL METER	

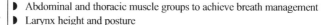

I-25

Exercise I-25: Ascending major triad (I-III-V), portamento, with consistent resonance and volume

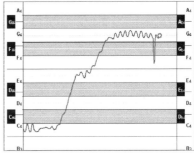

AIM	To sing an ascending major triad, portamento, in mid-voice, on a specified vowel, with pitch accuracy, consistent resonance and consistent volume.
OBJECTIVES	▶ To develop management of pitch, vowel articulation and volume when singing connected intervals. Of importance is learning the aural and kinaesthetic skills necessary to make the distinction between major and minor thirds. ▶ To build the aural and kinaesthetic memory necessary for this task.
PHYSICAL INVOLVEMENT	▶ Abdominal and thoracic muscle groups to achieve breath management ▶ Larynx height and posture ▶ Articulators, including pharynx, velum (soft palate), tongue, lips and jaw, for appropriate vowel formation and vocal resonance
INSTRUCTIONS	1 Play the target notes in sequence from the lowest note 2 Mentally hear the continuous series of notes contained between the target pitches, and sung on the chosen vowel 3 Breathe the correct vowel shape 4 Position the larynx 5 Activate breath support 6 Start to sing 7 Gradually increase breath pressure in order to increase pitch, while keeping the vowel shape 8 Ensure that breath pressure and vowel quality are maintained to the end of the exercise
PITCH DISPLAY	Sing each interval through the range of notes by directing the blue pitch line from the centre of the lowest note to the centre of the middle note, and then to the centre of the highest note, with minimal deviation. The optimal display is two connected, steadily ascending diagonal lines. Check that each interval is accurate. [Sometimes there is a tendency to modify ascending intervals.]
SPECTROGRAM	The Spectrogram should exhibit the same pattern of resonances throughout the exercise.
LEVEL METER	The volume should remain consistent throughout the exercise. *Note: Where intervals traverse register changes, this is an especially useful skill to encourage.*

/a/

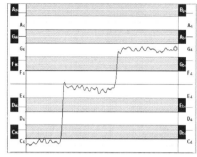

AIM	To sing an ascending major triad, legato, in mid-voice, on a specified vowel, with pitch accuracy, consistent resonance and consistent volume.
OBJECTIVES	▶ To develop management of pitch, vowel articulation and volume when singing connected intervals. Of importance is learning the aural and kinaesthetic skills necessary to make the distinction between major and minor thirds. ▶ To enhance legato capability ▶ To build the aural and kinaesthetic memory necessary for this task.
PHYSICAL INVOLVEMENT	▶ Abdominal and thoracic muscle groups to achieve breath management ▶ Larynx height and posture ▶ Articulators, including pharynx, velum (soft palate), tongue, lips and jaw, for appropriate vowel formation

INSTRUCTIONS	1 Play the target notes in sequence from the lowest note
	2 Mentally hear these two intervals sung on the chosen vowel
	3 Breathe the correct vowel shape
	4 Position the larynx
	5 Activate breath support
	   6 Start to sing
	   7 Gradually increase breath pressure in order to increase pitch, while keeping connected tone and vowel shape

PITCH DISPLAY	Sing each interval by directing the blue pitch line from the centre of the lowest note to the centre of the middle note, and then to the centre of the highest note, with minimal deviation. Check that each interval is accurate. [Sometimes there is a tendency to modify ascending intervals.]
SPECTROGRAM	The Spectrogram should exhibit the same pattern of resonances throughout the exercise.
LEVEL METER	The volume should remain consistent throughout the exercise. *Note: Where intervals traverse register changes, this is an especially useful skill to encourage.*

Exercise I-27: Descending major triad (V-III-I)

/a/

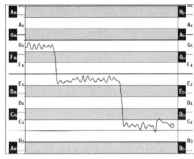

AIM	To sing a descending major triad, in mid-voice, on a specified vowel, with pitch accuracy, consistent resonance and consistent volume.

OBJECTIVES	▶ To develop management of pitch when singing a sequence of intervals. Of importance is learning the aural and kinaesthetic skills necessary to make the distinction between major and minor thirds. ▶ To build the aural and kinaesthetic memory necessary for this task.

PHYSICAL INVOLVEMENT	▶ Abdominal and thoracic muscle groups to achieve breath management ▶ Larynx height and posture ▶ Articulators, including pharynx, velum (soft palate), tongue, lips and jaw, for appropriate vowel formation and vocal resonance

INSTRUCTIONS	1 Play the target notes in sequence from the highest note 2 Mentally hear these two intervals, sung on the chosen vowel 3 Breathe the correct vowel shape 4 Position the larynx 5 Activate breath support	6 Start to sing 7 Maintain appropriate breath pressure for the descending pitch, while keeping the vowel shape 8 Ensure that breath pressure and vowel quality are maintained to the end of the exercise

PITCH DISPLAY	Sing each interval by directing the blue pitch line from the centre of the highest note to the centre of the middle note, and then to the centre of the lowest note, with minimal deviation. Check that each interval is accurate.

SPECTROGRAM	The Spectrogram should exhibit the same pattern of resonances throughout the exercise.

LEVEL METER	The volume should remain consistent throughout the exercise. *Note: Where intervals traverse register changes, this is an especially useful skill to encourage.*

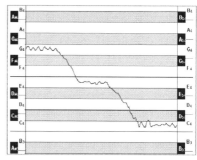

/a/

AIM	To sing a descending major triad, portamento, in mid-voice, on a specified vowel, with pitch accuracy, consistent resonance and consistent volume.
OBJECTIVES	▶ To develop management of pitch, vowel articulation and volume when singing connected intervals. Of importance is learning the aural and kinaesthetic skills necessary to make the distinction between major and minor thirds ▶ To enhance legato capability ▶ To build the aural and kinaesthetic memory necessary for this task.
PHYSICAL INVOLVEMENT	▶ Abdominal and thoracic muscle groups to achieve breath management ▶ Larynx height and posture ▶ Articulators, including pharynx, velum (soft palate), tongue, lips and jaw, for appropriate vowel formation and vocal resonance

INSTRUCTIONS	1 Play the target notes in sequence from the highest note 2 Mentally hear the continuous series of notes contained between the target pitches, and sung on the chosen vowel 3 Breathe the correct vowel shape	4 Position the larynx 5 Activate breath support 6 Start to sing 7 Maintain appropriate pressure for the descending pitch, while keeping the vowel shape 8 Ensure that breath pressure and vowel quality are maintained to the end of the exercise

PITCH DISPLAY	Sing each interval through the range of notes by directing the blue pitch line from the centre of the highest note to the centre of the middle note, and then to the centre of the lowest note, with minimal deviation. The optimal display is two connected, steadily descending diagonal lines. Check that each interval is accurate. [Sometimes there is a tendency to modify ascending intervals.]
SPECTROGRAM	The Spectrogram should exhibit the same pattern of resonances throughout the exercise.
LEVEL METER	The volume should remain consistent throughout the exercise. *Note: Where intervals traverse register changes, this is an especially useful skill to encourage.*

Exercise I-29: Descending major triad (V-III-I), legato

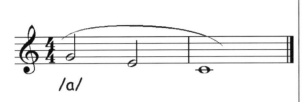

/a/

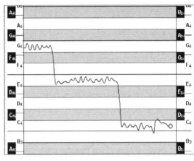

AIM	To sing a descending major triad, legato, in mid-voice, on a specified vowel, with pitch accuracy, consistent resonance and consistent volume.
OBJECTIVES	▶ To develop management of pitch, vowel articulation and volume when singing connected intervals. Of importance is learning the aural and kinaesthetic skills necessary to make the distinction between major and minor thirds. ▶ To enhance legato capability ▶ To build the aural and kinaesthetic memory necessary for this task.
PHYSICAL INVOLVEMENT	▶ Abdominal and thoracic muscle groups to achieve breath management ▶ Larynx height and posture ▶ Articulators, including pharynx, velum (soft palate), tongue, lips and jaw, for appropriate vowel formation
INSTRUCTIONS	1 Play the target notes in sequence from the highest note 2 Mentally hear these two intervals sung on the chosen vowel 3 Breathe the correct vowel shape 4 Position the larynx 5 Activate breath support 6 Start to sing 7 Maintain appropriate breath pressure for the descending pitch, while keeping connected tone and vowel shape
PITCH DISPLAY	Sing each interval by directing the blue pitch line from the centre of the highest note to the centre of the middle note, and then to the centre of the lowest note, with minimal deviation. Check that each interval is accurate.
SPECTROGRAM	The Spectrogram should exhibit the same pattern of resonances throughout the exercise.
LEVEL METER	The volume should remain consistent throughout the exercise. *Note: Where intervals traverse register changes, this is an especially useful skill to encourage.*

/a/

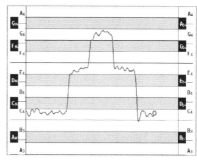

AIM	To sing an ascending and descending major triad, in mid-voice, on a specified vowel, with pitch accuracy.
OBJECTIVES	▶ To develop management of pitch when singing a sequence of intervals. Of importance is learning the aural and kinaesthetic skills necessary to make the distinction between major and minor thirds. ▶ To build the aural and kinaesthetic memory necessary for this task.
PHYSICAL INVOLVEMENT	▶ Abdominal and thoracic muscle groups to achieve breath management ▶ Larynx height and posture ▶ Articulators, including pharynx, velum (soft palate), tongue, lips and jaw, for appropriate vowel formation and vocal resonance

INSTRUCTIONS	1 Play the target notes in sequence from the lowest note 2 Mentally hear these two intervals, sung on the chosen vowel 3 Breathe the correct vowel shape 4 Position the larynx 5 Activate breath support 6 Start to sing	7 Increase breath pressure in order to increase pitch, while keeping the vowel shape 8 Maintain appropriate breath pressure for the descending pitch, while keeping the vowel shape 9 Ensure that breath pressure and vowel quality are maintained to the end of the exercise

PITCH DISPLAY	Sing each interval by directing the blue pitch line from the centre of the lowest note to the centre of the middle note, and then to the centre of the highest note, and then back again, with minimal deviation. Check that each interval is accurate. [Sometimes there is a tendency to modify rising intervals.]
SPECTROGRAM	
LEVEL METER	

Exercise I-31: Ascending and descending major triad, portamento, with consistent resonance and volume

/a/

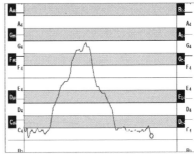

AIM	To sing an ascending and descending major triad, portamento, in mid-voice, on a specified vowel, with pitch accuracy, consistent resonance and consistent volume.
OBJECTIVES	▶ To develop management of pitch, vowel articulation and volume when singing connected intervals. Of importance is learning the aural and kinaesthetic skills necessary to make the distinction between major and minor thirds. ▶ To enhance legato capability ▶ To build the aural and kinaesthetic memory necessary for this task.
PHYSICAL INVOLVEMENT	▶ Abdominal and thoracic muscle groups to achieve breath management ▶ Larynx height and posture ▶ Articulators, including pharynx, velum (soft palate), tongue, lips and jaw, for appropriate vowel formation and vocal resonance
INSTRUCTIONS	1 Play the target notes in sequence from the lowest note 2 Mentally hear the continuous series of notes contained between the target pitches, and sung on the chosen vowel 3 Breathe the correct vowel shape 4 Position the larynx 5 Activate breath support	6 Start to sing 7 Gradually increase breath pressure in order to increase pitch, while maintaining the vowel shape 8 Maintain appropriate breath pressure as the pitch descends, while keeping the vowel shape 9 Ensure that breath pressure and vowel quality are maintained to the end of the exercise
PITCH DISPLAY	Sing each interval through the range of notes by directing the blue pitch line from the centre of the lowest note to the centre of the middle note, and then to the centre of the highest note, and back again, with minimal deviation. The optimal display is two connected, steadily ascending diagonal lines, then two connected, steadily descending lines. Check that each interval is accurate. [Sometimes there is a tendency to modify ascending intervals.]
SPECTROGRAM	The Spectrogram should exhibit the same pattern of resonances throughout the exercise.
LEVEL METER	The volume should remain consistent throughout the exercise. *Note: Where intervals traverse register changes, this is an especially useful skill to encourage.*

Exercise I-32: Ascending and descending major triad, legato

/a/

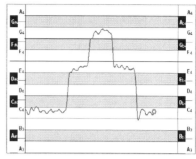

AIM	To sing an ascending and descending major triad, legato, in mid-voice, on a specified vowel, with pitch accuracy, consistent resonance and consistent volume.
OBJECTIVES	▶ To develop management of pitch, vowel articulation and volume when singing connected intervals. Of importance is learning the aural and kinaesthetic skills necessary to make the distinction between major and minor thirds. ▶ To enhance legato capability. ▶ To build the aural and kinaesthetic memory necessary for this task.
PHYSICAL INVOLVEMENT	▶ Abdominal and thoracic muscle groups to achieve breath management ▶ Larynx height and posture ▶ Articulators, including pharynx, velum (soft palate), tongue, lips and jaw, for appropriate vowel formation and vocal resonance
INSTRUCTIONS	1 Play the target notes in sequence from the lowest note 2 Mentally hear these two intervals sung on the chosen vowel 3 Breathe the correct vowel shape 4 Position the larynx 5 Activate breath support	6 Start to sing 7 Gradually increase breath pressure in order to increase pitch, while keeping connected tone and vowel shape 8 Maintain appropriate breath pressure as the pitch descends, while keeping connected tone and vowel shape
PITCH DISPLAY	Sing each interval by directing the blue pitch line from the centre of the lowest note to the centre of the middle note, and then to the centre of the highest note, and back again, with minimal deviation. Check that each interval is accurate. [Sometimes there is a tendency to modify ascending intervals.]
SPECTROGRAM	The Spectrogram should exhibit the same pattern of resonances throughout the exercise.
LEVEL METER	The volume should remain consistent throughout the exercise. *Note: Where intervals traverse register changes, this is an especially useful skill to encourage.*

Exercise I-33: Ascending minor triad

/a/

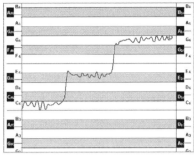

AIM	To sing an ascending minor triad, in mid-voice, on a specified vowel, with pitch accuracy.
OBJECTIVES	▶ To develop management of pitch when singing a sequence of intervals. Of importance is learning the aural and kinaesthetic skills necessary to make the distinction between major and minor thirds. ▶ To build the aural and kinaesthetic memory necessary for this task.
PHYSICAL INVOLVEMENT	▶ Abdominal and thoracic muscle groups to achieve breath management ▶ Larynx height and posture ▶ Articulators, including pharynx, velum (soft palate), tongue, lips and jaw, for appropriate vowel formation and vocal resonance

INSTRUCTIONS	1 Play the target notes in sequence from the lowest note 2 Mentally hear these two intervals, sung on the chosen vowel 3 Breathe the correct vowel shape 4 Position the larynx 5 Activate breath support	6 Start to sing 7 Increase breath pressure in order to increase pitch, while keeping the vowel shape 8 Ensure that breath pressure and vowel quality are maintained to the end of the exercise

PITCH DISPLAY	Sing each interval by directing the blue pitch line from the centre of the lowest note to the centre of the middle note, and then to the centre of the highest note, with minimal deviation. Check that each interval is accurate. [Sometimes there is a tendency to modify rising intervals.]
SPECTROGRAM	
LEVEL METER	

Sing&See

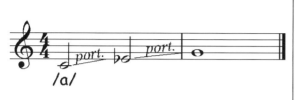

/a/

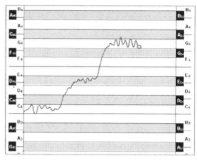

AIM 	To sing an ascending minor triad, portamento, in mid-voice, on a specified vowel, with pitch accuracy, consistent resonance and consistent volume.
OBJECTIVES 	▶ To develop management of pitch, vowel articulation and volume when singing connected intervals. Of importance is learning the aural and kinaesthetic skills necessary to make the distinction between major and minor thirds. ▶ To enhance legato capability. ▶ To build the aural and kinaesthetic memory necessary for this task.
PHYSICAL INVOLVEMENT 	▶ Abdominal and thoracic muscle groups to achieve breath management ▶ Larynx height and posture ▶ Articulators, including pharynx, velum (soft palate), tongue, lips and jaw, for appropriate vowel formation and vocal resonance
INSTRUCTIONS 	1 Play the target notes in sequence from the lowest note 2 Mentally hear the continuous series of notes contained between the target pitches, and sung on the chosen vowel 3 Breathe the correct vowel shape 4 Position the larynx 5 Activate breath support 6 Start to sing 7 Gradually increase breath pressure in order to increase pitch, while keeping the vowel shape 8 Ensure that breath pressure and vowel quality are maintained to the end of the exercise
PITCH DISPLAY 	Sing the intervals through the range of notes by directing the blue pitch line from the centre of the lowest note to the centre of the middle note, and then to the centre of the highest note, with minimal deviation. The optimal display is two connected, steadily ascending diagonal lines. Check that each interval is accurate. [Sometimes there is a tendency to modify ascending intervals.]
SPECTROGRAM 	The Spectrogram should exhibit the same pattern of resonances throughout the exercise.
LEVEL METER	The volume should remain consistent throughout the exercise. *Note: Where intervals traverse register changes, this is an especially useful skill to encourage.*

Exercise I-35: Ascending minor triad, legato

/a/

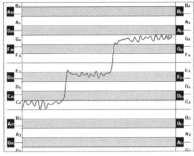

AIM	To sing an ascending minor triad, legato, in mid-voice, on a specified vowel, with pitch accuracy, consistent resonance and consistent volume.
OBJECTIVES	▶ To develop management of pitch, vowel articulation and volume when singing connected intervals. Of importance is learning the aural and kinaesthetic skills necessary to make the distinction between major and minor thirds. ▶ To enhance legato capability. ▶ To build the aural and kinaesthetic memory necessary for this task.
PHYSICAL INVOLVEMENT	▶ Abdominal and thoracic muscle groups to achieve breath management ▶ Larynx height and posture ▶ Articulators, including pharynx, velum (soft palate), tongue, lips and mandible, for appropriate vowel formation and vocal resonance
INSTRUCTIONS	1 Play the target notes in sequence from the lowest note 2 Mentally hear these two intervals sung on the chosen vowel 3 Breathe the correct vowel shape 4 Position the larynx 5 Activate breath support 6 Start to sing 7 Gradually increase breath pressure in order to increase pitch, while keeping connected tone and vowel shape
PITCH DISPLAY	Sing each interval by directing the blue pitch line from the centre of the lowest note to the centre of the middle note, and then to the centre of the highest note, with minimal deviation. Check that each interval is accurate. [Sometimes there is a tendency to modify ascending intervals.]
SPECTROGRAM	The Spectrogram should exhibit the same pattern of resonances throughout the exercise.
LEVEL METER	The volume should remain consistent throughout the exercise. *Note: Where intervals traverse register changes, this is an especially useful skill to encourage.*

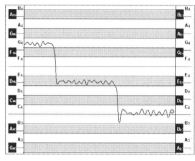

/a/

AIM	To sing a descending minor triad in mid-voice, on a specified vowel, with pitch accuracy.
OBJECTIVES	▶ To develop management of pitch when singing a sequence of intervals. Of importance is learning the aural and kinaesthetic skills necessary to make the distinction between major and minor thirds. ▶ To build the aural and kinaesthetic memory necessary for this task.
PHYSICAL INVOLVEMENT	▶ Abdominal and thoracic muscle groups to achieve breath management ▶ Larynx height and posture ▶ Articulators, including pharynx, velum (soft palate), tongue, lips and jaw, for appropriate vowel formation and vocal resonance

INSTRUCTIONS	1 Play the target notes in sequence from the highest note 2 Mentally hear these two intervals sung on the chosen vowel 3 Breathe the correct vowel shape 4 Position the larynx 5 Activate breath support	6 Start to sing 7 Maintain appropriate breath pressure as the pitch descends, while keeping the vowel shape 8 Ensure that breath pressure and vowel quality are maintained to the end of the exercise

PITCH DISPLAY	Sing each interval by directing the blue pitch line from the centre of the highest note to the centre of the middle note, and then to the centre of the lowest note, with minimal deviation. Check that each interval is accurate.
SPECTROGRAM	
LEVEL METER	

Exercise I-37: Descending minor triad, portamento, with consistent resonance and volume

I-37

/a/

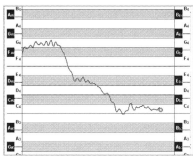

AIM	To sing a descending minor triad, portamento, in mid-voice, on a specified vowel, with pitch accuracy, consistent resonance and consistent volume.
OBJECTIVES	▶ To develop management of pitch, vowel articulation and volume when singing connected intervals. Of importance is learning the aural and kinaesthetic skills necessary to make the distinction between major and minor thirds ▶ To enhance legato capability. ▶ To build the aural and kinaesthetic memory necessary for this task.
PHYSICAL INVOLVEMENT	▶ Abdominal and thoracic muscle groups to achieve breath management ▶ Larynx height and posture ▶ Articulators, including pharynx, velum (soft palate), tongue, lips and jaw, for appropriate vowel formation and vocal resonance

INSTRUCTIONS	1 Play the target notes in sequence from the highest note 2 Mentally hear the continous series of notes contained between the target pitches, and sung on the chosen vowel 3 Breathe the correct vowel shape 4 Position the larynx	5 Activate breath support 6 Start to sing 7 Maintain appropriate breath pressure as the pitch descends, while keeping the vowel shape 8 Ensure that breath pressure and vowel quality are maintained to the end of the exercise

PITCH DISPLAY	Sing the intervals through the range of notes by directing the blue pitch line from the centre of the highest note to the centre of the middle note, and then to the centre of the lowest note, with minimal deviation. The optimal display is two connected, steadily descending diagonal lines. Check that each interval is accurate.
SPECTROGRAM	The Spectrogram should exhibit the same pattern of resonances throughout the exercise.
LEVEL METER	The volume should remain consistent throughout the exercise. *Note: Where intervals traverse register changes, this is an especially useful skill to encourage.*

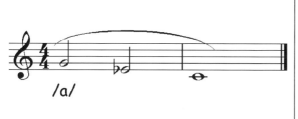

/a/

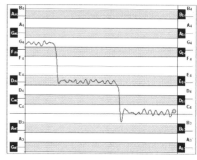

AIM	To sing a descending minor triad, legato, in mid-voice, on a specified vowel, with pitch accuracy, consistent resonance and consistent volume.
OBJECTIVES	▶ To develop management of pitch, vowel articulation and volume when singing connected intervals. Of importance is learning the aural and kinaesthetic skills necessary to make the distinction between major and minor thirds. ▶ To enhance legato capability. ▶ To build the aural and kinaesthetic memory necessary for this task.
PHYSICAL INVOLVEMENT	▶ Abdominal and thoracic muscle groups to achieve breath management ▶ Larynx height and posture ▶ Articulators, including pharynx, velum (soft palate), tongue, lips and jaw, for appropriate vowel formation and vocal resonance

INSTRUCTIONS	1 Play the target notes in sequence from the highest note	6 Start to sing	
	2 Mentally hear these two intervals sung on the chosen vowel	7 Maintain appropriate breath pressure as the pitch descends, while keeping connected tone and vowel shape	
	3 Breathe the correct vowel shape		
	4 Position the larynx		
	5 Activate breath support		

PITCH DISPLAY	Sing the intervals through the range of notes by directing the blue pitch line from the centre of the highest note to the centre of the middle note, and then to the centre of the lowest note, with minimal deviation. Check that each interval is accurate.
SPECTROGRAM	The Spectrogram should exhibit the same pattern of resonances throughout the exercise.
LEVEL METER	The volume should remain consistent throughout the exercise. *Note: Where intervals traverse register changes, this is an especially useful skill to encourage.*

/a/

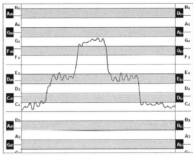

AIM	To sing an ascending and descending minor triad, in mid-voice, on a specified vowel, with pitch accuracy.
OBJECTIVES	▶ To develop management of pitch when singing a sequence of intervals. Of importance is learning the aural and kinaesthetic skills necessary to make the distinction between major and minor thirds. ▶ To build the aural and kinaesthetic memory necessary for this task.
PHYSICAL INVOLVEMENT	▶ Abdominal and thoracic muscle groups to achieve breath management ▶ Larynx height and posture ▶ Articulators, including pharynx, velum (soft palate), tongue, lips and jaw, for appropriate vowel formation and vocal resonance

INSTRUCTIONS			
	1	Play the target notes in sequence from the lowest note	7	Increase breath pressure in order to increase pitch, while keeping the vowel shape
	2	Mentally hear these two intervals sung on the chosen vowel	8	Maintain appropriate breath pressure as the pitch descends, while keeping the vowel shape
	3	Breathe the correct vowel shape		
	4	Position the larynx	9	Ensure that breath pressure and vowel quality are maintained to the end of the exercise
	5	Activate breath support		
	6	Start to sing		

PITCH DISPLAY	Sing each interval by directing the blue pitch line from the centre of the lowest note to the centre of the middle note, and then to the centre of the highest note, and then back again, with minimal deviation. Check that each interval is accurate. [Sometimes there is a tendency to modify rising intervals.]
SPECTROGRAM	
LEVEL METER	

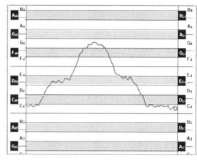

/a/

AIM	To sing an ascending and descending minor triad, portamento, in mid-voice, on a specified vowel, with pitch accuracy, consistent resonance and consistent volume.
OBJECTIVES	▶ To develop management of pitch, vowel articulation and volume when singing connected intervals. Of importance is learning the aural and kinaesthetic skills necessary to make the distinction between major and minor thirds. ▶ To enhance legato capability. ▶ To build the aural and kinaesthetic memory necessary for this task.
PHYSICAL INVOLVEMENT	▶ Abdominal and thoracic muscle groups to achieve breath management ▶ Larynx height and posture ▶ Articulators, including pharynx, velum (soft palate), tongue, lips and jaw, for appropriate vowel formation and vocal resonance
INSTRUCTIONS	1 Play the target notes in sequence from the lowest note 2 Mentally hear the continuous series of notes contained between the target pitches, and sung on the chosen vowel 3 Breathe the correct vowel shape 4 Position the larynx 5 Activate breath support 6 Start to sing 7 Gradually increase breath pressure in order to increase pitch, while keeping the vowel shape 8 Maintain appropriate breath pressure as the pitch descends, while keeping the vowel shape 9 Ensure that breath pressure and vowel quality are maintained to the end of the exercise
PITCH DISPLAY	Sing each interval through the range of notes by directing the blue pitch line from the centre of the lowest note to the centre of the middle note, and then to the centre of the highest note, and back again, with minimal deviation. The optimal display is two connected, steadily ascending diagonal lines, then two connected, steadily descending lines. Check that each interval is accurate. [Sometimes there is a tendency to modify ascending intervals.]
SPECTROGRAM	The Spectrogram should exhibit the same pattern of resonances throughout the exercise.
LEVEL METER	The volume should remain consistent throughout the exercise. *Note: Where intervals traverse register changes, this is an especially useful skill to encourage.*

Exercise I-41: Ascending and descending minor triad, legato

/a/

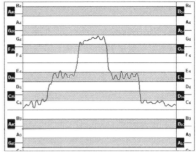

AIM	To sing an ascending and descending minor triad, legato, in mid-voice, on a specified vowel, with pitch accuracy, consistent resonance and consistent volume.
OBJECTIVES	▶ To develop management of pitch, vowel articulation and volume when singing connected intervals. Of importance is learning the aural and kinaesthetic skills necessary to make the distinction between major and minor thirds. ▶ To enhance legato capability. ▶ To build the aural and kinaesthetic memory necessary for this task.
PHYSICAL INVOLVEMENT	▶ Abdominal and thoracic muscle groups to achieve breath management ▶ Larynx height and posture ▶ Articulators, including pharynx, velum (soft palate), tongue, lips and jaw, for appropriate vowel formation and vocal resonance
INSTRUCTIONS	1 Play the target notes in sequence from the lowest note 2 Mentally hear these two intervals sung on the chosen vowel 3 Breathe the correct vowel shape 4 Position the larynx 5 Activate breath support 6 Start to sing 7 Gradually increase breath pressure in order to increase pitch, while keeping connected tone and vowel shape 8 Maintain appropriate breath pressure for the descending pitch, while keeping connected tone and vowel shape
PITCH DISPLAY	Sing each interval by directing the blue pitch line from the centre of the lowest note to the centre of the middle note, and then to the centre of the highest note, and back again, with minimal deviation. Check that each interval is accurate. [Sometimes there is a tendency to modify ascending intervals.]
SPECTROGRAM	The Spectrogram should exhibit the same pattern of resonances throughout the exercise.
LEVEL METER	The volume should remain consistent throughout the exercise. *Note: Where intervals traverse register changes, this is an especially useful skill to encourage.*

Exercise I-42: Ascending octave

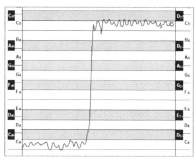

AIM	To sing an ascending octave, in mid-voice, on a specified vowel, with pitch accuracy.
OBJECTIVES	▶ To develop pitch management when singing octaves. ▶ To build recognition of the unique acoustic quality of the octave: the higher note is double the frequency of the lower. ▶ To build the aural and kinaesthetic memory necessary for this task.
PHYSICAL INVOLVEMENT	▶ Abdominal and thoracic muscle groups to achieve breath management ▶ Larynx height and posture ▶ Articulators, including pharynx, velum (soft palate), tongue, lips and jaw, for appropriate vowel formation and vocal resonance
INSTRUCTIONS	1 Play the target notes 2 Mentally hear this interval sung on the chosen vowel 3 Breathe the correct vowel shape 4 Position the larynx 5 Activate breath support 6 Start to sing 7 Increase breath pressure in order to increase pitch, while keeping the vowel shape
PITCH DISPLAY	Sing the octave interval by directing the blue pitch line from the centre of the lower note to the centre of the higher note, with minimal deviation.
SPECTROGRAM	
LEVEL METER	

Exercise I-43: Ascending octave, portamento, with consistent resonance and volume

I-43

/a/

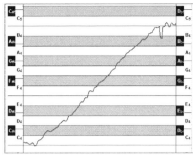

AIM	To sing an ascending octave, portamento, in mid-voice, on a specified vowel, with pitch accuracy, consistent resonance and consistent volume.
OBJECTIVES	▶ To develop management of pitch, vowel articulation and volume when singing octaves ▶ To build recognition of the unique acoustic quality of the octave: the higher note is double the frequency of the lower. ▶ To enhance legato capability. ▶ To build the aural and kinaesthetic memory necessary for this task.
PHYSICAL INVOLVEMENT	▶ Abdominal and thoracic muscle groups to achieve breath management ▶ Larynx height and posture ▶ Articulators, including pharynx, velum (soft palate), tongue, lips and jaw, for appropriate vowel formation and vocal resonance
INSTRUCTIONS	1 Play the target notes 2 Mentally hear the continuous series of notes contained between the target pitches, and sung on the chosen vowel 3 Breathe the correct vowel shape 4 Position the larynx	5 Activate breath support 6 Start to sing 7 Gradually increase breath pressure in order to increase pitch, while keeping the vowel shape

PITCH DISPLAY	Sing the octave interval through the range of notes from the centre of the lower note to the centre of the higher note, with minimal deviation. The optimal display is a steadily ascending diagonal line.
SPECTROGRAM	The Spectrogram should exhibit the same pattern of resonances throughout the exercise.
LEVEL METER	The volume should remain consistent throughout the exercise. *Note: Where intervals traverse register changes, this is an especially useful skill to encourage.*

Exercise I-44: Ascending octave, legato

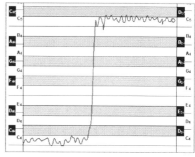

AIM	To sing an ascending octave, legato, in mid-voice, on a specified vowel, with pitch accuracy, consistent resonance and consistent volume.
OBJECTIVES	▶ To develop management of pitch, vowel articulation and volume when singing octaves. ▶ To build recognition of the unique acoustic quality of the octave: the higher note is double the frequency of the lower. ▶ To enhance legato capability. ▶ To build the aural and kinaesthetic memory necessary for this task.
PHYSICAL INVOLVEMENT	▶ Abdominal and thoracic muscle groups to achieve breath management ▶ Larynx height and posture ▶ Articulators, including pharynx, velum (soft palate), tongue, lips and jaw, for appropriate vowel formation and vocal resonance
INSTRUCTIONS	1 Play the target notes 2 Mentally hear this interval sung on the chosen vowel 3 Breathe the correct vowel shape 4 Position the larynx 5 Activate breath support 6 Start to sing	7 Gradually increase breath pressure in order to increase pitch, while keeping connected tone and vowel shape
PITCH DISPLAY	Sing the octave interval by directing the blue pitch line from the centre of the lower note to the centre of the higher note, with minimal deviation.
SPECTROGRAM	The Spectrogram should exhibit the same pattern of resonances throughout the exercise.
LEVEL METER	The volume should remain consistent throughout the exercise. *Note: Where intervals traverse register changes, this is an especially useful skill to encourage.*

/a/

Exercise I-45: Descending octave

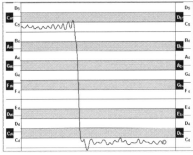

/a/

AIM	To sing a descending octave, in mid-voice, on a specified vowel, and with pitch accuracy.
OBJECTIVES	▶ To develop pitch management when singing octaves. ▶ To build recognition of the unique acoustic quality of the octave: the higher note is double the frequency of the lower. ▶ To build the aural and kinaesthetic memory necessary for this task.
PHYSICAL INVOLVEMENT	▶ Abdominal and thoracic muscle groups to achieve breath management ▶ Larynx height and posture ▶ Articulators, including pharynx, velum (soft palate), tongue, lips and jaw, for appropriate vowel formation and vocal resonance
INSTRUCTIONS	1 Play the target notes 2 Mentally hear this interval sung on the chosen vowel 3 Breathe the correct vowel shape 4 Position the larynx 5 Activate breath support 6 Start to sing || 7 Maintain appropriate breath pressure for the descending pitch, while keeping the vowel shape
PITCH DISPLAY	Sing the octave interval by directing the blue pitch line from the centre of the higher note to the centre of the lower note, with minimal deviation.
SPECTROGRAM	
LEVEL METER	

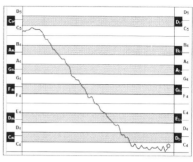

AIM	To sing a descending octave, portamento, in mid-voice, on a specified vowel, with pitch accuracy, consistent resonance and consistent volume.
OBJECTIVES	▶ To develop management of pitch, vowel articulation and volume when singing octaves. ▶ To build recognition of the unique acoustic quality of the octave: the higher note is double the frequency of the lower. ▶ To enhance legato capability. ▶ To build the aural and kinaesthetic memory necessary for this task.
PHYSICAL INVOLVEMENT	▶ Abdominal and thoracic muscle groups to achieve breath management ▶ Larynx height and posture ▶ Articulators, including pharynx, velum (soft palate), tongue, lips and jaw, for appropriate vowel formation and vocal resonance
INSTRUCTIONS	1 Play the target notes 2 Mentally hear the continuous series of notes contained between the target pitches, and sung on the chosen vowel 3 Breathe the correct vowel shape 4 Position the larynx 5 Activate breath support	6 Start to sing 7 Maintain appropriate breath pressure for the descending pitch, while keeping the vowel shape 8 Ensure that breath pressure and vowel quality are maintained to the end of the exercise.
PITCH DISPLAY	Sing the octave interval through the range of notes from the centre of the higher note to the centre of the lower note, with minimal deviation. The optimal display is a steadily descending diagonal line.
SPECTROGRAM	The Spectrogram should exhibit the same pattern of resonances throughout the exercise.
LEVEL METER	The volume should remain consistent throughout the exercise. *Note: Where intervals traverse register changes, this is an especially useful skill to encourage.*

Exercise I-47: Descending octave, legato

/a/

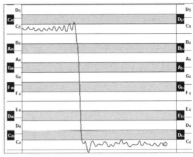

AIM	To sing a descending octave, legato, in mid-voice, on a specified vowel, with pitch accuracy, consistent resonance and consistent volume.
OBJECTIVES	▶ To develop management of pitch, vowel articulation and volume when singing octaves. ▶ To build recognition of the unique acoustic quality of the octave: the higher note is double the frequency of the lower. ▶ To enhance legato capability. ▶ To build the aural and kinaesthetic memory necessary for this task.
PHYSICAL INVOLVEMENT	▶ Abdominal and thoracic muscle groups to achieve breath management ▶ Larynx height and posture ▶ Articulators, including pharynx, velum (soft palate), tongue, lips and jaw, for appropriate vowel formation and vocal resonance
INSTRUCTIONS	1 Play the target notes 2 Mentally hear the interval sung on the chosen vowel 3 Breathe the correct vowel shape 4 Position the larynx 5 Activate breath support 6 Start to sing	7 Maintain appropriate breath pressure for the descending pitch, while keeping connected tone, and vowel shape 8 Ensure that breath pressure and vowel quality are maintained to the end of the exercise

PITCH DISPLAY	Ssing the octave interval by directing the blue pitch line from the centre of the higher note to the centre of the lower note, with minimal deviation.
SPECTROGRAM	The Spectrogram should exhibit the same pattern of resonances throughout the exercise. *Note: This is an essential skill for classical singing styles; for other styles, variations in resonance may be desirable.*
LEVEL METER	The volume should remain consistent throughout the exercise. *Note: Where intervals traverse register changes, this is an especially useful skill to encourage.*

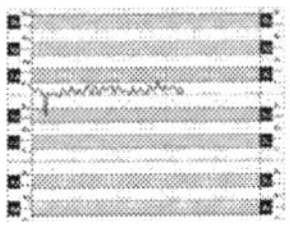

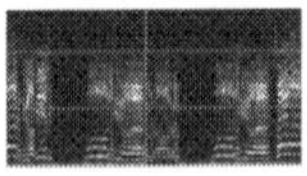

/a/

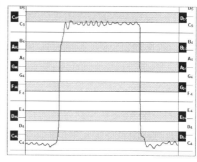

AIM	To sing an ascending and descending octave, in mid-voice, on a specified vowel, with pitch accuracy.
OBJECTIVES	▶ To develop management of pitch when singing octaves. ▶ To build recognition of the unique acoustic quality of the octave: the higher note is double the frequency of the lower. ▶ To build the aural and kinaesthetic memory necessary for this task.
PHYSICAL INVOLVEMENT	▶ Abdominal and thoracic muscle groups to achieve breath management ▶ Larynx height and posture ▶ Articulators, including pharynx, velum (soft palate), tongue, lips and jaw, for appropriate vowel formation and vocal resonance
INSTRUCTIONS	1 Play the target notes in sequence from the lowest note 2 Mentally hear the sequence of intervals sung on the chosen vowel 3 Breathe the correct vowel shape 4 Position the larynx 5 Activate breath support 6 Start to sing 7 Increase breath pressure in order to increase pitch, while maintaining the vowel shape 8 Maintain appropriate breath pressure for the descending pitch, while keeping the vowel shape 9 Ensure that breath pressure and vowel quality are maintained to the end of the exercise
PITCH DISPLAY	Sing each interval by directing the blue pitch line from the centre of the lowest note to the centre of the highest note, and then back again, with minimal deviation. Check that each interval is accurate. [Sometimes there is a tendency to modify rising intervals.]
SPECTROGRAM	
LEVEL METER	

Exercise I-49: Ascending and descending octave, portamento, with consistent resonance and volume

I-49

/a/

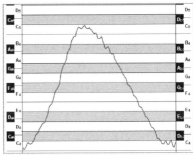

AIM	To sing an ascending and descending octave, portamento, in mid-voice, on a specified vowel, with pitch accuracy, consistent resonance and consistent volume.
OBJECTIVES	▶ To develop management of pitch, vowel articulation and volume when singing a sequence of intervals. ▶ To build recognition of the unique acoustic quality of the octave: the higher note is double the frequency of the lower. ▶ To enhance legato capability. ▶ To build the aural and kinaesthetic memory necessary for this task.
PHYSICAL INVOLVEMENT	▶ Abdominal and thoracic muscle groups to achieve breath management ▶ Larynx height and posture ▶ Articulators, including pharynx, velum (soft palate), tongue, lips and jaw, for appropriate vowel formation and vocal resonance
INSTRUCTIONS	1 Play the target notes in sequence from the lowest note 2 Mentally hear the continuous series of notes contained between the target pitches, and sung on the chosen vowel 3 Breathe the correct vowel shape 4 Position the larynx 5 Activate breath support 6 Start to sing 7 Gradually increase breath pressure in order to increase pitch, while maintaining the vowel shape 8 Maintain appropriate breath pressure for the descending pitch, while keeping the vowel shape 9 Ensure that breath pressure and vowel quality are maintained to the end of the exercise
PITCH DISPLAY	Sing each interval through the range of notes by directing the blue pitch line from the centre of the lowest note to the centre of the highest note, and back again, with minimal deviation.. The optimal display is a smoothly ascending diagonal line connected to a smoothly descending diagonal line of equal length and angle. Check that each interval is accurate. [Sometimes there is a tendency to modify ascending intervals.]
SPECTROGRAM	The Spectrogram should exhibit the same pattern of resonances throughout the exercise.
LEVEL METER	The volume should remain consistent throughout the exercise. *Note: Where intervals traverse register changes, this is an especially useful skill to encourage.*

Exercise I-50: Ascending and descending octave, legato

/a/

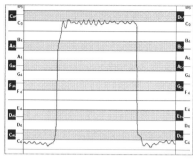

AIM	To sing an ascending and descending octave, legato, in mid-voice, on a specified vowel, with pitch accuracy, consistent resonance and consistent volume.
OBJECTIVES	▶ To develop management of pitch, vowel articulation and volume when singing a sequence of intervals. ▶ To build recognition of the unique acoustic quality of the octave: the higher note is double the frequency of the lower. ▶ To enhance legato capability. ▶ To build the aural and kinaesthetic memory necessary for this task.
PHYSICAL INVOLVEMENT	▶ Abdominal and thoracic muscle groups to achieve breath management ▶ Larynx height and posture ▶ Articulators, including pharynx, velum (soft palate), tongue, lips and jaw, for appropriate vowel formation and vocal resonance
INSTRUCTIONS	1 Play the target notes in sequence from the lower note 2 Mentally hear the sequence of intervals sung on the chosen vowel 3 Breathe the correct vowel shape 4 Position the larynx 5 Activate breath support 6 Start to sing 7 Gradually increase breath pressure in order to increase pitch, while maintaining the vowel shape 8 Maintain appropriate breath pressure for the descending pitch, while keeping connected tone and vowel shape
PITCH DISPLAY	Sing each interval by directing the blue pitch line from the centre of the lowest note to the centre of the highest note, and back again, with minimal deviation. Check that each interval is accurate. [Sometimes there is a tendency to modify ascending intervals.]
SPECTROGRAM 	The Spectrogram should exhibit the same pattern of resonances throughout the exercise.
LEVEL METER	The volume should remain consistent throughout the exercise. *Note: Where intervals traverse register changes, this is an especially useful skill to encourage.*

Exercise I-51: Arpeggio- I-III-V-VIII sequence

/a/

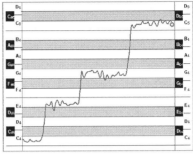

AIM	To sing an ascending arpeggio over an octave, on a specified vowel, with pitch accuracy.
OBJECTIVES 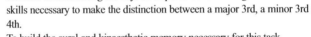	▶ To develop management of pitch when singing arpeggios. This sequence of intervals represents a spread chord in root position. If the root is regarded as the tonic, then the ability to sing this sequence of intervals accurately is essential in establishing the key. Of importance is learning the aural and kinaesthetic skills necessary to make the distinction between a major 3rd, a minor 3rd and a perfect 4th. ▶ To build the aural and kinaesthetic memory necessary for this task.
PHYSICAL INVOLVEMENT	▶ Abdominal and thoracic muscle groups to achieve breath management ▶ Larynx height and posture ▶ Articulators, including pharynx, velum (soft palate), tongue, lips and jaw, for appropriate vowel formation and vocal resonance

INSTRUCTIONS	1 Play the arpeggio 2 Mentally hear these three intervals in sequence sung on the chosen vowel 3 Breathe the correct vowel shape 4 Position the larynx 5 Activate breath support 6 Start to sing	7 Increase breath pressure in order to increase pitch, while keeping the vowel shape

PITCH DISPLAY	Sing each interval by directing the blue pitch line from the centre of the lowest note to the centre of each following note, with minimal deviation. Check that each interval is accurate. [Sometimes there is a tendency to modify rising intervals.]
SPECTROGRAM	
LEVEL METER	

/a/

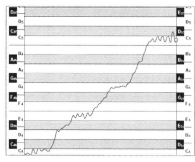

AIM	To sing a I-III-V-VIII sequence, portamento, on a specified vowel, with pitch accuracy, consistent resonance and consistent volume.
OBJECTIVES	▶ To develop management of pitch, vowel articulation and volume, when singing arpeggios. This sequence of intervals represents a spread chord in root position. If the root is regarded as the tonic, then the ability to sing this sequence of intervals accurately is essential in establishing the key. Of importance is learning the aural and kinaesthetic skills necessary to make the distinction between a major 3rd, a minor 3rd and a perfect 4th. ▶ To enhance legato capability. ▶ To build the aural and kinaesthetic memory necessary for this task.
PHYSICAL INVOLVEMENT	▶ Abdominal and thoracic muscle groups to achieve breath management ▶ Larynx height and posture ▶ Articulators, including pharynx, velum (soft palate), tongue, lips and jaw, for appropriate vowel formation and vocal resonance
INSTRUCTIONS	1 Play the arpeggio 2 Mentally hear the continuous series of notes contained between the target pitches, and sung on the chosen vowel 3 Breathe the correct vowel shape 4 Position the larynx	5 Activate breath support 6 Start to sing 7 Gradually increase breath pressure in order to increase pitch, while keeping connected tone and vowel shape
PITCH DISPLAY	Sing the arpeggio through the range of notes by directing the blue pitch line from the centre of the lowest note to the centre of each following note, with minimal deviation. The optimal display is three connected, steadily ascending diagonal lines. Check that each interval is accurate. [Sometimes there is a tendency to modify ascending intervals.]
SPECTROGRAM	The Spectrogram should exhibit the same pattern of resonances throughout the exercise.
LEVEL METER	The volume should remain consistent throughout the exercise. *Note: Where intervals traverse register changes, this is an especially useful skill to encourage.*

Exercise I-53: Arpeggio - I-III-V-VIII sequence, legato

/a/

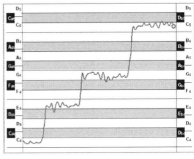

Section	Content
AIM	To sing an ascending arpeggio over an octave, legato, on a specified vowel, with pitch accuracy, consistent resonance and consistent volume.
OBJECTIVES	▶ To develop management of pitch, vowel articulation and volume when singing arpeggios. This sequence of intervals represents a spread chord in root position. If the root is regarded as the tonic, then the ability to sing this sequence of intervals accurately is essential in establishing the key. Of importance is learning the aural and kinaesthetic skills necessary to make the distinction between a major 3rd, a minor 3rd and a perfect 4th. ▶ To enhance legato capability. ▶ To build the aural and kinaesthetic memory necessary for this task.
PHYSICAL INVOLVEMENT	▶ Abdominal and thoracic muscle groups to achieve breath management ▶ Larynx height and posture ▶ Articulators, including pharynx, velum (soft palate), tongue, lips and jaw, for appropriate vowel formation and vocal resonance
INSTRUCTIONS	1 Play the arpeggio 2 Mentally hear these three intervals in sequence sung on the chosen vowel 3 Breathe the correct vowel shape 4 Position the larynx 5 Activate breath support 6 Start to sing 7 Gradually increase breath pressure in order to increase pitch, while keeping connected tone and vowel shape
PITCH DISPLAY	Sing each interval by directing the blue pitch line from the centre of the lowest note to the centre of each following note, with minimal deviation. Check that each interval is accurate. [Sometimes there is a tendency to modify ascending intervals.]
SPECTROGRAM	The Spectrogram should exhibit the same pattern of resonances throughout the exercise.
LEVEL METER	The volume should remain consistent throughout the exercise. *Note: Where intervals traverse register changes, this is an especially useful skill to encourage.*

Exercise I-54: Arpeggio - VIII-V-III-I sequence

/a/

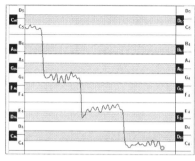

AIM	To sing a descending arpeggio over an octave, on a specified vowel, with pitch accuracy.
OBJECTIVES	▶ To develop management of pitch when singing arpeggios. This sequence of intervals represents a spread chord in root position. If the root is regarded as the tonic, then the ability to sing this sequence of intervals accurately is essential in establishing the key. Of importance is learning the aural and kinaesthetic skills necessary to make the distinction between a perfect 4th, a minor 3rd and a major 3rd. ▶ To build the aural and kinaesthetic memory necessary for this task.
PHYSICAL INVOLVEMENT	▶ Abdominal and thoracic muscle groups to achieve breath management ▶ Larynx height and posture ▶ Articulators, including pharynx, velum (soft palate), tongue, lips and jaw, for appropriate vowel formation and vocal resonance

INSTRUCTIONS	1 Play the arpeggio 2 Mentally hear these three intervals in sequence sung on the chosen vowel 3 Breathe the correct vowel shape 4 Position the larynx 5 Activate breath support 6 Start to sing	7 Maintain appropriate breath pressure for the descending pitch, while keeping the vowel shape

PITCH DISPLAY	Sing each interval by directing the blue pitch line from the centre of the highest note to the centre of each following note, with minimal deviation. Check that each interval is accurate.
SPECTROGRAM	
LEVEL METER	

Exercise I-55: Arpeggio - VIII-V-III-I sequence, portamento, with consistent resonance and volume

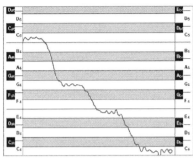

AIM	To sing an VIII-V-III-I sequence, portamento, on a specified vowel, with pitch accuracy, consistent resonance and consistent volume.
OBJECTIVES	▶ To develop management of pitch, vowel articulation and volume, when singing arpeggios. This sequence of intervals represents a spread chord in root position. If the root is regarded as the tonic, then the ability to sing this sequence of intervals accurately is essential in establishing the key. Of importance is learning the aural and kinaesthetic skills necessary to make the distinction between a perfect 4th, a minor 3rd and a major 3rd. ▶ To enhance legato capability. ▶ To build the aural and kinaesthetic memory necessary for this task.
PHYSICAL INVOLVEMENT	▶ Abdominal and thoracic muscle groups to achieve breath management ▶ Larynx height and posture ▶ Articulators, including pharynx, velum (soft palate), tongue, lips and jaw, for appropriate vowel formation and vocal resonance
INSTRUCTIONS	1 Play the arpeggio 2 Mentally hear the continuous series of notes contained between the target pitches, and sung on the chosen vowel 3 Breathe the correct vowel shape 4 Position the larynx	5 Activate breath support 6 Start to sing 7 Maintain appropriate breath pressure for the descending pitch, while keeping connected tone and vowel shape
PITCH DISPLAY	Sing the arpeggio through the range of notes by directing the blue pitch line from the centre of the highest note to the centre of each following note, with minimal deviation. The optimal display is three connected, steadily descending diagonal lines. Check that each interval is accurate.
SPECTROGRAM	The Spectrogram should exhibit the same pattern of resonances throughout the exercise.
LEVEL METER	The volume should remain consistent throughout the exercise. *Note: Where intervals traverse register changes, this is an especially useful skill to encourage.*

/a/

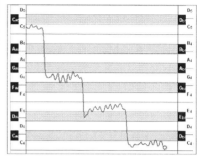

AIM	To sing a descending arpeggio over an octave, legato, on a specified vowel, with pitch accuracy, consistent resonance and consistent volume.
OBJECTIVES	▶ To develop management of pitch, vowel articulation and volume when singing arpeggios. ▶ This sequence of intervals represents a spread chord in root position. If the root is regarded as the tonic, then the ability to sing this sequence of intervals accurately is essential in establishing the key. Of importance is learning the aural and kinaesthetic skills necessary to make the distinction between a perfect 4th, a minor 3rd and a major 3rd. ▶ To enhance legato capability. ▶ To build the aural and kinaesthetic memory necessary for this task.
PHYSICAL INVOLVEMENT	▶ Abdominal and thoracic muscle groups to achieve breath management ▶ Larynx height and posture ▶ Articulators, including pharynx, velum (soft palate), tongue, lips and jaw, for appropriate vowel formation and vocal resonance
INSTRUCTIONS	1 Play the arpeggio 2 Mentally hear these three intervals in sequence sung on the chosen vowel 3 Breathe the correct vowel shape 4 Position the larynx 5 Activate breath support 6 Start to sing 7 Maintain appropriate breath pressure for the descending pitch while keeping connected tone and vowel shape
PITCH DISPLAY	Sing each interval by directing the blue pitch line from the centre of the highest note to the centre of each following note, with minimal deviation. Check that each interval is accurate.
SPECTROGRAM	The Spectrogram should exhibit the same pattern of resonances throughout the exercise.
LEVEL METER	The volume should remain consistent throughout the exercise. *Note: Where intervals traverse register changes, this is an especially useful skill to encourage.*

Exercise I-57: Arpeggio - I-III-V-VIII-V-III-I sequence

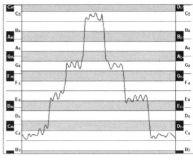

AIM	To sing an ascending and descending arpeggio over an octave, on a specified vowel, with pitch accuracy.
OBJECTIVES	▶ To develop management of pitch when singing arpeggios. This sequence of intervals represents a spread chord in root position. If the root is regarded as the tonic, then the ability to sing this sequence of intervals accurately is essential in establishing the key. Of importance is learning the aural and kinaesthetic skills necessary to make the distinction between three different intervals. ▶ To build the aural and kinaesthetic memory necessary for this task.
PHYSICAL INVOLVEMENT	▶ Abdominal and thoracic muscle groups to achieve breath management ▶ Larynx height and posture ▶ Articulators, including pharynx, velum (soft palate), tongue, lips and jaw, for appropriate vowel formation and vocal resonance
INSTRUCTIONS	1 Play the arpeggio 2 Mentally hear the arpeggio sung on the chosen vowel 3 Breathe the correct vowel shape 4 Position the larynx 5 Activate breath support 6 Start to sing	7 Increase breath pressure in order to increase pitch, while keeping the vowel shape 8 Maintain appropriate breath pressure for the descending pitch, while keeping the vowel shape
PITCH DISPLAY	Sing each interval by directing the blue pitch line from the centre of the lowest note to the centre of the three subsequent notes, and then back again, with minimal deviation. Check that each interval is accurate. [Sometimes there is a tendency to modify rising intervals.]
SPECTROGRAM	
LEVEL METER	

Exercise I-58: Arpeggio - I-III-V-VIII-V-III-I sequence, portamento, with consistent resonance and volume

I-58

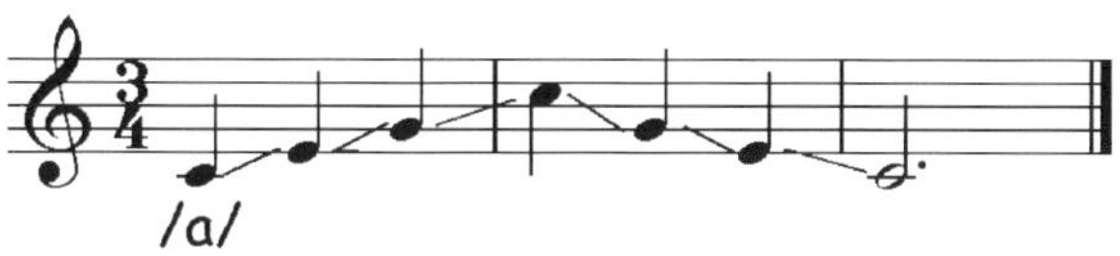

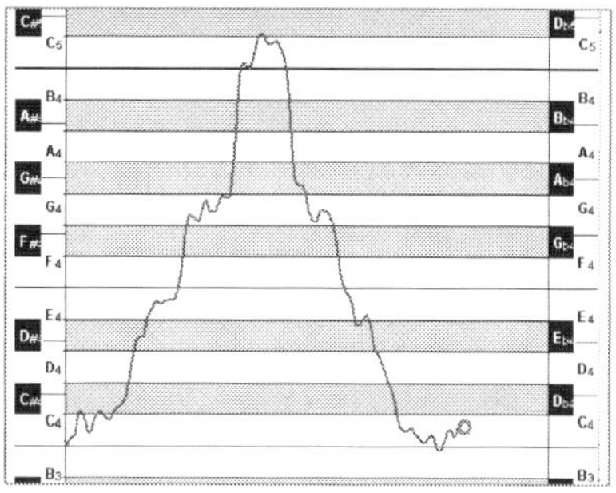

AIM

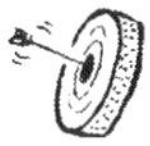

To sing an ascending and descending arpeggio over an octave, portamento, on a specified vowel, with pitch accuracy, consistent resonance and consistent volume.

OBJECTIVES

- To develop management of pitch, vowel articulation and volume, when singing arpeggios. This sequence of intervals represents a spread chord in root position. If the root is regarded as the tonic, then the ability to sing this sequence of intervals accurately is essential in establishing the key.
  Of importance is learning the aural and kinaesthetic skills necessary to make the distinction between thre different intervals.
- To enhance legato capability.
- To build the aural and kinaesthetic memory necessary for this task.

PHYSICAL INVOLVEMENT

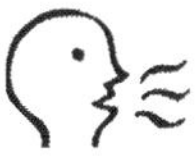

- Abdominal and thoracic muscle groups to achieve breath management
- Larynx height and posture
- Articulators, including pharynx, velum (soft palate), tongue, lips and jaw, for appropriate vowel formation and vocal resonance

INSTRUCTIONS

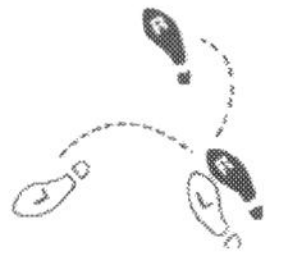

1. Play the arpeggio
2. Mentally hear the continuous series of notes contained between the target pitches, and sung on the chosen vowel
3. Breathe the correct vowel shape
4. Position the larynx
5. Activate breath support
6. Start to sing
7. Gradually increase breath pressure in order to increase pitch, while keeping connected tone and vowel shape
8. Maintain appropriate breath pressure for the descending pitch, while keeping connected tone and vowel shape

PITCH DISPLAY

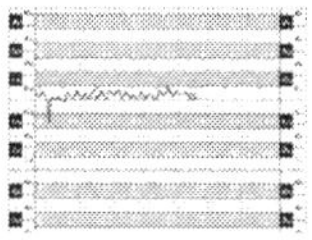

Sing the arpeggio through the range of notes by directing the blue pitch line from the centre of the lowest note to the centre of the three subsequent notes, and then back again, with minimal deviation. The optimal display is three connected, steadily ascending diagonal lines, then three connected, steadily descending diagonal lines. Check that each interval is accurate. [Sometimes there is a tendency to modify ascending intervals.]

SPECTROGRAM

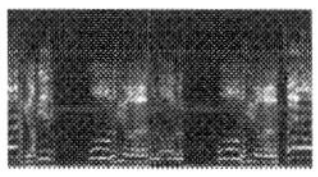

The Spectrogram should exhibit the same pattern of resonances throughout the exercise.

LEVEL METER

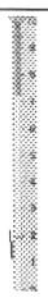

The volume should remain consistent throughout the exercise.
Note: Where intervals traverse register changes, this is an especially useful skill to encourage.

Exercise I-59: Arpeggio - I-III-V-VIII-V-III-I sequence, staccato

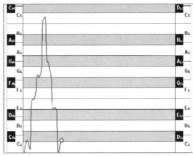

AIM	To sing an ascending and descending arpeggio over an octave, staccato, on a specified vowel, with pitch accuracy.
OBJECTIVES	▶ To develop management of pitch, vowel articulation and volume, when singing staccato arpeggios. This sequence of intervals represents a spread chord in root position. If the root is regarded as the tonic, then the ability to sing this sequence of intervals accurately is essential in establishing the key. Of importance is learning the aural and kinaesthetic skills necessary to make the distinction between three different intervals. ▶ To build the aural and kinaesthetic memory necessary for this task.
PHYSICAL INVOLVEMENT	▶ Abdominal and thoracic muscle groups to achieve breath management ▶ Larynx height and posture ▶ Articulators, including pharynx, velum (soft palate), tongue, lips and jaw, for appropriate vowel formation and vocal resonance
INSTRUCTIONS	1 Play the arpeggio 7 Increase breath pressure in order to increase pitch, while keeping the vowel shape 2 Mentally hear the arpeggio sung on the chosen vowel 3 Breathe the correct vowel shape 8 Maintain appropriate pressure for the descending pitch, while keeping the vowel shape 4 Position the larynx 5 Activate breath support 6 Start to sing
PITCH DISPLAY	Sing the arpeggio clearly and accurately by directing the blue pitch line from the centre of the first note to the centre of each following note, with minimal deviation. The optimal display will show minimal, clean horizontal lines in an upward, then equally downward, diagonal.
SPECTROGRAM	
LEVEL METER	

96   *Sing&See*

/a/

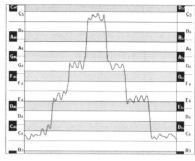

AIM	To sing an ascending and descending arpeggio over an octave, legato, on a specified vowel, with pitch accuracy, consistent resonance and consistent volume.
OBJECTIVES	▶ To develop management of pitch, vowel articulation and volume, when singing arpeggios. This sequence of intervals represents a spread chord in root position. If the root is regarded as the tonic, then the ability to sing this sequence of intervals accurately is essential in establishing the key. Of importance is learning the aural and kinaesthetic skills necessary to make the distinction between three different intervals. ▶ To enhance legato capability. ▶ To build the aural and kinaesthetic memory necessary for this task.
PHYSICAL INVOLVEMENT	▶ Abdominal and thoracic muscle groups to achieve breath management ▶ Larynx height and posture ▶ Articulators, including pharynx, velum (soft palate), tongue, lips and jaw, for appropriate vowel formation and vocal resonance
INSTRUCTIONS	1 Play the target notes 2 Mentally hear the arpeggio sung on the chosen vowel 3 Breathe the correct vowel shape 4 Position the larynx 5 Activate breath support 6 Start to sing 7 Gradually increase breath pressure in order to increase pitch, while keeping connected tone and vowel shape 8 Maintain appropriate breath pressure for the descending pitch, while keeping connected tone and vowel shape
PITCH DISPLAY	Sing the arpeggio by directing the blue pitch line from the centre of the lowest note to the centre of the three subsequent notes, and then back again, with minimal deviation. Check that each interval is accurate. [Sometimes there is a tendency to modify ascending intervals.]
SPECTROGRAM	The Spectrogram should exhibit the same pattern of resonances throughout the exercise.
LEVEL METER	The volume should remain consistent throughout the exercise. *Note: Where intervals traverse register changes, this is an especially useful skill to encourage.*

Exercise I-61: Arpeggio - I-III-V-VIII-V-III-I sequence, staccato and then legato

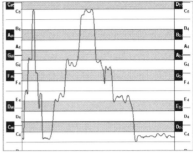

/a/

AIM	To sing an ascending and descending arpeggio over an octave, first staccato, and then legato, on a specified vowel, with pitch accuracy, consistent resonance and consistent volume.
OBJECTIVES 	▶ To develop management of pitch, vowel articulation and volume, when singing an ascending and descending arpeggio. This sequence of intervals represents a spread chord in root position. If the root is regarded as the tonic, then the ability to sing this sequence of intervals accurately is essential in establishing the key. Of importance is learning the aural and kinaesthetic skills necessary to make the distinction between three different intervals. ▶ To enhance legato capability. ▶ To build the aural and kinaesthetic memory necessary for this task.
PHYSICAL INVOLVEMENT	▶ Abdominal and thoracic muscle groups to achieve breath management ▶ Larynx height and posture ▶ Articulators, including pharynx, velum (soft palate), tongue, lips and jaw, for appropriate vowel formation and vocal resonance
INSTRUCTIONS	1 Play the arpeggio 2 Mentally hear the arpeggio sung on the chosen vowel 3 Breathe the correct vowel shape 4 Position the larynx 5 Activate breath support 6 Start to sing 7 Gradually increase breath pressure in order to increase pitch, while keeping the vowel shape 8 Maintain appropriate breath pressure for the descending pitch, while keeping the vowel shape.
PITCH DISPLAY	Sing the arpeggio by directing the blue pitch line from the centre of the first note to the centre of each following note, with minimal deviation. For both staccato and legato, the optimal display will show minimal, clean horizontal lines in an upward, then equally downward, diagonal.
SPECTROGRAM	The Spectrogram should exhibit the same pattern of resonances throughout the exercise.
LEVEL METER	The volume should remain consistent throughout the exercise. *Note: Where intervals traverse register changes, this is an especially useful skill to encourage.*

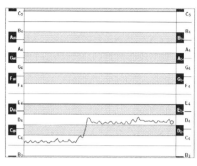

AIM	To sing an ascending major second, in mid-voice, on a specified vowel, with pitch accuracy.
OBJECTIVES	▶ To develop management of pitch when singing intervals. ▶ To build the aural and kinaesthetic memory necessary for this task.
PHYSICAL INVOLVEMENT	▶ Abdominal and thoracic muscle groups to achieve breath management ▶ Larynx height and posture ▶ Articulators, including pharynx, velum (soft palate), tongue, lips and jaw, for appropriate vowel formation and vocal resonance
INSTRUCTIONS	1 Play the target notes 2 Mentally hear this interval sung on the chosen vowel 3 Breathe the correct vowel shape 4 Position the larynx 5 Activate breath support 6 Start to sing 7 Increase breath pressure in order to increase pitch, while keeping the vowel shape
PITCH DISPLAY	Sing the interval by directing the blue pitch line from the centre of the lower note to the centre of the higher note, with minimal deviation.
SPECTROGRAM	
LEVEL METER	

Exercise I-63: Ascending major second, legato

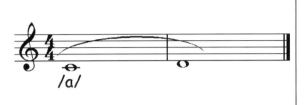

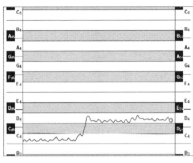

AIM	To sing a ascending major second, legato, in mid-voice, on a specified vowel and with pitch accuracy, consistent resonance and consistent volume.
OBJECTIVES	▶ To develop management of pitch, vowel articulation and volume when singing intervals. ▶ To build the aural and kinaesthetic memory necessary for this task.
PHYSICAL INVOLVEMENT	▶ Abdominal and thoracic muscle groups to achieve breath management ▶ Larynx height and posture ▶ Articulators, including pharynx, velum (soft palate), tongue, lips and jaw, for appropriate vowel formation and vocal resonance

INSTRUCTIONS	1 Play the target notes 2 Mentally hear this interval sung on the chosen vowel 3 Breathe the correct vowel shape 4 Position the larynx 5 Activate breath support 6 Start to sing	7 Gradually increase breath pressure in order to increase pitch while keeping connected tone and vowel shape

PITCH DISPLAY	Sing the interval by directing the blue pitch line from the centre of the lower note to the centre of the higher note, with minimal deviation.
SPECTROGRAM	The Spectrogram should exhibit the same pattern of resonances throughout the exercise. *Note: This is an essential skill for classical singing styles; for other styles, variations in resonance may be desirable.*
LEVEL METER	The volume should remain consistent throughout the exercise. *Note: Where intervals traverse register changes, this is an especially useful skill to encourage.*

/a/

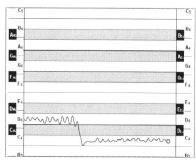

AIM	To sing a descending major second in mid-voice, on a specified vowel, with pitch accuracy.
OBJECTIVES	▶ To develop management of pitch when singing intervals. ▶ To build the aural and kinaesthetic memory necessary for this task.
PHYSICAL INVOLVEMENT	▶ Abdominal and thoracic muscle groups to achieve breath management ▶ Larynx height and posture ▶ Articulators, including pharynx, velum (soft palate), tongue, lips and jaw, for appropriate vowel formation and vocal resonance
INSTRUCTIONS	1 Play the target notes 2 Mentally hear this interval sung on the chosen vowel 3 Breathe the correct vowel shape 4 Position the larynx 5 Activate breath support 6 Start to sing 7 Maintain appropriate breath pressure for the descending pitch, while keeping the vowel shape
PITCH DISPLAY 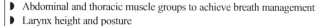	Sing the interval by directing the blue pitch line from the centre of the higher note to the centre of the lower note, with minimal deviation.
SPECTROGRAM	
LEVEL METER	

Exercise I-65: Descending major second, legato

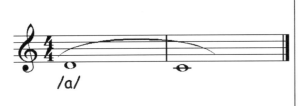

/a/

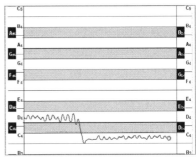

AIM	To sing a descending major second, legato, in mid-voice, on a specified vowel, with pitch accuracy, consistent resonance and consistent volume.
OBJECTIVES	▶ To develop management of pitch, vowel articulation and volume when singing intervals. ▶ To enhance legato capability. ▶ To build the aural and kinaesthetic memory necessary for this task.
PHYSICAL INVOLVEMENT	▶ Abdominal and thoracic muscle groups to achieve breath management ▶ Larynx height and posture ▶ Articulators, including pharynx, velum (soft palate), tongue, lips and jaw, for appropriate vowel formation
INSTRUCTIONS	1 Play the target notes 2 Mentally hear this interval sung on the chosen vowel 3 Breathe the correct vowel shape 4 Position the larynx 5 Activate breath support 6 Start to sing	7 Maintain appropriate breath pressure for the descending pitch while keeping connected tone and vowel shape
PITCH DISPLAY	Sing the interval by directing the blue pitch line from the centre of the higher note to the centre of the lower note, with minimal deviation.
SPECTROGRAM	The Spectrogram should exhibit the same pattern of resonances throughout the exercise. *Note: This is an essential skill for classical singing styles; for other styles, variations in resonance may be desirable.*
LEVEL METER	The volume should remain consistent throughout the exercise. *Note: Where intervals traverse register changes, this is an especially useful skill to encourage.*

Exercise I-66: Ascending minor second (semitone)

/a/

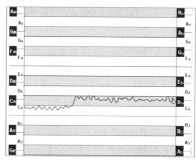

AIM	To sing an ascending minor second (semitone), in mid-voice, on a specified vowel, with pitch accuracy.
OBJECTIVES	▶ To develop management of pitch when singing intervals. ▶ To build the aural and kinaesthetic memory necessary for this task.
PHYSICAL INVOLVEMENT 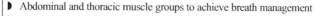	▶ Abdominal and thoracic muscle groups to achieve breath management ▶ Larynx height and posture ▶ Articulators, including pharynx, velum (soft palate), tongue, lips and jaw, for appropriate vowel formation and vocal resonance
INSTRUCTIONS	1 Play the target notes 2 Mentally hear this interval sung on the chosen vowel 3 Breathe the correct vowel shape 4 Position the larynx 5 Activate breath support 6 Start to sing 7 Increase breath pressure in order to increase pitch, while keeping the vowel shape
PITCH DISPLAY	Sing the interval by directing the blue pitch line from the centre of the lower note to the centre of the higher note, with minimal deviation.
SPECTROGRAM	
LEVEL METER	

Exercise I-67: Ascending minor second (semitone), legato

I-67

/a/

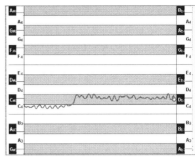

AIM	To sing an ascending minor second (semitone), legato, in mid-voice, on a specified vowel and with pitch accuracy, consistent resonance and consistent volume.
OBJECTIVES	▶ To develop management of pitch, vowel articulation and volume when singing intervals. ▶ To enhance legato capability. ▶ To build the aural and kinaesthetic memory necessary for this task.
PHYSICAL INVOLVEMENT	▶ Abdominal and thoracic muscle groups to achieve breath management ▶ Larynx height and posture ▶ Articulators, including pharynx, velum (soft palate), tongue, lips and jaw, for appropriate vowel formation and vocal resonance
INSTRUCTIONS	1 Play the target notes 2 Mentally hear this interval sung on the chosen vowel 3 Breathe the correct vowel shape 4 Position the larynx 5 Activate breath support 6 Start to sing	7 Gradually increase breath pressure in order to increase pitch while keeping connected tone and vowel shape
PITCH DISPLAY	Sing the interval by directing the blue pitch line from the centre of the lower note to the centre of the higher note, with minimal deviation.
SPECTROGRAM	The Spectrogram should exhibit the same pattern of resonances throughout the exercise. *Note: This is an essential skill for classical singing styles; for other styles, variations in resonance may be desirable.*
LEVEL METER	The volume should remain consistent throughout the exercise. *Note: Where intervals traverse register changes, this is an especially useful skill to encourage.*

/a/

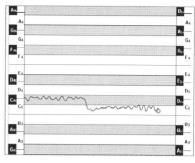

AIM	To sing a descending minor second (semitone), in mid-voice, on a specified vowel, with pitch accuracy.
OBJECTIVES	▶ To develop management of pitch when singing intervals. ▶ To build the aural and kinaesthetic memory necessary for this task.
PHYSICAL INVOLVEMENT	▶ Abdominal and thoracic muscle groups to achieve breath management ▶ Larynx height and posture ▶ Articulators, including pharynx, velum (soft palate), tongue, lips and jaw, for appropriate vowel formation and vocal resonance

INSTRUCTIONS	1 Play the target notes 2 Mentally hear this interval sung on the chosen vowel 3 Breathe the correct vowel shape 4 Position the larynx 5 Activate breath support 6 Start to sing	7 Maintain appropriate breath pressure for the descending pitch, while keeping the vowel shape

PITCH DISPLAY	Sing the interval by directing the blue pitch line from the centre of the higher note to the centre of the lower note, with minimal deviation.
SPECTROGRAM	
LEVEL METER	

Exercise I-69: Descending minor second (semitone), legato

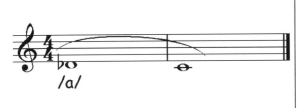

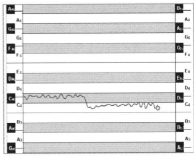

/a/

AIM	To sing a descending minor second (semitone) in mid-voice, on a specified vowel, with pitch accuracy, consistent resonance and consistent volume.
OBJECTIVES	▶ To develop management of pitch, vowel articulation and volume when singing intervals. ▶ To enhance legato capability ▶ To build the aural and kinaesthetic memory necessary for this task.
PHYSICAL INVOLVEMENT	▶ Abdominal and thoracic muscle groups to achieve breath management ▶ Larynx height and posture ▶ Articulators, including pharynx, velum (soft palate), tongue, lips and mandible, for appropriate vowel formation and vocal resonance
INSTRUCTIONS	1 Play the target notes 2 Mentally hear this interval sung on the chosen vowel 3 Breathe the correct vowel shape 4 Position the larynx 5 Activate breath support 6 Start to sing 7 Maintain appropriate breath pressure for the descending pitch while keeping connected tone and vowel shape
PITCH DISPLAY	Sing the interval by directing the blue pitch line from the centre of the higher note to the centre of the lower note, with minimal deviation.
SPECTROGRAM	The Spectrogram should exhibit the same pattern of resonances throughout the exercise. *Note: This is an essential skill for classical singing styles; for other styles, variations in resonance may be desirable.*
LEVEL METER	The volume should remain consistent throughout the exercise. *Note: Where intervals traverse register changes, this is an especially useful skill to encourage.*

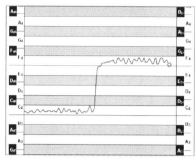

AIM	To sing an ascending perfect fourth, in mid-voice, on a specified vowel, with pitch accuracy.
OBJECTIVES	▶ To develop management of pitch when singing intervals. ▶ To build the aural and kinaesthetic memory necessary for this task.
PHYSICAL INVOLVEMENT	▶ Abdominal and thoracic muscle groups to achieve breath management ▶ Larynx height and posture ▶ Articulators, including pharynx, velum (soft palate), tongue, lips and jaw, for appropriate vowel formation and vocal resonance
INSTRUCTIONS	1 Play the target notes 2 Mentally hear this interval sung on the chosen vowel 3 Breathe the correct vowel shape 4 Position the larynx 5 Activate breath support 6 Start to sing 7 Increase breath pressure in order to increase pitch, while keeping the vowel shape
PITCH DISPLAY	Sing the interval by directing the blue pitch line from the centre of the lower note to the centre of the higher note, with minimal deviation.
SPECTROGRAM	
LEVEL METER	

Exercise I-71: Ascending perfect fourth, portamento, with consistent resonance and volume

/a/

port.

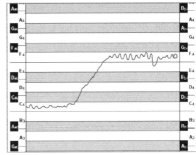

AIM	To sing an ascending perfect fourth, portamento, in mid-voice, on a specified vowel, with pitch accuracy, consistent resonance and consistent volume.	
OBJECTIVES	▶ To develop management of pitch, vowel articulation and volume when singing intervals. ▶ To enhance legato capability. ▶ To build the aural and kinaesthetic memory necessary for this task.	
PHYSICAL INVOLVEMENT	▶ Abdominal and thoracic muscle groups to achieve breath management ▶ Larynx height and posture ▶ Articulators, including pharynx, velum (soft palate), tongue, lips and jaw, for appropriate vowel formation and vocal resonance	
INSTRUCTIONS	1 Play the target notes 2 Mentally hear the continuous series of notes contained between the target pitches, and sung on the chosen vowel 3 Breathe the correct vowel shape 4 Position the larynx	5 Activate breath support 6 Start to sing 7 Gradually increase breath pressure in order to increase pitch, while keeping connected tone and vowel shape
PITCH DISPLAY	Sing the interval through the range of notes to the centre of the higher note, with minimal deviation. The optimal display is a steadily ascending diagonal line.	
SPECTROGRAM	The Spectrogram should exhibit the same pattern of resonances throughout the exercise.	
LEVEL METER	The volume should remain consistent throughout the exercise. *Note: Where intervals traverse register changes, this is an especially useful skill to encourage.*	

/a/

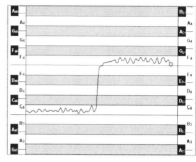

AIM	To sing an ascending perfect fourth, legato, in mid-voice, on a specified vowel and with pitch accuracy, consistent resonance and consistent volume.
OBJECTIVES	▶ To develop management of pitch, vowel articulation and volume when singing intervals. ▶ To enhance legato capability. ▶ To build the aural and kinaesthetic memory necessary for this task.
PHYSICAL INVOLVEMENT	▶ Abdominal and thoracic muscle groups to achieve breath management ▶ Larynx height and posture ▶ Articulators, including pharynx, velum (soft palate), tongue, lips and jaw, for appropriate vowel formation and vocal resonance
INSTRUCTIONS	1 Play the target notes 2 Mentally hear this interval sung on the chosen vowel 3 Breathe the correct vowel shape 4 Position the larynx 5 Activate breath support 6 Start to sing 7 Gradually increase breath pressure in order to increase pitch, while keeping connected tone and vowel shape
PITCH DISPLAY	Sing the interval by directing the blue pitch line from the centre of the lower note to the centre of the higher note, with minimal deviation.
SPECTROGRAM	The Spectrogram should exhibit the same pattern of resonances throughout the exercise. *Note: This is an essential skill for classical singing styles; for other styles, variations in resonance may be desirable.*
LEVEL METER	The volume should remain consistent throughout the exercise. *Note: Where intervals traverse register changes, this is an especially useful skill to encourage.*

Exercise I-73: Ascending major sixth

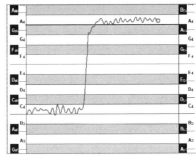

/a/

AIM	To sing an ascending major sixth, in mid-voice, on a specified vowel, with pitch accuracy.
OBJECTIVES	▶ To develop management of pitch when singing intervals. ▶ To build the aural and kinaesthetic memory necessary for this task.
PHYSICAL INVOLVEMENT	▶ Abdominal and thoracic muscle groups to achieve breath management ▶ Larynx height and posture ▶ Articulators, including pharynx, velum (soft palate), tongue, lips and jaw, for appropriate vowel formation and vocal resonance
INSTRUCTIONS	1 Play the target notes 2 Mentally hear this interval sung on the chosen vowel 3 Breathe the correct vowel shape 4 Position the larynx 5 Activate breath support 6 Start to sing 7 Increase breath pressure in order to increase pitch, while keeping the vowel shape
PITCH DISPLAY	Sing the interval by directing the blue pitch line from the centre of the lower note to the centre of the higher note, with minimal deviation.
SPECTROGRAM	
LEVEL METER	

Exercise I-74: Ascending major sixth, portamento, with consistent resonance and volume

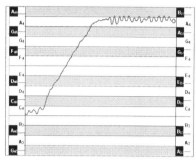

AIM	To sing an ascending major sixth, portamento, in mid-voice, on a specified vowel, with pitch accuracy, consistent resonance and consistent volume.
OBJECTIVES	▶ To develop management of pitch, vowel articulation and volume when singing intervals. ▶ To enhance legato capability. ▶ To build the aural and kinaesthetic memory necessary for this task.
PHYSICAL INVOLVEMENT	▶ Abdominal and thoracic muscle groups to achieve breath management ▶ Larynx height and posture ▶ Articulators, including pharynx, velum (soft palate), tongue, lips and jaw, for appropriate vowel formation and vocal resonance
INSTRUCTIONS	1 Play the target notes 2 Mentally hear the continuous series of notes contained between the target pitches, and sung on the chosen vowel 3 Breathe the correct vowel shape 4 Position the larynx 5 Activate breath support 6 Start to sing 7 Increase breath pressure in order to increase pitch, while keeping the vowel shape
PITCH DISPLAY	Sing the interval through the range of notes to the centre of the higher note, with minimal deviation. The optimal display is a steadily ascending diagonal line.
SPECTROGRAM	The Spectrogram should exhibit the same pattern of resonances throughout the exercise.
LEVEL METER	The volume should remain consistent throughout the exercise. *Note: Where intervals traverse register changes, this is an especially useful skill to encourage.*

Exercise I-75: Ascending major sixth, legato

/a/

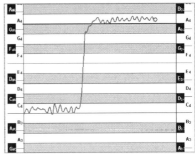

AIM	To sing an ascending major sixth, legato, in mid-voice, on a specified vowel and with pitch accuracy, consistent resonance and consistent volume.
OBJECTIVES	▶ To develop management of pitch, vowel articulation and volume when singing intervals. ▶ To enhance legato capability ▶ To build the aural and kinaesthetic memory necessary for this task.
PHYSICAL INVOLVEMENT	▶ Abdominal and thoracic muscle groups to achieve breath management ▶ Larynx height and posture ▶ Articulators, including pharynx, velum (soft palate), tongue, lips and jaw, for appropriate vowel formation

INSTRUCTIONS

1 Play the target notes 2 Mentally hear this interval sung on the chosen vowel 3 Breathe the correct vowel shape 4 Position the larynx 5 Activate breath support 6 Start to sing	7 Gradually increase breath pressure in order to increase pitch, while keeping connected tone and vowel shape

PITCH DISPLAY	Sing the interval by directing the blue pitch line from the centre of the lower note to the centre of the higher note, with minimal deviation.
SPECTROGRAM	The Spectrogram should exhibit the same pattern of resonances throughout the exercise. *Note: This is an essential skill for classical singing styles; for other styles, variations in resonance may be desirable.*
LEVEL METER	The volume should remain consistent throughout the exercise. *Note: Where intervals traverse register changes, this is an especially useful skill to encourage.*

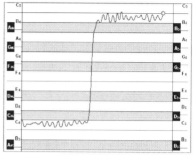

AIM	To sing an ascending major seventh, in mid-voice, on a specified vowel, with pitch accuracy.
OBJECTIVES	▶ To develop management of pitch when singing intervals. ▶ To build the aural and kinaesthetic memory necessary for this task.
PHYSICAL INVOLVEMENT	▶ Abdominal and thoracic muscle groups to achieve breath management ▶ Larynx height and posture ▶ Articulators, including pharynx, velum (soft palate), tongue, lips and jaw, for appropriate vowel formation and vocal resonance
INSTRUCTIONS	1 Play the target notes 2 Mentally hear this interval sung on the chosen vowel 3 Breathe the correct vowel shape 4 Position the larynx 5 Activate breath support 6 Start to sing 7 Increase breath pressure in order to increase pitch, while keeping the vowel shape
PITCH DISPLAY	Sing the interval by directing the blue pitch line from the centre of the lower note to the centre of the higher note, with minimal deviation.
SPECTROGRAM	
LEVEL METER	

Exercise I-77: Ascending major seventh, portamento, with consistent resonance and volume

/a/

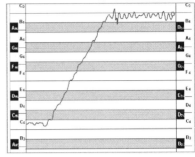

AIM	To sing an ascending major seventh, portamento, in mid-voice, on a specified vowel, with pitch accuracy, consistent resonance and consistent volume.
OBJECTIVES 	▶ To develop management of pitch, vowel articulation and volume when singing intervals. ▶ To enhance legato capability. ▶ To build the aural and kinaesthetic memory necessary for this task.
PHYSICAL INVOLVEMENT	▶ Abdominal and thoracic muscle groups to achieve breath management ▶ Larynx height and posture ▶ Articulators, including pharynx, velum (soft palate), tongue, lips and jaw, for appropriate vowel formation and vocal resonance
INSTRUCTIONS	1 Play the target notes 2 Mentally hear the continuous series of notes contained between the target pitches, and sung on the chosen vowel 3 Breathe the correct vowel shape 4 Position the larynx	5 Activate breath support 6 Start to sing 7 Increase breath pressure in order to increase pitch, while keeping the vowel shape
PITCH DISPLAY	Sing the interval through the range of notes to the centre of the higher note, with minimal deviation. The optimal display is a steadily ascending diagonal line.
SPECTROGRAM	The Spectrogram should exhibit the same pattern of resonances throughout the exercise.
LEVEL METER	The volume should remain consistent throughout the exercise. *Note: Where intervals traverse register changes, this is an especially useful skill to encourage.*

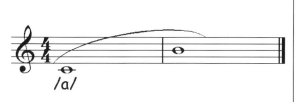

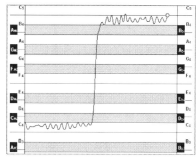

/a/

AIM	To sing an ascending major seventh, legato, in mid-voice, on a specified vowel, with pitch accuracy, consistent resonance and consistent volume.
OBJECTIVES	▶ To develop management of pitch, vowel articulation and volume when singing intervals. ▶ To enhance legato capability. ▶ To build the aural and kinaesthetic memory necessary for this task.
PHYSICAL INVOLVEMENT	▶ Abdominal and thoracic muscle groups to achieve breath management ▶ Larynx height and posture ▶ Articulators, including pharynx, velum (soft palate), tongue, lips and jaw, for appropriate vowel formation and vocal resonance
INSTRUCTIONS	1 Play the target notes 2 Mentally hear this interval sung on the chosen vowel 3 Breathe the correct vowel shape 4 Position the larynx 5 Activate breath support 6 Start to sing	7 Gradually increase breath pressure in order to increase pitch while keeping connected tone and vowel shape
PITCH DISPLAY	Sing the interval by directing the blue pitch line from the centre of the lower note to the centre of the higher note, with minimal deviation.
SPECTROGRAM	The Spectrogram should exhibit the same pattern of resonances throughout the exercise. *Note: This is an essential skill for classical singing styles; for other styles, variations in resonance may be desirable.*
LEVEL METER	The volume should remain consistent throughout the exercise. *Note: Where intervals traverse register changes, this is an especially useful skill to encourage.*

Exercise I-79: Descending perfect fourth

/a/

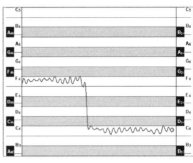

AIM	To sing a descending perfect fourth, in mid-voice, on a specified vowel, with pitch accuracy.
OBJECTIVES	▶ To develop management of pitch when singing intervals. ▶ To build the aural and kinaesthetic memory necessary for this task.
PHYSICAL INVOLVEMENT	▶ Abdominal and thoracic muscle groups to achieve breath management ▶ Larynx height and posture ▶ Articulators, including pharynx, velum (soft palate), tongue, lips and jaw, for appropriate vowel formation and vocal resonance
INSTRUCTIONS	1 Play the target notes 2 Mentally hear this interval sung on the chosen vowel 3 Breathe the correct vowel shape 4 Position the larynx 5 Activate breath support 6 Start to sing 7 Maintain appropriate breath pressure for the descending pitch, while keeping the vowel shape
PITCH DISPLAY	Sing the interval by directing the blue pitch line from the centre of the higher note to the centre of the lower note, with minimal deviation.
SPECTROGRAM	
LEVEL METER	

Exercise I-80: Descending perfect fourth, portamento, with consistent resonance and volume

/a/   *port.*

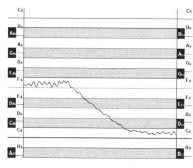

AIM	To sing a descending perfect fourth, portamento, in mid-voice, on a specified vowel, with pitch accuracy, consistent resonance and consistent volume.
OBJECTIVES	▶ To develop management of pitch, vowel articulation and volume when singing intervals. ▶ To enhance legato capability. ▶ To build the aural and kinaesthetic memory necessary for this task.
PHYSICAL INVOLVEMENT	▶ Abdominal and thoracic muscle groups to achieve breath management ▶ Larynx height and posture ▶ Articulators, including pharynx, velum (soft palate), tongue, lips and jaw, for appropriate vowel formation and vocal resonance
INSTRUCTIONS	1 Play the target notes 2 Mentally hear the continuous series of notes contained between the target pitches, and sung on the chosen vowel 3 Breathe the correct vowel shape 4 Position the larynx 5 Activate breath support 6 Start to sing 7 Maintain appropriate breath pressure for the descending pitch, while keeping the vowel shape
PITCH DISPLAY	Sing the interval through the range of notes to the centre of the lower note, with minimal deviation. The optimal display is a steadily descending diagonal line.
SPECTROGRAM	The Spectrogram should exhibit the same pattern of resonances throughout the exercise.
LEVEL METER	The volume should remain consistent throughout the exercise. *Note: Where intervals traverse register changes, this is an especially useful skill to encourage.*

Exercise I-81: Descending perfect fourth, legato

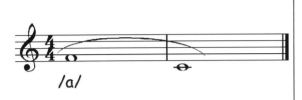

/a/

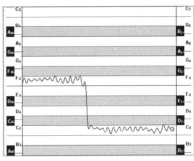

AIM	To sing a descending perfect fourth, legato, in mid-voice, on a specified vowel and with pitch accuracy, consistent resonance and consistent volume.
OBJECTIVES	▶ To develop management of pitch, vowel articulation and volume when singing intervals. ▶ To enhance legato capability. ▶ To build the aural and kinaesthetic memory necessary for this task.
PHYSICAL INVOLVEMENT	▶ Abdominal and thoracic muscle groups to achieve breath management ▶ Larynx height and posture ▶ Articulators, including pharynx, velum (soft palate), tongue, lips and jaw, for appropriate vowel formation and vocal resonance
INSTRUCTIONS	1 Play the target notes 2 Mentally hear this interval sung on the chosen vowel 3 Breathe the correct vowel shape 4 Position the larynx 5 Activate breath support 6 Start to sing	7 Maintain appropriate breath pressure for the descending pitch, while keeping the vowel shape
PITCH DISPLAY	Sing the interval by directing the blue pitch line from the centre of the higher note to the centre of the lower note, with minimal deviation.
SPECTROGRAM	The Spectrogram should exhibit the same pattern of resonances throughout the exercise. *Note: This is an essential skill for classical singing styles; for other styles, variations in resonance may be desirable.*
LEVEL METER	The volume should remain consistent throughout the exercise. *Note: Where intervals traverse register changes, this is an especially useful skill to encourage.*

/a/

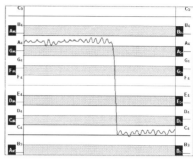

AIM	To sing a descending major sixth, in mid-voice, on a specified vowel, with pitch accuracy.

OBJECTIVES	▶ To develop management of pitch when singing intervals. ▶ To build the aural and kinaesthetic memory necessary for this task.

PHYSICAL INVOLVEMENT	▶ Abdominal and thoracic muscle groups to achieve breath management for pitch and portamento ▶ Larynx height and posture ▶ Articulators, including pharynx, velum (soft palate), tongue, lips and jaw, for appropriate vowel formation and vocal resonance

INSTRUCTIONS	1 Play the target notes 2 Mentally hear this interval sung on the chosen vowel 3 Breathe the correct vowel shape 4 Position the larynx 5 Activate breath support 6 Start to sing	7 Maintain appropriate breath pressure for the descending pitch, while keeping the vowel shape

PITCH DISPLAY	Sing the interval by directing the blue pitch line from the centre of the higher note to the centre of the lower note, with minimal deviation.

SPECTROGRAM	

LEVEL METER	

Exercise I-83: Descending major sixth, portamento, with consistent resonance and volume

/a/

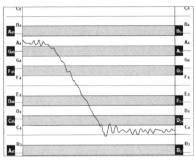

AIM	To sing a descending major sixth, *portamento*, in mid-voice, on a specified vowel, with pitch accuracy, consistent resonance and consistent volume.
OBJECTIVES	▶ To develop management of pitch, vowel articulation and volume when singing intervals. ▶ To enhance legato capability. ▶ To build the aural and kinaesthetic memory necessary for this task.
PHYSICAL INVOLVEMENT	▶ Abdominal and thoracic muscle groups to achieve breath management ▶ Larynx height and posture ▶ Articulators, including pharynx, velum (soft palate), tongue, lips and jaw, for appropriate vowel formation and vocal resonance
INSTRUCTIONS	1 Play the target notes 2 Mentally hear the continuous series of notes contained between the target pitches, and sung on the chosen vowel 3 Breathe the correct vowel shape 4 Position the larynx 5 Activate breath support 6 Start to sing 7 Maintain appropriate breath pressure as the pitch descends, while keeping the vowel shape
PITCH DISPLAY	Sing the interval through the range of notes to the centre of the lower note, with minimal deviation. The optimal display is a steadily descending diagonal line
SPECTROGRAM	The Spectrogram should exhibit the same pattern of resonances throughout the exercise.
LEVEL METER	The volume should remain consistent throughout the exercise. *Note: Where intervals traverse register changes, this is an especially useful skill to encourage.*

Sing&See

/a/

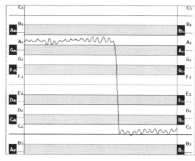

AIM	To sing a descending major sixth, legato, in mid-voice, on a specified vowel, with pitch accuracy, consistent resonance and consistent volume.
OBJECTIVES	▶ To develop management of pitch, vowel articulation and volume when singing intervals ▶ To enhance legato capability. ▶ To build the aural and kinaesthetic memory necessary for this task.
PHYSICAL INVOLVEMENT	▶ Abdominal and thoracic muscle groups to achieve breath management ▶ Larynx height and posture ▶ Articulators, including pharynx, velum (soft palate), tongue, lips and jaw, for appropriate vowel formation and vocal resonance
INSTRUCTIONS	1 Play the target notes 2 Mentally hear this interval sung on the chosen vowel 3 Breathe the correct vowel shape 4 Position the larynx 5 Activate breath support 6 Start to sing	7 Maintain appropriate breath pressure for the descending pitch, while keeping the vowel shape
PITCH DISPLAY	Sing the interval by directing the blue pitch line from the centre of the higher note to the centre of the lower note, with minimal deviation.
SPECTROGRAM	The Spectrogram should exhibit the same pattern of resonances throughout the exercise. *Note: This is an essential skill for classical singing styles; for other styles, variations in resonance may be desirable.*
LEVEL METER	The volume should remain consistent throughout the exercise. *Note: Where intervals traverse register changes, this is an especially useful skill to encourage.*

Exercise I-85: Descending major seventh

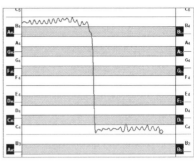

/a/

AIM	To sing a descending major seventh, in mid-voice, on a specified vowel, with pitch accuracy.
OBJECTIVES	▶ To develop management of pitch when singing intervals. ▶ To build the aural and kinaesthetic memory necessary for this task.
PHYSICAL INVOLVEMENT	▶ Abdominal and thoracic muscle groups to achieve breath management ▶ Larynx height and posture ▶ Articulators, including pharynx, velum (soft palate), tongue, lips and jaw, for appropriate vowel formation and vocal resonance
INSTRUCTIONS	1 Play the target notes 2 Mentally hear this interval sung on the chosen vowel 3 Breathe the correct vowel shape 4 Position the larynx 5 Activate breath support 6 Start to sing 7 Maintain appropriate breath pressure for the descending pitch, while keeping the vowel shape
PITCH DISPLAY	Sing the interval by directing the blue pitch line from the centre of the higher note to the centre of the lower note, with minimal deviation.
SPECTROGRAM	
LEVEL METER	

Exercise I-86: Descending major seventh, portamento, with consistent resonance and volume

/a/

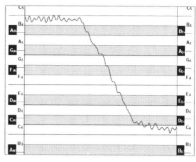

AIM	To sing a descending major seventh, portamento, in mid-voice, on a specified vowel, with pitch accuracy, consistent resonance and consistent volume.
OBJECTIVES	▶ To develop management of pitch, vowel articulation and volume when singing intervals. ▶ To enhance legato capability. ▶ To build the aural and kinaesthetic memory necessary for this task.
PHYSICAL INVOLVEMENT	▶ Abdominal and thoracic muscle groups to achieve breath management ▶ Larynx height and posture ▶ Articulators, including pharynx, velum (soft palate), tongue, lips and jaw, for appropriate vowel formation and vocal resonance
INSTRUCTIONS	1 Play the target notes 2 Mentally hear the continuous series of notes contained between the target pitches, and sung on the chosen vowel 3 Breathe the correct vowel shape 4 Position the larynx 5 Activate breath support 6 Start to sing 7 Maintain appropriate breath pressure for the descending pitch, while keeping the vowel shape
PITCH DISPLAY	Sing the interval through the range of notes to the centre of the lower note, with minimal deviation. The optimal display is a steadily descending diagonal line.
SPECTROGRAM	The Spectrogram should exhibit the same pattern of resonances throughout the exercise.
LEVEL METER	The volume should remain consistent throughout the exercise. *Note: Where intervals traverse register changes, this is an especially useful skill to encourage.*

Exercise I-87: Descending major seventh, legato

/a/

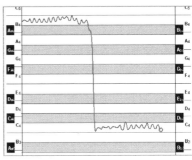

AIM	To sing a descending major seventh, legato, in mid-voice, on a specified vowel, with pitch accuracy, consistent resonance and consistent volume.
OBJECTIVES 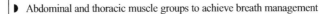	▶ To develop management of pitch, vowel articulation and volume when singing intervals. ▶ To enhance legato capability. ▶ To build the aural and kinaesthetic memory necessary for this task.
PHYSICAL INVOLVEMENT	▶ Abdominal and thoracic muscle groups to achieve breath management ▶ Larynx height and posture ▶ Articulators, including pharynx, velum (soft palate), tongue, lips and jaw, for appropriate vowel formation and vocal resonance
INSTRUCTIONS	1 Play the target notes 2 Mentally hear this interval sung on the chosen vowel 3 Breathe the correct vowel shape 4 Position the larynx 5 Activate breath support 6 Start to sing 7 Maintain appropriate breath pressure for the descending pitch while keeping connected tone and vowel shape
PITCH DISPLAY	Sing the interval by directing the blue pitch line from the centre of the higher note to the centre of the lower note, with minimal deviation.
SPECTROGRAM	The Spectrogram should exhibit the same pattern of resonances throughout the exercise. *Note: This is an essential skill for classical singing styles; for other styles, variations in resonance may be desirable.*
LEVEL METER	The volume should remain consistent throughout the exercise. *Note: Where intervals traverse register changes, this is an especially useful skill to encourage.*

Exercise S-1: Ascending chromatic scale

S-1

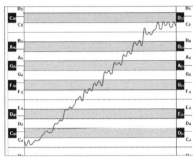

AIM	To sing an ascending chromatic scale on a specified vowel, with accurate pitch.
OBJECTIVES	▶ To develop management of pitch when singing an ascending chromatic scale. Musically, it is important that the semitones are equidistant. Vocally, this may require particular attention through register changes and on different vowels. ▶ To build the aural and kinaesthetic memory necessary for this task.
PHYSICAL INVOLVEMENT	▶ Abdominal and thoracic muscle groups to achieve breath management ▶ Larynx height and posture ▶ Articulators, including pharynx, velum (soft palate), tongue, lips and jaw, for appropriate vowel formation and vocal resonance

INSTRUCTIONS	1 Play the scale 2 Mentally hear the scale sung on the chosen vowel 3 Breathe the correct vowel shape 4 Position the larynx 5 Activate breath support 6 Start to sing	7 Increase breath pressure in order to increase pitch, while keeping the vowel shape

PITCH DISPLAY	Sing the scale by directing the blue pitch line from the centre of the lowest note to the centre of each following note. The optimal display will show minimal, clean horizontal in an upward diagonal.
SPECTROGRAM	
LEVEL METER	

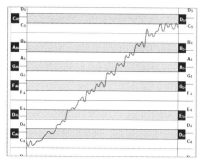

AIM	To sing an ascending chromatic scale, legato, on a specified vowel, while maintaining pitch accuracy, consistent resonance and consistent volume.
OBJECTIVES	▶ To develop management of pitch, vowel articulation and volume, when singing an ascending chromatic major scale. Musically, it is important that the semitones are equidistant. Vocally, this may require particular attention through register changes and on different vowels. ▶ To enhance legato capability. ▶ To build the aural and kinaesthetic memory necessary for this task.
PHYSICAL INVOLVEMENT	▶ Abdominal and thoracic muscle groups to achieve breath management ▶ Larynx height and posture ▶ Articulators, including pharynx, velum (soft palate), tongue, lips and jaw, for appropriate vowel formation and vocal resonance
INSTRUCTIONS	1 Play the scale 2 Mentally hear the scale sung on the chosen vowel 3 Breathe the correct vowel shape 4 Position the larynx 5 Activate breath support 6 Start to sing 7 Gradually increase breath pressure in order to increase pitch, while keeping connected tone and vowel shape.
PITCH DISPLAY	Sing the scale by directing the blue pitch line from the centre of the lowest note to the centre of each following note, with minimal deviation. The optimal display will show minimal, clean horizontal lines in an upward diagonal.
SPECTROGRAM	The Spectrogram should exhibit the same pattern of resonances throughout the exercise.
LEVEL METER	The volume should remain consistent throughout the exercise. *Note: Where intervals traverse register changes, this is an especially useful skill to encourage.*

Exercise S-3: Descending chromatic scale

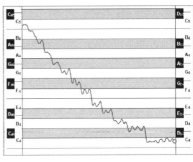

AIM	To sing a descending chromatic scale on a specified vowel, with accurate pitch.
OBJECTIVES	▶ To develop management of pitch when singing a descending chromatic scale. Musically, it is important that the semitones are equidistant. Vocally, this may require particular attention through register changes and on different vowels. ▶ To build the aural and kinaesthetic memory necessary for this task.
PHYSICAL INVOLVEMENT	▶ Abdominal and thoracic muscle groups to achieve breath management ▶ Larynx height and posture ▶ Articulators, including pharynx, velum (soft palate), tongue, lips and jaw, for appropriate vowel formation and vocal resonance

INSTRUCTIONS	1 Play the scale 2 Mentally hear the scale sung on the chosen vowel 3 Breathe the correct vowel shape 4 Position the larynx 5 Activate breath support 6 Start to sing	7 Maintain appropriate breath pressure for the descending pitch while keeping the vowel shape

PITCH DISPLAY	Sing the scale by directing the blue pitch line from the centre of the highest note to the centre of each following note. The optimal display will show minimal, clean horizontal in a downward diagonal.

SPECTROGRAM	

LEVEL METER	

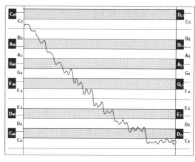

/a/

AIM	To sing a descending chromatic scale, legato, on a specified vowel, with pitch accuracy, consistent resonance and consistent volume.
OBJECTIVES	▶ To develop management of pitch, vowel articulation and volume, when singing a descending chromatic scale. Musically, it is important that the semitones are equidistant. Vocally, this may require particular attention through register changes and on different vowels. ▶ To enhance legato capability. ▶ To build the aural and kinaesthetic memory necessary for this task.
PHYSICAL INVOLVEMENT	▶ Abdominal and thoracic muscle groups to achieve breath management ▶ Larynx height and posture ▶ Articulators, including pharynx, velum (soft palate), tongue, lips and jaw, for appropriate vowel formation and vocal resonance
INSTRUCTIONS	1 Play the scale 2 Mentally hear the scale sung on the chosen vowel 3 Breathe the correct vowel shape 4 Position the larynx 5 Activate breath support 6 Start to sing	7 Maintain appropriate pressure for the descending pitch, while keeping connected tone and vowel shape
PITCH DISPLAY	Sing the scale by directing the blue pitch line from the centre of the highest note to the centre of each following note, with minimal deviation. The optimal display will show minimal, clean horizontal lines in a downward diagonal.
SPECTROGRAM	The Spectrogram should exhibit the same pattern of resonances throughout the exercise.
LEVEL METER	The volume should remain consistent throughout the exercise. *Note: Where intervals traverse register changes, this is an especially useful skill to encourage.*

Exercise S-5: Ascending and descending chromatic scale

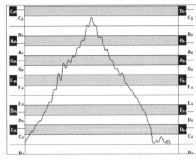

AIM	To sing an ascending and descending chromatic scale on a specified vowel, with accurate pitch.
OBJECTIVES 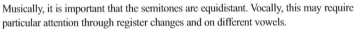	▶ To develop management of pitch when singing an ascending and descending chromatic scale. Musically, it is important that the semitones are equidistant. Vocally, this may require particular attention through register changes and on different vowels. ▶ To build the aural and kinaesthetic memory necessary for this task.
PHYSICAL INVOLVEMENT 	▶ Abdominal and thoracic muscle groups to achieve breath management ▶ Larynx height and posture ▶ Articulators, including pharynx, velum (soft palate), tongue, lips and jaw, for appropriate vowel formation and vocal resonance
INSTRUCTIONS	1 Play the scale 2 Mentally hear the scale sung on the chosen vowel 3 Breathe the correct vowel shape 4 Position the larynx 5 Activate breath support 6 Start to sing 7 Increase breath pressure in order to increase pitch, while keeping the vowel shape 8 Maintain appropriate breath pressure for the descending pitch, while keeping the vowel shape
PITCH DISPLAY 	Sing the scale by directing the blue pitch line from the centre of the first note to the centre of each following note. The optimal display will show minimal, clean horizontal lines in an upward, then equally downward, diagonal.
SPECTROGRAM	
LEVEL METER	

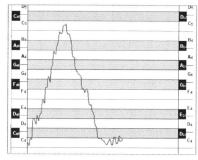

AIM	To sing an ascending and descending chromatic scale, staccato, on a specified vowel, with accurate pitch.
OBJECTIVES	▶ To develop management of pitch when singing an ascending and descending chromatic scale staccato. Musically, it is important that the semitones are equidistant. Vocally, this may require particular attention through register changes and on different vowels. ▶ To build the aural and kinaesthetic memory necessary for this task.
PHYSICAL INVOLVEMENT	▶ Abdominal and thoracic muscle groups to achieve breath management ▶ Larynx height and posture ▶ Articulators, including pharynx, velum (soft palate), tongue, lips and jaw, for appropriate vowel formation and vocal resonance

INSTRUCTIONS	1 Play the scale 2 Mentally hear the scale sung on the chosen vowel 3 Breathe the correct vowel shape 4 Position the larynx 5 Activate breath support 6 Start to sing	7 Pay attention to precise onset and offset while increasing breath pressure for each ascending pitch and keeping vowel shape 8 Pay attention to precise onset and offset while maintaining appropriate breath pressure for each descending pitch and keeping vowel shape

PITCH DISPLAY	Sing the scale by directing the blue pitch line from the centre of the first note to the centre of each following note with minimal deviation. The optimal display will show minimal, clean horizontal lines in an upward, then equally downward, diagonal.
SPECTROGRAM	
LEVEL METER	

Exercise S-7: Ascending and descending chromatic scale, legato

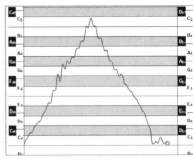

AIM	To sing an ascending and descending chromatic scale, legato, on a specified vowel, with pitch accuracy, consistent resonance and consistent volume.
OBJECTIVES	▶ To develop management of pitch, vowel articulation and volume, when singing an ascending and descending chromatic scale. Musically, it is important that the semitones are equidistant. Vocally, this may require particular attention through register changes and on different vowels. ▶ To enhance legato capability. ▶ To build the aural and kinaesthetic memory necessary for this task.
PHYSICAL INVOLVEMENT	▶ Abdominal and thoracic muscle groups to achieve breath management ▶ Larynx height and posture ▶ Articulators, including pharynx, velum (soft palate), tongue, lips and jaw, for appropriate vowel formation and vocal resonance
INSTRUCTIONS	1 Play the scale 2 Mentally hear the scale sung on the chosen vowel 3 Breathe the correct vowel shape 4 Position the larynx 5 Activate breath support 6 Start to sing 7 Gradually increase breath pressure in order to increase pitch, while keeping connected tone and vowel shape 8 Maintain appropriate breath pressure for the descending pitch, while keeping connected tone and vowel shape
PITCH DISPLAY	Sing the scale by directing the blue pitch line from the centre of the first note to the centre of each following note, with minimal deviation. The optimal display will show minimal, clean horizontal lines in an upward, then equally downward, diagonal.
SPECTROGRAM	The Spectrogram should exhibit the same pattern of resonances throughout the exercise.
LEVEL METER	The volume should remain consistent throughout the exercise. *Note: Where intervals traverse register changes, this is an especially useful skill to encourage.*

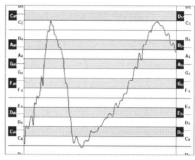

AIM	To sing an ascending and descending chromatic scale, first staccato, and then legato, on a specified vowel, with pitch accuracy, consistent resonance and consistent volume.
OBJECTIVES	▶ To develop management of pitch, vowel articulation and volume, when singing an ascending and descending chromatic scale. Musically, it is important that the semitones are equidistant. Vocally, this may require particular attention through register changes and on different vowels. ▶ To enhance staccato and legato capability. ▶ To build the aural and kinaesthetic memory necessary for this task.
PHYSICAL INVOLVEMENT	▶ Abdominal and thoracic muscle groups to achieve breath management ▶ Larynx height and posture ▶ Articulators, including pharynx, velum (soft palate), tongue, lips and jaw, for appropriate vowel formation and vocal resonance
INSTRUCTIONS	1 Play the scale 2 Mentally hear the scale sung on the chosen vowel 3 Breathe the correct vowel shape 4 Position the larynx 5 Activate breath support 6 Start to sing 7 For the staccato, pay attention to precise onset and offset while increasing breath pressure for each ascending pitch and maintaining appropriate breath pressure for each descending pitch 8 For the legato, keep connected tone and vowel shape while gradually increasing breath pressure for ascending pitch and maintaining appropriate breath pressure for descending pitch
PITCH DISPLAY	Sing the scale by directing the blue pitch line from the centre of the first note to the centre of each following note, with minimal deviation. For both staccato and legato, the optimal display will show minimal, clean horizontal lines in upward, then equally downward, diagonals.
SPECTROGRAM	The Spectrogram should exhibit the same pattern of resonances throughout the exercise.
LEVEL METER	The volume should remain consistent throughout the exercise. *Note: Where intervals traverse register changes, this is an especially useful skill to encourage.*

Exercise S-9: Ascending whole-tone scale

/a/

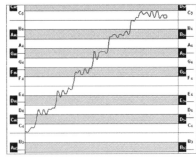

AIM	To sing an ascending whole-tone scale on a specified vowel, with accurate pitch.
OBJECTIVES	▶ To develop management of pitch when singing an ascending whole-tone scale. Musically, it is important that the tones are equidistant. Vocally, this may require particular attention through register changes and on different vowels. ▶ To build the aural and kinaesthetic memory necessary for this task.
PHYSICAL INVOLVEMENT	▶ Abdominal and thoracic muscle groups to achieve breath management ▶ Larynx height and posture ▶ Articulators, including pharynx, velum (soft palate), tongue, lips and jaw, for appropriate vowel formation and vocal resonance

INSTRUCTIONS	1 Play the scale 2 Mentally hear the scale sung on the chosen vowel 3 Breathe the correct vowel shape 4 Position the larynx 5 Activate breath support 6 Start to sing	7 Increase breath pressure in order to increase pitch, while keeping the vowel shape

PITCH DISPLAY	Sing the scale by directing the blue pitch line from the centre of the lowest note to the centre of each following note. The optimal display will show minimal, clean horizontal lines in an upward diagonal.
SPECTROGRAM	
LEVEL METER	

/a/

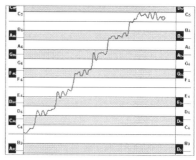

AIM	To sing an ascending whole-tone scale, legato, on a specified vowel, with pitch accuracy, consistent resonance and consistent volume.
OBJECTIVES	▶ To develop management of pitch, vowel articulation and volume, when singing an ascending whole-tone scale. Musically, it is important that the tones are equidistant. Vocally, this may require particular attention through register changes and on different vowels ▶ To enhance legato capability. ▶ To build the aural and kinaesthetic memory necessary for this task.
PHYSICAL INVOLVEMENT	▶ Abdominal and thoracic muscle groups to achieve breath management ▶ Larynx height and posture ▶ Articulators, including pharynx, velum (soft palate), tongue, lips and jaw, for appropriate vowel formation and vocal resonance
INSTRUCTIONS	1 Play the scale 2 Mentally hear the scale sung on the chosen vowel 3 Breathe the correct vowel shape 4 Position the larynx 5 Activate breath support 6 Start to sing	7 Gradually increase breath pressure in order to increase pitch, while keeping connected tone and vowel shape
PITCH DISPLAY	Sing the scale by directing the blue pitch line from the centre of the lowest note to the centre of each following note, with minimal deviation and no breaks in the line. The optimal display will show minimal, clean horizontal lines in an upward diagonal.
SPECTROGRAM	The Spectrogram should exhibit the same pattern of resonances throughout the exercise.
LEVEL METER	The volume should remain consistent throughout the exercise. *Note: Where intervals traverse register changes, this is an especially useful skill to encourage.*

Exercise S-11: Descending whole-tone scale

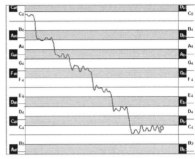

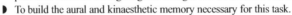

AIM	To sing a descending whole-tone scale on a specified vowel, with accurate pitch.
OBJECTIVES	▶ To develop management of pitch when singing a descending whole-tone scale. Musically, it is important that the tones are equidistant. Vocally, this may require particular attention through register changes and on different vowels. ▶ To build the aural and kinaesthetic memory necessary for this task.
PHYSICAL INVOLVEMENT	▶ Abdominal and thoracic muscle groups to achieve breath management ▶ Larynx height and posture ▶ Articulators, including pharynx, velum (soft palate), tongue, lips and jaw, for appropriate vowel formation and vocal resonance

INSTRUCTIONS	1 Play the scale 2 Mentally hear the scale sung on the chosen vowel 3 Breathe the correct vowel shape 4 Position the larynx 5 Activate breath support 6 Start to sing	7 Increase breath pressure in order to increase pitch, while keeping the vowel shape

PITCH DISPLAY	Sing the scale by directing the blue pitch line from the centre of the highest note to the centre of each following note. The optimal display will show minimal, clean horizontal lines in a downward diagonal.

SPECTROGRAM	

LEVEL METER	

Exercise S-12: Descending whole-tone scale, legato

S-12

/a/

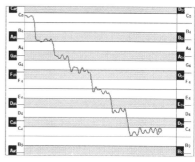

AIM	To sing a descending whole-tone scale, legato, on a specified vowel, with pitch accuracy, consistent resonance and consistent volume.
OBJECTIVES	▶ To develop management of pitch, vowel articulation and volume, when singing a descending whole-tone scale. Musically, it is important that the tones are equidistant. Vocally, this may require particular attention through register changes and on different vowels. ▶ To enhance legato capability. ▶ To build the aural and kinaesthetic memory necessary for this task.
PHYSICAL INVOLVEMENT	▶ Abdominal and thoracic muscle groups to achieve breath management ▶ Larynx height and posture ▶ Articulators, including pharynx, velum (soft palate), tongue, lips and jaw, for appropriate vowel formation and vocal resonance
INSTRUCTIONS	1 Play the scale 2 Mentally hear the scale sung on the chosen vowel 3 Breathe the correct vowel shape 4 Position the larynx 5 Activate breath support 6 Start to sing 7 Gradually increase breath pressure in order to increase pitch, while keeping connected tone and vowel shape 8 Maintain appropriate pressure for the descending pitch, while keeping connected tone and vowel shape
PITCH DISPLAY	Sing the scale by directing the blue pitch line from the centre of the highest note to the centre of each following note, with minimal deviation. The optimal display will show minimal, clean horizontal lines in a downward diagonal.
SPECTROGRAM	The Spectrogram should exhibit the same pattern of resonances throughout the exercise.
LEVEL METER	The volume should remain consistent throughout the exercise. *Note: Where intervals traverse register changes, this is an especially useful skill to encourage.*

Exercise S-13: Ascending and descending whole-tone scale

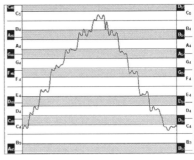

/a/

AIM	To sing an ascending and descending whole-tone scale on a specified vowel, with accurate pitch.
OBJECTIVES	▶ To develop management of pitch when singing an ascending and descending whole-tone scale. Musically, it is important that the tones are equidistant. Vocally, this may require particular attention through register changes and on different vowels. ▶ To build the aural and kinaesthetic memory necessary for this task.
PHYSICAL INVOLVEMENT	▶ Abdominal and thoracic muscle groups to achieve breath management ▶ Larynx height and posture ▶ Articulators, including pharynx, velum (soft palate), tongue, lips and jaw, for appropriate vowel formation and vocal resonance

INSTRUCTIONS	1 Play the scale 2 Mentally hear the scale sung on the chosen vowel 3 Breathe the correct vowel shape 4 Position the larynx 5 Activate breath support 6 Start to sing	7 Increase breath pressure in order to increase pitch, while keeping the vowel shape 8 Maintain appropriate breath pressure for the descending pitch, while keeping the vowel shape

PITCH DISPLAY	Sing the scale by directing the blue pitch line from the centre of the first note to the centre of each following note. The optimal display will show minimal, clean horizontal lines in an upward, then equally downward, diagonal.
SPECTROGRAM	
LEVEL METER	

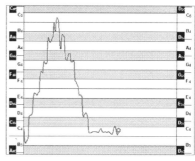

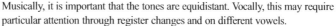

AIM	To sing an ascending and descending whole-tone scale, staccato, on a specified vowel, with accurate pitch.
OBJECTIVES	▶ To develop management of pitch when singing an ascending and descending whole-tone scale staccato. Musically, it is important that the tones are equidistant. Vocally, this may require particular attention through register changes and on different vowels. ▶ To build the aural and kinaesthetic memory necessary for this task.
PHYSICAL INVOLVEMENT	▶ Abdominal and thoracic muscle groups to achieve breath management ▶ Larynx height and posture ▶ Articulators, including pharynx, velum (soft palate), tongue, lips and jaw, for appropriate vowel formation and vocal resonance
INSTRUCTIONS	1 Play the scale 2 Mentally hear the scale sung on the chosen vowel 3 Breathe the correct vowel shape 4 Position the larynx 5 Activate breath support 6 Start to sing 7 Pay attention to precise onset and offset while increasing breath pressure for each ascending pitch and keeping vowel shape 8 Pay attention to precise onset and offset while maintaining appropriate breath pressure for each descending pitch and keeping vowel shape
PITCH DISPLAY	Sing the scale clearly and accurately by directing the blue pitch line from the centre of the first note to the centre of each following note. The optimal display will show minimal, clean horizontal lines in an upward, then equally downward, diagonal.
SPECTROGRAM	
LEVEL METER	

Exercise S-15: Ascending and descending whole-tone scale, legato

/a/

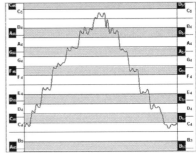

AIM	To sing an ascending and descending whole-tone scale, legato, on a specified vowel, with pitch accuracy, consistent resonance and consistent volume.
OBJECTIVES	▶ To develop management of pitch, vowel articulation and volume, when singing an ascending and descending whole-tone scale. Musically, it is important that the tones are equidistant. Vocally, this may require particular attention through register changes and on different vowels. ▶ To enhance legato capability. ▶ To build the aural and kinaesthetic memory necessary for this task.
PHYSICAL INVOLVEMENT	▶ Abdominal and thoracic muscle groups to achieve breath management ▶ Larynx height and posture ▶ Articulators, including pharynx, velum (soft palate), tongue, lips and jaw, for appropriate vowel formation and vocal resonance

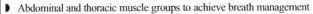

INSTRUCTIONS	1 Play the scale 2 Mentally hear the scale sung on the chosen vowel 3 Breathe the correct vowel shape 4 Position the larynx 5 Activate breath support 6 Start to sing	7 Gradually increase breath pressure in order to increase pitch, while keeping connected tone and vowel shape 8 Maintain appropriate breath pressure for the descending pitch while keeping connected tone and vowel shape

PITCH DISPLAY	Sing the scale by directing the blue pitch line from the centre of the first note to the centre of each following note, with minimal deviation. The optimal display will show minimal, clean horizontal lines in an upward, then equally downward, diagonal.
SPECTROGRAM	The Spectrogram should exhibit the same pattern of resonances throughout the exercise.
LEVEL METER	The volume should remain consistent throughout the exercise. *Note: Where intervals traverse register changes, this is an especially useful skill to encourage.*

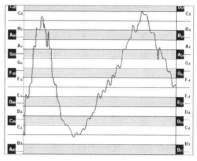

AIM	To sing an ascending and descending whole-tone scale, first staccato and then legato, on a specified vowel, with pitch accuracy, consistent resonance and consistent volume.
OBJECTIVES	▶ To develop management of pitch, vowel articulation and volume, when singing an ascending and descending whole-tone scale. Musically, it is important that the tones are equidistant. Vocally, this may require particular attention through register changes and on different vowels. ▶ To enhance staccato and legato capability. ▶ To build the aural and kinaesthetic memory necessary for this task.
PHYSICAL INVOLVEMENT	▶ Abdominal and thoracic muscle groups to achieve breath management ▶ Larynx height and posture ▶ Articulators, including pharynx, velum (soft palate), tongue, lips and jaw, for appropriate vowel formation and vocal resonance
INSTRUCTIONS	1 Play the scale 2 Mentally hear the scale sung on the chosen vowel 3 Breathe the correct vowel shape 4 Position the larynx 5 Activate breath support 6 Start to sing 7 For the staccato, pay attention to precise onset and offset while increasing breath pressure for each ascending pitch and maintaining appropriate breath pressure for each descending pitch 8 For the legato, keep connected tone and vowel shape while gradually increasing breath pressure for ascending pitch and maintaining appropriate breath pressure for descending pitch
PITCH DISPLAY	Sing the scale by directing the blue pitch line from the centre of the first note to the centre of each following note, with minimal deviation. For both staccato and legato, the optimal display will show minimal, clean horizontal lines in upward, then equally downward, diagonals.
SPECTROGRAM	The Spectrogram should exhibit the same pattern of resonances throughout the exercise.
LEVEL METER	The volume should remain consistent throughout the exercise. *Note: Where intervals traverse register changes, this is an especially useful skill to encourage.*

S-17 Exercise S-17: Ascending and descending pentatonic (TTmin.3T) scale

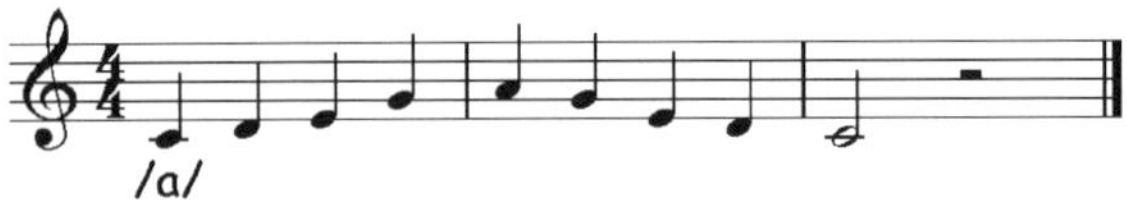

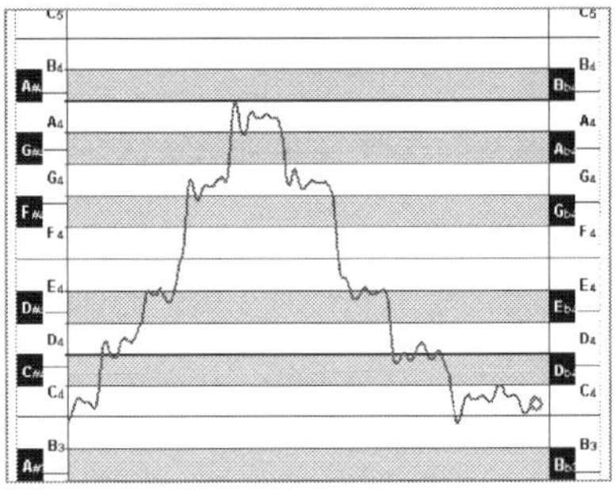

AIM

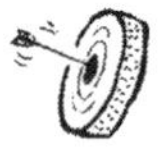

To sing an ascending and descending pentatonic scale on a specified vowel, with accurate pitch.

OBJECTIVES

- To develop management of pitch when singing an ascending and descending pentatonic scale.
  In defining this scale, the accuracy of the minor 3rd is particularly important.
- To build the aural and kinaesthetic memory necessary for this task.

PHYSICAL INVOLVEMENT

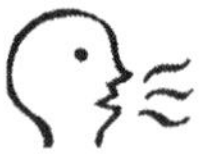

- Abdominal and thoracic muscle groups to achieve breath management
- Larynx height and posture
- Articulators, including pharynx, velum (soft palate), tongue, lips and jaw, for appropriate vowel formation and vocal resonance

INSTRUCTIONS

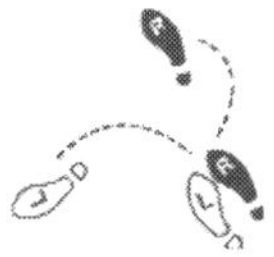

1. Play the pentachord
2. Mentally hear the sequence sung on the chosen vowel
3. Breathe the correct vowel shape
4. Position the larynx
5. Activate breath support
6. Start to sing
7. Increase breath pressure in order to increase pitch, while keeping the vowel shape
8. Maintain appropriate pressure for the descending pitch, while keeping the vowel shape

PITCH DISPLAY

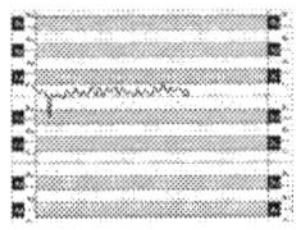

Sing the scale by directing the blue pitch line from the centre of the first note to the centre of each following note. The optimal display will show minimal, clean horizontal lines in an upward, then equally downward, diagonal.

SPECTROGRAM

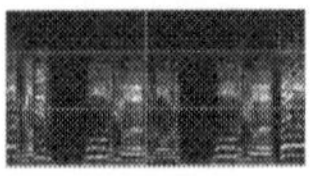

The Spectrogram should exhibit the same pattern of resonances throughout the exercise.

LEVEL METER

The volume should remain consistent throughout the exercise.
Note: Where intervals traverse register changes, this is an especially useful skill to encourage.

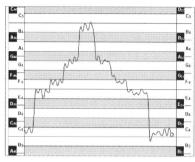

/a/

AIM	To sing an ascending and descending pentatonic scale on a specified vowel, with accurate pitch.
OBJECTIVES	▶ To develop management of pitch when singing an ascending and descending pentatonic scale. In defining this scale, the accuracy of the major 3rds is particularly important. ▶ To build the aural and kinaesthetic memory necessary for this task.
PHYSICAL INVOLVEMENT	▶ Abdominal and thoracic muscle groups to achieve breath management ▶ Larynx height and posture ▶ Articulators, including pharynx, velum (soft palate), tongue, lips and jaw, for appropriate vowel formation and vocal resonance
INSTRUCTIONS	1 Play the pentachord 2 Mentally hear the sequence sung on the chosen vowel 3 Breathe the correct vowel shape 4 Position the larynx 5 Activate breath support 6 Start to sing 7 Increase breath pressure in order to increase pitch, while keeping the vowel shape 8 Maintain appropriate pressure as the pitch descends, while keeping the vowel shape
PITCH DISPLAY	Sing the scale by directing the blue pitch line from the centre of the first note to the centre of each following note. The optimal display will show minimal, clean horizontal lines in an upward, then equally downward, diagonal.
SPECTROGRAM	
LEVEL METER	

Exercise S-19: Ascending and descending pentatonic (maj.3 S maj.3 T) scale

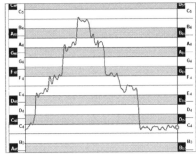

AIM	To sing an ascending and descending pentatonic scale on a specified vowel, with accurate pitch.

OBJECTIVES	▶ To develop management of pitch when singing an ascending and descending pentatonic scale. In defining this scale, the accuracy of the major 3rds is particularly important. ▶ To build the aural and kinaesthetic memory necessary for this task.

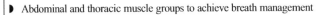

PHYSICAL INVOLVEMENT	▶ Abdominal and thoracic muscle groups to achieve breath management ▶ Larynx height and posture ▶ Articulators, including pharynx, velum (soft palate), tongue, lips and jaw, for appropriate vowel formation and vocal resonance

INSTRUCTIONS	1 Play the pentachord 2 Mentally hear the sequence sung on the chosen vowel 3 Breathe the correct vowel shape 4 Position the larynx 5 Activate breath support 6 Start to sing	7 Increase breath pressure in order to increase pitch, while keeping the vowel shape 8 Maintain appropriate pressure as the pitch descends, while keeping the vowel shape

PITCH DISPLAY	Sing the scale by directing the blue pitch line from the centre of the first note to the centre of each following note. The optimal display will show minimal, clean horizontal lines in an upward, then equally downward, diagonal.

SPECTROGRAM	

LEVEL METER	

Exercise S-20 : Ascending and descending pentachord (TTST)

/a/

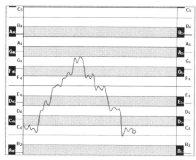

AIM	To sing an ascending and descending pentachord (Tone-Tone-Semitone-Tone) on a specified vowel, with accurate pitch.
OBJECTIVES	▶ To develop management of pitch when singing an ascending and descending pentachord. Of importance is the distinction between tones and semitones. ▶ To build the aural and kinaesthetic memory necessary for this task.
PHYSICAL INVOLVEMENT	▶ Abdominal and thoracic muscle groups to achieve breath management ▶ Larynx height and posture ▶ Articulators, including pharynx, velum (soft palate), tongue, lips and jaw, for appropriate vowel formation and vocal resonance
INSTRUCTIONS	1 Play the pentachord 2 Mentally hear the sequence sung on the chosen vowel 3 Breathe the correct vowel shape 4 Position the larynx 5 Activate breath support 6 Start to sing 7 Increase breath pressure in order to increase pitch, while keeping the vowel shape 8 Maintain appropriate pressure as the pitch descends, while keeping the vowel shape
PITCH DISPLAY	Sing the sequence by directing the blue pitch line from the centre of the first note to the centre of each following note, with minimal deviation. The optimal display will show minimal, clean horizontal lines in an upward, then equally downward, diagonal.
SPECTROGRAM	
LEVEL METER	

Exercise S-21: Ascending and descending pentachord (TSTT)

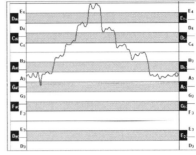

AIM	To sing an ascending and descending pentachord (Tone-Semitone-Tone-Tone) on a specified vowel, with accurate pitch.
OBJECTIVES	▶ To develop management of pitch when singing an ascending and descending pentachords. Of importance is the distinction between tones and semitones. ▶ To build the aural and kinaesthetic memory necessary for this task.
PHYSICAL INVOLVEMENT	▶ Abdominal and thoracic muscle groups to achieve breath management ▶ Larynx height and posture ▶ Articulators, including pharynx, velum (soft palate), tongue, lips and jaw, for appropriate vowel formation and vocal resonance
INSTRUCTIONS	1 Play the pentachord 2 Mentally hear the sequence sung on the chosen vowel 3 Breathe the correct vowel shape 4 Position the larynx 5 Activate breath support 6 Start to sing 7 Increase breath pressure in order to increase pitch, while keeping the vowel shape 8 Maintain appropriate pressure as the pitch descends, while keeping the vowel shape
PITCH DISPLAY	Sing the sequence by directing the blue pitch line from the centre of the lowest note to the centre of each following note. The optimal display will show minimal, clean horizontal lines in an upward, then equally downward, diagonal.
SPECTROGRAM	
LEVEL METER	

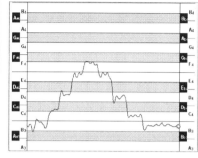

AIM	To sing an ascending and descending pentachord (Semitone-Tone-Tone-Tone) on a specified vowel, with accurate pitch.
OBJECTIVES	▶ To develop management of pitch when singing ascending and descending pentachords. Of importance is the distinction between tones and semitones. ▶ To build the aural and kinaesthetic memory necessary for this task.
PHYSICAL INVOLVEMENT	▶ Abdominal and thoracic muscle groups to achieve breath management ▶ Larynx height and posture ▶ Articulators, including pharynx, velum (soft palate), tongue, lips and jaw, for appropriate vowel formation and vocal resonance
INSTRUCTIONS	1 Play the pentachord 2 Mentally hear the sequence sung on the chosen vowel 3 Breathe the correct vowel shape 4 Position the larynx 5 Activate breath support 6 Start to sing	7 Increase breath pressure in order to increase pitch, while keeping the vowel shape 8 Maintain appropriate pressure as the pitch descends, while keeping the vowel shape
PITCH DISPLAY	Sing the sequence by directing the blue pitch line from the centre of the lowest note to the centre of each following note. The optimal display will show minimal, clean horizontal lines in an upward, then equally downward, diagonal.
SPECTROGRAM	
LEVEL METER	

S-23

Exercise S-23: Ascending and descending pentachord (TTST+)

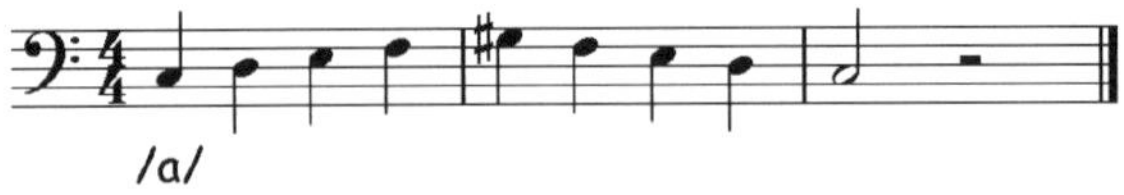

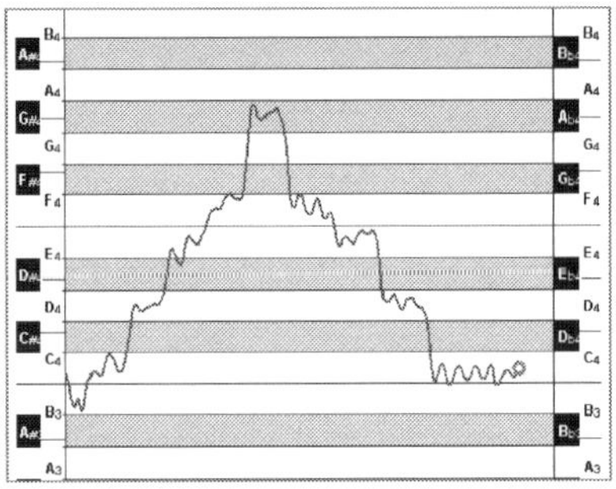

AIM

To sing an ascending and descending pentachord (Tone-Tone-Semitone-Augmented Tone) on a specified vowel, with accurate pitch.

OBJECTIVES

- To develop management of pitch when singing ascending and descending pentachords. Of importance is the distinction between tones and semitones.
- To build the aural and kinaesthetic memory necessary for this task.

PHYSICAL INVOLVEMENT

- Abdominal and thoracic muscle groups to achieve breath management
- Larynx height and posture
- Articulators, including pharynx, velum (soft palate), tongue, lips and jaw, for appropriate vowel formation and vocal resonance

INSTRUCTIONS

1. Play the pentachord
2. Mentally hear the sequence sung on the chosen vowel
3. Breathe the correct vowel shape
4. Position the larynx
5. Activate breath support
6. Start to sing
7. Increase breath pressure in order to increase pitch, while keeping the vowel shape
8. Maintain appropriate pressure as the pitch descends, while keeping the vowel shape

PITCH DISPLAY

Sing the sequence by directing the blue pitch line from the centre of the lowest note to the centre of each following note. The optimal display will show minimal, clean horizontal lines in an upward, then equally downward, diagonal.

SPECTROGRAM

LEVEL METER

/a/

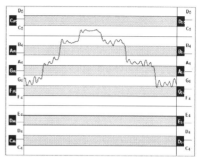

AIM	To sing an ascending and descending tetrachord (Tone-Tone-Semitone) on a specified vowel, with accurate pitch.
OBJECTIVES	▶ To develop management of pitch when singing an ascending and descending tetrachord Of importance is the distinction between tones and semitones. ▶ To build the aural and kinaesthetic memory necessary for this task.
PHYSICAL INVOLVEMENT	▶ Abdominal and thoracic muscle groups to achieve breath management ▶ Larynx height and posture ▶ Articulators, including pharynx, velum (soft palate), tongue, lips and jaw, for appropriate vowel formation and vocal resonance
INSTRUCTIONS	1 Play the tetrachord 2 Mentally hear the sequence sung on the chosen vowel 3 Breathe the correct vowel shape 4 Position the larynx 5 Activate breath support 6 Start to sing 7 Increase breath pressure in order to increase pitch, while keeping the vowel shape 8 Maintain appropriate breath pressure for the descending pitch while keeping the vowel shape
PITCH DISPLAY	Sing the sequence by directing the blue pitch line from the centre of the first note to the centre of each following note, with minimal deviation. The optimal display will show minimal, clean horizontal lines in an upward, then equally downward, diagonal.
SPECTROGRAM	
LEVEL METER	

Exercise S-25: Ascending and descending tetrachord (TST)

/a/

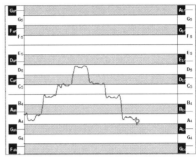

AIM	To sing an ascending and descending tetrachord (Tone-Semitone-Tone) on a specified vowel, with accurate pitch.
OBJECTIVES	▶ To develop management of pitch when singing an ascending and descending tetrachord. Of importance is the distinction between tones and semitones ▶ To build the aural and kinaesthetic memory necessary for this task.
PHYSICAL INVOLVEMENT	▶ Abdominal and thoracic muscle groups to achieve breath management ▶ Larynx height and posture ▶ Articulators, including pharynx, velum (soft palate), tongue, lips and jaw, for appropriate vowel formation and vocal resonance

INSTRUCTIONS	1 Play the tetrachord 2 Mentally hear the sequence sung on the chosen vowel 3 Breathe the correct vowel shape 4 Position the larynx 5 Activate breath support 6 Start to sing		7 Increase breath pressure in order to increase pitch, while keeping the vowel shape 8 Maintain appropriate pressure as the pitch descends, while keeping the vowel shape

PITCH DISPLAY	Sing the sequence by directing the blue pitch line from the centre of the lowest note to the centre of each following note. The optimal display will show minimal, clean horizontal lines in an upward, and then equally downward, diagonal.
SPECTROGRAM	
LEVEL METER	

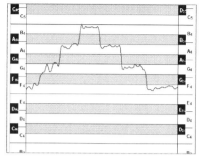

AIM	To sing an ascending and descending tetrachord (Tone-Tone-Tone) on a specified vowel, with accurate pitch.
OBJECTIVES	▸ To develop management of pitch when singing an ascending and descending tetrachord. Of importance is the distinction between tones and semitones. ▸ To build the aural and kinaesthetic memory necessary for this task.
PHYSICAL INVOLVEMENT	▸ Abdominal and thoracic muscle groups to achieve breath management ▸ Larynx height and posture ▸ Articulators, including pharynx, velum (soft palate), tongue, lips and jaw, for appropriate vowel formation and vocal resonance
INSTRUCTIONS	1 Play the tetrachord 2 Mentally hear the sequence sung on the chosen vowel 3 Breathe the correct vowel shape 4 Position the larynx 5 Activate breath support 6 Start to sing 7 Increase breath pressure in order to increase pitch, while keeping the vowel shape 8 Maintain appropriate breath pressure for the descending pitch, while keeping the vowel shape
PITCH DISPLAY	Sing the sequence by directing the blue pitch line from the centre of the lowest note to the centre of each following note. The optimal display will show minimal, clean horizontal lines in an upward, and then equally downward, diagonal.
SPECTROGRAM	
LEVEL METER	

Exercise S-27: Ascending and descending tetrachord (STT)

/a/

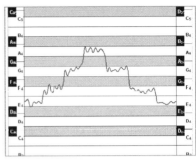

AIM	To sing an ascending and descending tetrachord (Tone-Tone-Semitone) on a specified vowel, with accurate pitch.
OBJECTIVES	▶ To develop management of pitch when singing an ascending and descending tetrachord. Of importance is the distinction between tones and semitones. ▶ To build the aural and kinaesthetic memory necessary for this task.
PHYSICAL INVOLVEMENT	▶ Abdominal and thoracic muscle groups to achieve breath management ▶ Larynx height and posture ▶ Articulators, including pharynx, velum (soft palate), tongue, lips and jaw, for appropriate vowel formation and vocal resonance
INSTRUCTIONS	1 Play the tetrachord 2 Mentally hear the sequence sung on the chosen vowel 3 Breathe the correct vowel shape 4 Position the larynx 5 Activate breath support 6 Start to sing 7 Increase breath pressure in order to increase pitch, while keeping the vowel shape 8 Maintain appropriate pressure for the descending pitch, while keeping the vowel shape
PITCH DISPLAY	Sing the sequence by directing the blue pitch line from the centre of the lowest note to the centre of each following note. The optimal display will show minimal, clean horizontal lines in an upward, and then equally downward, diagonal.
SPECTROGRAM	
LEVEL METER	

/α/

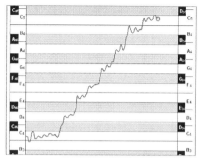

AIM	To sing an ascending major scale on a specified vowel, with accurate pitch.
OBJECTIVES	▶ To develop management of pitch when singing an ascending major scale. Of importance is the distinction between major and minor seconds, since it is the patterns of tones and semitones which constitute the scale. ▶ To build the aural and kinaesthetic memory necessary for this task.
PHYSICAL INVOLVEMENT	▶ Abdominal and thoracic muscle groups to achieve breath management ▶ Larynx height and posture ▶ Articulators, including pharynx, velum (soft palate), tongue, lips and jaw, for appropriate vowel formation and vocal resonance

INSTRUCTIONS	1 Play the scale 2 Mentally hear the scale sung on the chosen vowel 3 Breathe the correct vowel shape 4 Position the larynx 5 Activate breath support 6 Start to sing		7 Increase breath pressure in order to increase pitch, while keeping the vowel shape

PITCH DISPLAY	Sing the scale by directing the blue pitch line from the centre of the lowest note to the centre of each following note. The optimal display will show minimal, clean horizontal lines in an upward diagonal.
SPECTROGRAM	
LEVEL METER	

Exercise S-29: Ascending major scale, legato

/a/

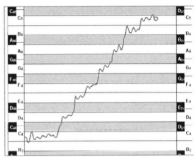

AIM	To sing an ascending major scale, legato, on a specified vowel, with pitch accuracy, consistent resonance and consistent volume.
OBJECTIVES	▶ To develop management of pitch, vowel articulation and volume, when singing an ascending major scale Of importance is the distinction between major and minor seconds, since it is the patterns of tones and semitones which constitute the scale. ▶ To enhance legato capability. ▶ To build the aural and kinaesthetic memory necessary for this task.
PHYSICAL INVOLVEMENT	▶ Abdominal and thoracic muscle groups to achieve breath management ▶ Larynx height and posture ▶ Articulators, including pharynx, velum (soft palate), tongue, lips and jaw, for appropriate vowel formation and vocal resonance

INSTRUCTIONS	1 Play the scale 2 Mentally hear the scale sung on the chosen vowel 3 Breathe the correct vowel shape 4 Position the larynx 5 Activate breath support 6 Start to sing	7 Gradually increase breath pressure in order to increase pitch, while keeping connected tone and vowel shape

PITCH DISPLAY	Sing the scale by directing the blue pitch line from the centre of the lowest note to the centre of each following note, with minimal deviation. The optimal display will show minimal, clean horizontal lines in an upward diagonal.
SPECTROGRAM	The Spectrogram should exhibit the same pattern of resonances throughout the exercise.
LEVEL METER	The volume should remain consistent throughout the exercise. *Note: Where intervals traverse register changes, this is an especially useful skill to encourage.*

/a/

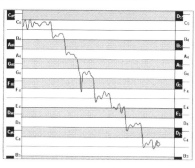

AIM	To sing a descending major scale on a specified vowel, with accurate pitch.
OBJECTIVES	▶ To develop management of pitch when singing a descending major scale. Of importance is the distinction between major and minor seconds, since it is the patterns of tones and semitones which constitute the scale. ▶ To build the aural and kinaesthetic memory necessary for this task.
PHYSICAL INVOLVEMENT	▶ Abdominal and thoracic muscle groups to achieve breath management ▶ Larynx height and posture ▶ Articulators, including pharynx, velum (soft palate), tongue, lips and jaw, for appropriate vowel formation and vocal resonance

<table>
<tr><td rowspan="2">INSTRUCTIONS
</td><td>1 Play the scale
2 Mentally hear the scale sung on the chosen vowel
3 Breathe the correct vowel shape
4 Position the larynx
5 Activate breath support
6 Start to sing</td><td>7 Maintain appropriate breath pressure for the descending pitch, while keeping the vowel shape</td></tr>
</table>

PITCH DISPLAY	Sing the scale by directing the blue pitch line from the centre of the highest note to the centre of each following note. The optimal display will show minimal, clean horizontal lines in a downward diagonal.
SPECTROGRAM	
LEVEL METER	

Exercise S-31: Descending major scale, legato

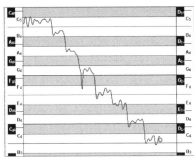

/a/

AIM	To sing a descending major scale, legato, on a specified vowel, with pitch accuracy, consistent resonance and consistent volume.
OBJECTIVES	▶ To develop management of pitch, vowel articulation and volume, when singing a descending major scale. Of importance is the distinction between major and minor seconds, since it is the patterns of tones and semitones which constitute the scale. ▶ To enhance legato capability. ▶ To build the aural and kinaesthetic memory necessary for this task.
PHYSICAL INVOLVEMENT	▶ Abdominal and thoracic muscle groups to achieve breath management ▶ Larynx height and posture ▶ Articulators, including pharynx, velum (soft palate), tongue, lips and jaw, for appropriate vowel formation and vocal resonance
INSTRUCTIONS	1 Play the scale 2 Mentally hear the scale sung on the chosen vowel 3 Breathe the correct vowel shape 4 Position the larynx 5 Activate breath support 6 Start to sing	7 Increase breath pressure in order to increase pitch, while maintaining the vowel shape 8 Maintain appropriate pressure as the pitch descends, while keeping the vowel shape
PITCH DISPLAY	Sing the scale by directing the blue pitch line from the centre of the highest note to the centre of each following note. The optimal display will show minimal, clean horizontal lines in a downward diagonal.
SPECTROGRAM	The Spectrogram should exhibit the same pattern of resonances throughout the exercise.
LEVEL METER	The volume should remain consistent throughout the exercise. *Note: Where intervals traverse register changes, this is an especially useful skill to encourage.*

/a/

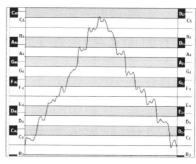

AIM	To sing an ascending and descending major scale on a specified vowel, with accurate pitch.
OBJECTIVES	▶ To develop management of pitch when singing an ascending and descending major scale. Of importance is the distinction between major and minor seconds, since it is the patterns of tones and semitones which constitute the scale. ▶ To build the aural and kinaesthetic memory necessary for this task.
PHYSICAL INVOLVEMENT	▶ Abdominal and thoracic muscle groups to achieve breath management ▶ Larynx height and posture ▶ Articulators, including pharynx, velum (soft palate), tongue, lips and jaw, for appropriate vowel formation and vocal resonance

INSTRUCTIONS

1 Play the scale
2 Mentally hear the scale sung on the chosen vowel
3 Breathe the correct vowel shape
4 Position the larynx
5 Activate breath support
6 Start to sing

7 Increase breath pressure in order to increase pitch, while keeping the vowel shape
8 Maintain appropriate pressure for the descending pitch, while keeping the vowel shape

PITCH DISPLAY	Sing the scale by directing the blue pitch line from the centre of the first note to the centre of each following note. The optimal display will show minimal, clean horizontal lines in an upward, then equally downward, diagonal.
SPECTROGRAM	
LEVEL METER	

Exercise S-33: Ascending and descending major scale, staccato

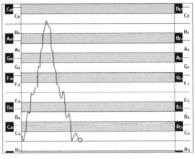

/a/

AIM	To sing an ascending and descending major scale, staccato, on a specified vowel, with accurate pitch.

OBJECTIVES	▶ To develop management of pitch when singing an ascending and descending major scale, staccato. Of importance is the distinction between major and minor seconds, since it is the patterns of tones and semitones which constitute the scale ▶ To build the aural and kinaesthetic memory necessary for this task.

PHYSICAL INVOLVEMENT	▶ Abdominal and thoracic muscle groups to achieve breath management ▶ Larynx height and posture ▶ Articulators, including pharynx, velum (soft palate), tongue, lips and jaw, for appropriate vowel formation and vocal resonance

INSTRUCTIONS	1 Play the scale 2 Mentally hear the scale sung on the chosen vowel 3 Breathe the correct vowel shape 4 Position the larynx 5 Activate breath support 6 Start to sing	7 Pay attention to precise onset and offset while increasing breath pressure for each ascending pitch and keeping the vowel shape 8 Pay attention to precise onset and offset while maintaining appropriate breath pressure for each descending pitch and keeping the vowel shape

PITCH DISPLAY	Sing the scale by directing the blue pitch line from the centre of the first note to the centre of each following note, with minimal deviation. The optimal display will show minimal, clean horizontal lines in an upward, then equally downward, diagonal.

SPECTROGRAM	

LEVEL METER	

Exercise S-34: Ascending and descending major scale, legato

/a/

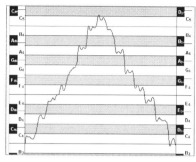

AIM	To sing an ascending and descending major scale, legato, on a specified vowel, with pitch accuracy, consistent resonance and consistent volume.

OBJECTIVES	▶ To develop management of pitch, vowel articulation and volume, when singing an ascending and descending major scale. Of importance is the distinction between major and minor seconds, since it is the patterns of tones and semitones which constitute the scale. ▶ To enhance legato capability. ▶ To build the aural and kinaesthetic memory necessary for this task.

PHYSICAL INVOLVEMENT 	▶ Abdominal and thoracic muscle groups to achieve breath management ▶ Larynx height and posture ▶ Articulators, including pharynx, velum (soft palate), tongue, lips and jaw, for appropriate vowel formation and vocal resonance

INSTRUCTIONS 	1 Play the scale 2 Mentally hear the scale sung on the chosen vowel 3 Breathe the correct vowel shape 4 Position the larynx 5 Activate breath support 6 Start to sing	7 Increase breath pressure in order to increase pitch, while maintaining the vowel shape 8 Maintain appropriate pressure for the descending pitch, while keeping the vowel shape

PITCH DISPLAY 	Sing the scale by directing the blue pitch line from the centre of the first note to the centre of each following note, with minimal deviation. The optimal display will show minimal, clean horizontal lines in an upward, then equally downward, diagonal.

SPECTROGRAM 	The Spectrogram should exhibit the same pattern of resonances throughout the exercise.

LEVEL METER	The volume should remain consistent throughout the exercise. *Note: Where intervals traverse register changes, this is an especially useful skill to encourage.*

Exercise S-35: Ascending and descending major scale, staccato, and then legato

/a/

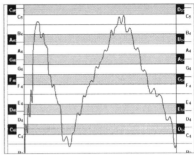

AIM	To sing an ascending and descending major scale, staccato, and then legato, on a specified vowel, with pitch accuracy, consistent resonance and consistent volume.
OBJECTIVES	▶ To develop management of pitch, vowel articulation and volume, when singing an ascending and descending major scale with both staccato and legato techniques. Of importance is the distinction between major and minor seconds, since it is the patterns of tones and semitones which constitute the scale. ▶ To enhance staccato and legato capability. ▶ To build the aural and kinaesthetic memory necessary for this task.
PHYSICAL INVOLVEMENT	▶ Abdominal and thoracic muscle groups to achieve breath management ▶ Larynx height and posture ▶ Articulators, including pharynx, velum (soft palate), tongue, lips and jaw, for appropriate vowel formation and vocal resonance
INSTRUCTIONS	1 Play the scale 2 Mentally hear the scale sung on the chosen vowel 3 Breathe the correct vowel shape 4 Position the larynx 5 Activate breath support 6 Start to sing 7 For the staccato, pay attention to precise	onset and offset while increasing breath pressure for each ascending pitch and maintaining appropriate breath pressure for each descending pitch 8 For the legato, keep connected tone and vowel shape while gradually increasing breath pressure for ascending pitch and maintaining appropriate breath pressure for descending pitch
PITCH DISPLAY	Sing the scale by directing the blue pitch line from the centre of the first note to the centre of each following note, with minimal deviation. For both staccato and legato, the optimal display will show minimal, clean horizontal lines in an upward, then equally downward, diagonal.
SPECTROGRAM	The Spectrogram should exhibit the same pattern of resonances throughout the exercise.
LEVEL METER	The volume should remain consistent throughout the exercise. *Note: Where intervals traverse register changes, this is an especially useful skill to encourage.*

Exercise S-36: Ascending Mixolydian mode (TTST TST)

/a/

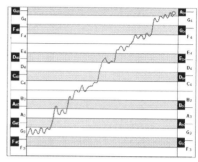

AIM	To sing an ascending Mixolydian mode on a specified vowel, with accurate pitch.
OBJECTIVES	▶ To develop management of pitch when singing an ascending Mixolydian mode. In order to distinguish this mode from the major scale, it is important to pay attention to the accuracy of the upper tetrachord, particularly the tone between the 7th degree and the final ▶ To build the aural and kinaesthetic memory necessary for this task.
PHYSICAL INVOLVEMENT	▶ Abdominal and thoracic muscle groups to achieve breath management ▶ Larynx height and posture ▶ Articulators, including pharynx, velum (soft palate), tongue, lips and jaw, for appropriate vowel formation and vocal resonance
INSTRUCTIONS	1 Play the mode 2 Mentally hear the mode sung on the chosen vowel 3 Breathe the correct vowel shape 4 Position the larynx 5 Activate breath support 6 Start to sing 7 Increase breath pressure in order to increase pitch, while keeping the vowel shape
PITCH DISPLAY	Sing the mode by directing the blue pitch line from the centre of the lowest note to the centre of each following note. The optimal display will show minimal, clean horizontal lines in an upward diagonal.
SPECTROGRAM	
LEVEL METER	

Exercise S-37: Ascending Mixolydian mode, legato

S-37

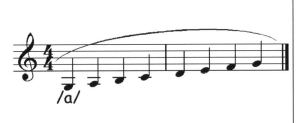

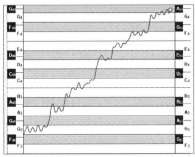

/a/

AIM	To sing an ascending Mixolydian mode, legato, on a specified vowel, with pitch accuracy, consistent resonance and consistent volume.
OBJECTIVES	▶ To develop management of pitch, vowel articulation and volume, when singing an ascending Mixolydian mode. In order to distinguish this mode from the major scale, it is important to pay attention to the accuracy of the upper tetrachord, particularly the tone between the 7th degree and the final. ▶ To enhance legato capability. ▶ To build the aural and kinaesthetic memory necessary for this task.
PHYSICAL INVOLVEMENT	▶ Abdominal and thoracic muscle groups to achieve breath management ▶ Larynx height and posture ▶ Articulators, including pharynx, velum (soft palate), tongue, lips and jaw, for appropriate vowel formation and vocal resonance
INSTRUCTIONS	1 Play the mode 2 Mentally hear the mode sung on the chosen vowel 3 Breathe the correct vowel shape 4 Position the larynx 5 Activate breath support 6 Start to sing	7 Increase breath pressure in order to increase pitch, while keeping the vowel shape
PITCH DISPLAY	Sing the mode by directing the blue pitch line from the centre of the lowest note to the centre of each following note, with minimal deviation. The optimal display will show minimal, clean horizontal lines in an upward diagonal.
SPECTROGRAM	The Spectrogram should exhibit the same pattern of resonances throughout the exercise.
LEVEL METER	The volume should remain consistent throughout the exercise. *Note: Where intervals traverse register changes, this is an especially useful skill to encourage.*

/a/

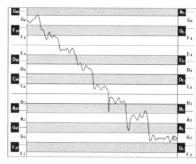

AIM	To sing a descending Mixolydian mode on a specified vowel, with accurate pitch.
OBJECTIVES	▶ To develop management of pitch when singing a descending Mixolydian mode. In order to distinguish this mode from the major scale, it is important to pay attention to the accuracy of the upper tetrachord, particularly the tone between the 7th degree and the final. ▶ To build the aural and kinaesthetic memory necessary for this task.
PHYSICAL INVOLVEMENT	▶ Abdominal and thoracic muscle groups to achieve breath management ▶ Larynx height and posture ▶ Articulators, including pharynx, velum (soft palate), tongue, lips and jaw, for appropriate vowel formation and vocal resonance

INSTRUCTIONS	1 Play the mode 2 Mentally hear the mode sung on the chosen vowel 3 Breathe the correct vowel shape 4 Position the larynx 5 Activate breath support 6 Start to sing		7 Maintain appropriate breath pressure for the descending pitch, while keeping the vowel shape

PITCH DISPLAY	Sing the mode by directing the blue pitch line from the centre of the highest note to the centre of each following note. The optimal display will show minimal, clean horizontal lines in a downward diagonal.
SPECTROGRAM	
LEVEL METER	

Exercise S-39: Descending Mixolydian mode, legato

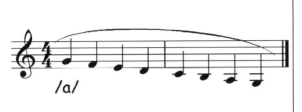

/a/

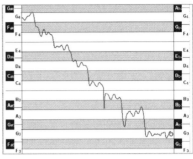

AIM	To sing a descending Mixolydian mode, legato, on a specified vowel, with pitch accuracy, consistent resonance and consistent volume.
OBJECTIVES	▶ To develop management of pitch, vowel articulation and volume, when singing a descending Mixolydian mode. In order to distinguish this mode from the major scale, it is important to pay attention to the accuracy of the upper tetrachord, particularly the tone between the 7th degree and the final. ▶ To enhance legato capability. ▶ To build the aural and kinaesthetic memory necessary for this task.
PHYSICAL INVOLVEMENT	▶ Abdominal and thoracic muscle groups to achieve breath management ▶ Larynx height and posture ▶ Articulators, including pharynx, velum (soft palate), tongue, lips and jaw, for appropriate vowel formation and vocal resonance
INSTRUCTIONS	1 Play the mode 2 Mentally hear the mode sung on the chosen vowel 3 Breathe the correct vowel shape 4 Position the larynx 5 Activate breath support 6 Start to sing 7 Increase breath pressure in order to increase pitch, while keeping the vowel shape 8 Maintain appropriate pressure for the descending pitch, while keeping the vowel shape
PITCH DISPLAY	Sing the mode by directing the blue pitch line from the centre of the highest note to the centre of each following note, with minimal deviation. The optimal display will show minimal, clean horizontal lines in a downward diagonal.
SPECTROGRAM	The Spectrogram should exhibit the same pattern of resonances throughout the exercise.
LEVEL METER	The volume should remain consistent throughout the exercise. *Note: Where intervals traverse register changes, this is an especially useful skill to encourage.*

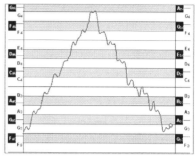

AIM	To sing an ascending and descending Mixolydian mode on a specified vowel, with accurate pitch.
OBJECTIVES	▶ To develop management of pitch when singing an ascending and descending Mixolydian mode. In order to distinguish this mode from the major scale, it is important to pay attention to the accuracy of the upper tetrachord, particularly the tone between the 7th degree and the final. ▶ To build the aural and kinaesthetic memory necessary for this task.
PHYSICAL INVOLVEMENT	▶ Abdominal and thoracic muscle groups to achieve breath management ▶ Larynx height and posture ▶ Articulators, including pharynx, velum (soft palate), tongue, lips and jaw, for appropriate vowel formation and vocal resonance
INSTRUCTIONS	1 Play the mode 2 Mentally hear the mode sung on the chosen vowel 3 Breathe the correct vowel shape 4 Position the larynx 5 Activate breath support 6 Start to sing 7 Increase breath pressure in order to increase pitch, while keeping the vowel shape 8 Maintain appropriate pressure for the descending pitch, while keeping the vowel shape
PITCH DISPLAY	Sing the mode by directing the blue pitch line from the centre of the first note to the centre of each following note. The optimal display will show minimal, clean horizontal lines in an upward, then equally downward, diagonal.
SPECTROGRAM 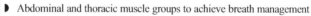	
LEVEL METER	

Exercise S-41: Ascending and descending Mixolydian mode, staccato

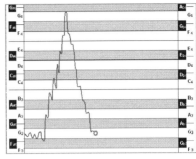

AIM	To sing an ascending and descending Mixolydian mode, staccato, on a specified vowel, with accurate pitch.
OBJECTIVES	▶ To develop management of pitch when singing an ascending and descending Mixolydian mode, staccato. In order to distinguish this mode from the major scale, it is important to pay attention to the accuracy of the upper tetrachord, particularly the tone between the 7th degree and the final. ▶ To build the aural and kinaesthetic memory necessary for this task.
PHYSICAL INVOLVEMENT	▶ Abdominal and thoracic muscle groups to achieve breath management ▶ Larynx height and posture ▶ Articulators, including pharynx, velum (soft palate), tongue, lips and jaw, for appropriate vowel formation and vocal resonance

INSTRUCTIONS	1 Play the mode 2 Mentally hear the mode sung on the chosen vowel 3 Breathe the correct vowel shape 4 Position the larynx 5 Activate breath support 6 Start to sing	7 Pay attention to precise onset and offset while increasing breath pressure for each ascending pitch and keeping the vowel shape 8 Pay attention to precise onset and offset while maintaining appropriate breath pressure for each descending pitch and keeping the vowel shape

PITCH DISPLAY	Sing the mode by directing the blue pitch line from the centre of the first note to the centre of each following note, with minimal deviation. The optimal display will show minimal, clean horizontal lines in an upward, then equally downward, diagonal.
SPECTROGRAM	
LEVEL METER	

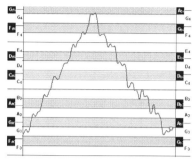

AIM	To sing an ascending and descending Mixolydian mode, legato, on a specified vowel, with pitch accuracy, consistent resonance and consistent volume.
OBJECTIVES	▶ To develop management of pitch, vowel articulation and volume, when singing an ascending and descending Mixolydian mode. In order to distinguish this mode from the major scale, it is important to pay attention to the accuracy of the upper tetrachord, particularly the tone between the 7th degree and the final. ▶ To enhance legato capability. ▶ To build the aural and kinaesthetic memory necessary for this task.
PHYSICAL INVOLVEMENT	▶ Abdominal and thoracic muscle groups to achieve breath management ▶ Larynx height and posture ▶ Articulators, including pharynx, velum (soft palate), tongue, lips and jaw, for appropriate vowel formation and vocal resonance
INSTRUCTIONS	1 Play the mode 2 Mentally hear the mode sung on the chosen vowel 3 Breathe the correct vowel shape 4 Position the larynx 5 Activate breath support 6 Start to sing 7 Gradually increase breath pressure in order to increase pitch, while keeping connected tone and vowel shape 8 Maintain appropriate breath pressure for the descending pitch while keeping connected tone and vowel shape
PITCH DISPLAY	Sing the mode by directing the blue pitch line from the centre of the first note to the centre of each following note, with minimal deviation. The optimal display will show minimal, clean horizontal lines in an upward, then equally downward, diagonal.
SPECTROGRAM	The Spectrogram should exhibit the same pattern of resonances throughout the exercise.
LEVEL METER	The volume should remain consistent throughout the exercise. *Note: Where intervals traverse register changes, this is an especially useful skill to encourage.*

Exercise S-43: Ascending and descending Mixolydian mode, staccato, and then legato

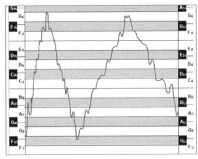

/a/

AIM	To sing an ascending and descending Mixolydian mode, staccato, and then legato, on a specified vowel, with pitch accuracy, consistent resonance and consistent volume.
OBJECTIVES	▶ To develop management of pitch, vowel articulation and volume, when singing an ascending and descending Mixolydian mode with both staccato and legato techniques. In order to distinguish this mode from the major scale, it is important to pay attention to the accuracy of the upper tetrachord, particularly the tone between the 7th degree and the final. ▶ To enhance staccato and legato capability. ▶ To build the aural and kinaesthetic memory necessary for this task.
PHYSICAL INVOLVEMENT	▶ Abdominal and thoracic muscle groups to achieve breath management ▶ Larynx height and posture ▶ Articulators, including pharynx, velum (soft palate), tongue, lips and jaw, for appropriate vowel formation and vocal resonance

INSTRUCTIONS	1 Play the mode 2 Mentally hear the mode sung on the chosen vowel 3 Breathe the correct vowel shape 4 Position the larynx 5 Activate breath support 6 Start to sing 7 For the staccato, pay attention to precise	onset and offset while increasing breath pressure for each ascending pitch and maintaining appropriate breath pressure for each descending pitch 8 For the legato, keep connected tone and vowel shape while gradually increasing breath pressure for ascending pitch and maintaining appropriate breath pressure for descending pitch

PITCH DISPLAY	Sing the mode by directing the blue pitch line from the centre of the first note to the centre of each following note, with minimal deviation. The optimal display will show minimal, clean horizontal lines in an upward, then equally downward, diagonal.
SPECTROGRAM	The Spectrogram should exhibit the same pattern of resonances throughout the exercise.
LEVEL METER	The volume should remain consistent throughout the exercise. *Note: Where intervals traverse register changes, this is an especially useful skill to encourage.*

/a/

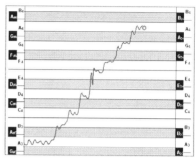

AIM	To sing an ascending natural minor scale on a specified vowel, with accurate pitch.
OBJECTIVES	▶ To develop management of pitch when singing an ascending natural minor scale. While the pentachord is the same as for the other minor scales, care needs to be taken to ensure the accuracy of the upper tetrachord, particularly the tone between the leading note and upper tonic. ▶ To build the aural and kinaesthetic memory necessary for this task.
PHYSICAL INVOLVEMENT	▶ Abdominal and thoracic muscle groups to achieve breath management ▶ Larynx height and posture ▶ Articulators, including pharynx, velum (soft palate), tongue, lips and jaw, for appropriate vowel formation and vocal resonance
INSTRUCTIONS	1 Play the scale 2 Mentally hear the scale sung on the chosen vowel 3 Breathe the correct vowel shape 4 Position the larynx 5 Activate breath support 6 Start to sing 7 Increase breath pressure in order to increase pitch, while keeping the vowel shape
PITCH DISPLAY	Sing the scale by directing the blue pitch line from the centre of the lowest note to the centre of each following note. The optimal display will show minimal, clean horizontal lines in an upward diagonal.
SPECTROGRAM	
LEVEL METER	

Exercise S-45: Ascending natural minor scale, legato

/a/

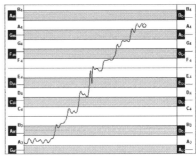

AIM	To sing an ascending natural minor scale, legato, on a specified vowel, with pitch accuracy, consistent resonance and consistent volume.
OBJECTIVES 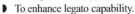	▶ To develop management of pitch, vowel articulation and volume, when singing an ascending natural minor scale. While the pentachord is the same as for the other minor scales, care needs to be taken to ensure the accuracy of the upper tetrachord, particularly the tone between the leading note and upper tonic. ▶ To enhance legato capability. ▶ To build the aural and kinaesthetic memory necessary for this task.
PHYSICAL INVOLVEMENT	▶ Abdominal and thoracic muscle groups to achieve breath management ▶ Larynx height and posture ▶ Articulators, including pharynx, velum (soft palate), tongue, lips and jaw, for appropriate vowel formation and vocal resonance
INSTRUCTIONS	1 Play the scale 2 Mentally hear the scale sung on the chosen vowel 3 Breathe the correct vowel shape 4 Position the larynx 5 Activate breath support 6 Start to sing 7 Increase breath pressure in order to increase pitch, while keeping the vowel shape
PITCH DISPLAY	Sing the scale by directing the blue pitch line from the centre of the lowest note to the centre of each following note, with minimal deviation. The optimal display will show minimal, clean horizontal lines in an upward diagonal.
SPECTROGRAM	The Spectrogram should exhibit the same pattern of resonances throughout the exercise.
LEVEL METER	The volume should remain consistent throughout the exercise. *Note: Where intervals traverse register changes, this is an especially useful skill to encourage.*

/a/

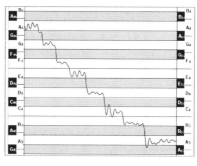

AIM	To sing a descending natural minor scale on a specified vowel, with accurate pitch.
OBJECTIVES	▶ To develop management of pitch when singing a descending natural minor scale. While the pentachord is the same as for the other minor scales, care needs to be taken to ensure the accuracy of the upper tetrachord, particularly the tone between the leading note and upper tonic. ▶ To build the aural and kinaesthetic memory necessary for this task.
PHYSICAL INVOLVEMENT	▶ Abdominal and thoracic muscle groups to achieve breath management ▶ Larynx height and posture ▶ Articulators, including pharynx, velum (soft palate), tongue, lips and jaw, for appropriate vowel formation and vocal resonance

INSTRUCTIONS

1 Play the scale 2 Mentally hear the scale sung on the chosen vowel 3 Breathe the correct vowel shape 4 Position the larynx 5 Activate breath support 6 Start to sing	7 Maintain appropriate breath pressure for the descending pitch, while keeping the vowel shape

PITCH DISPLAY	Sing the scale by directing the blue pitch line from the centre of the highest note to the centre of each following note. The optimal display will show minimal, clean horizontal lines in a downward diagonal.
SPECTROGRAM	
LEVEL METER	

Exercise S-47: Descending natural minor scale, legato

/a/

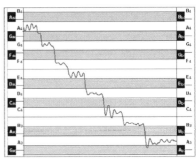

AIM	To sing a descending natural minor scale, legato, on a specified vowel, with pitch accuracy, consistent resonance and consistent volume.
OBJECTIVES	▶ To develop management of pitch, vowel articulation and volume, when singing a descending natural minor scale. While the pentachord is the same as for the other minor scales, care needs to be taken to ensure the accuracy of the upper tetrachord, particularly the tone between the leading note and upper tonic. ▶ To enhance legato capability. ▶ To build the aural and kinaesthetic memory necessary for this task.
PHYSICAL INVOLVEMENT	▶ Abdominal and thoracic muscle groups to achieve breath management ▶ Larynx height and posture ▶ Articulators, including pharynx, velum (soft palate), tongue, lips and jaw, for appropriate vowel formation and vocal resonance

INSTRUCTIONS	1 Play the scale 2 Mentally hear the scale sung on the chosen vowel 3 Breathe the correct vowel shape 4 Position the larynx 5 Activate breath support 6 Start to sing	7 Maintain appropriate pressure for the descending pitch, while keeping the vowel shape

PITCH DISPLAY	Sing the scale by directing the blue pitch line from the centre of the highest note to the centre of each following note, with minimal deviation. The optimal display will show minimal, clean horizontal lines in a downward diagonal.
SPECTROGRAM	The Spectrogram should exhibit the same pattern of resonances throughout the exercise.
LEVEL METER	The volume should remain consistent throughout the exercise. *Note: Where intervals traverse register changes, this is an especially useful skill to encourage.*

/a/

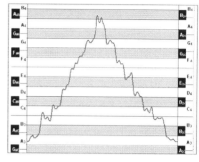

AIM	To sing an ascending and descending natural minor scale on a specified vowel, with accurate pitch.
OBJECTIVES	▸ To develop management of pitch when singing an ascending and descending natural minor scale. While the pentachord is the same as for the other minor scales, care needs to be taken to ensure the accuracy of the upper tetrachord, particularly the tone between the leading note and upper tonic. ▸ To build the aural and kinaesthetic memory necessary for this task.
PHYSICAL INVOLVEMENT	▸ Abdominal and thoracic muscle groups to achieve breath management ▸ Larynx height and posture ▸ Articulators, including pharynx, velum (soft palate), tongue, lips and jaw, for appropriate vowel formation and vocal resonance
INSTRUCTIONS	1 Play the scale 2 Mentally hear the scale sung on the chosen vowel 3 Breathe the correct vowel shape 4 Position the larynx 5 Activate breath support 6 Start to sing 7 Gradually increase breath pressure in order to increase pitch while keeping vowel shape 8 Maintain appropriate breath pressure for the descending pitch, while keeping the vowel shape
PITCH DISPLAY	Sing the scale by directing the blue pitch line from the centre of the first note to the centre of each following note. The optimal display will show minimal, clean horizontal lines in an upward, then equally downward, diagonal.
SPECTROGRAM	
LEVEL METER	

Exercise S-49: Ascending and descending natural minor scale, staccato

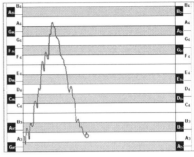

AIM	To sing an ascending and descending natural minor scale, staccato, on a specified vowel, with accurate pitch.
OBJECTIVES	▶ To develop management of pitch when singing an ascending and descending natural minor scale, staccato. While the pentachord is the same as for the other minor scales, care needs to be taken to ensure the accuracy of the upper tetrachord, particularly the tone between the leading note and upper tonic. ▶ To build the aural and kinaesthetic memory necessary for this task.
PHYSICAL INVOLVEMENT	▶ Abdominal and thoracic muscle groups to achieve breath management ▶ Larynx height and posture ▶ Articulators, including pharynx, velum (soft palate), tongue, lips and jaw, for appropriate vowel formation and vocal resonance
INSTRUCTIONS	1 Play the scale 2 Mentally hear the scale sung on the chosen vowel 3 Breathe the correct vowel shape 4 Position the larynx 5 Activate breath support 6 Start to sing 7 Pay attention to precise onset and offset while increasing breath pressure for each ascending pitch and keeping the vowel shape 8 Pay attention to precise onset and offset while maintaining appropriate breath pressure for each descending pitch and keeping the vowel shape
PITCH DISPLAY	Sing the scale by directing the blue pitch line from the centre of the first note to the centre of each following note, with minimal deviation The optimal display will show minimal, clean horizontal lines in an upward, then equally downward, diagonal.
SPECTROGRAM	
LEVEL METER	

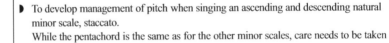

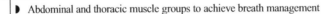

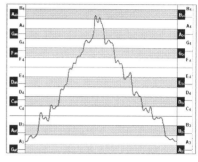

AIM	To sing an ascending and descending natural minor scale, legato, on a specified vowel, with pitch accuracy, consistent resonance and consistent volume.

OBJECTIVES	▶ To develop management of pitch, vowel articulation and volume, when singing an ascending and descending natural minor scale. While the pentachord is the same as for the other minor scales, care needs to be taken to ensure the accuracy of the upper tetrachord, particularly the tone between the leading note and upper tonic. ▶ To enhance legato capability. ▶ To build the aural and kinaesthetic memory necessary for this task.

PHYSICAL INVOLVEMENT	▶ Abdominal and thoracic muscle groups to achieve breath management ▶ Larynx height and posture ▶ Articulators, including pharynx, velum (soft palate), tongue, lips and jaw, for appropriate vowel formation and vocal resonance

INSTRUCTIONS	1 Play the scale 2 Mentally hear the scale sung on the chosen vowel 3 Breathe the correct vowel shape 4 Position the larynx 5 Activate breath support 6 Start to sing	7 Increase breath pressure in order to increase pitch, while keeping the vowel shape 8 Maintain appropriate pressure for the descending pitch, while keeping the vowel shape

PITCH DISPLAY	Sing the scale by directing the blue pitch line from the centre of the first note to the centre of each following note, with minimal deviation. The optimal display will show minimal, clean horizontal lines in an upward, then equally downward, diagonal.

SPECTROGRAM	The Spectrogram should exhibit the same pattern of resonances throughout the exercise.

LEVEL METER	The volume should remain consistent throughout the exercise. *Note: Where intervals traverse register changes, this is an especially useful skill to encourage.*

Exercise S-51: Ascending and descending natural minor scale, staccato, and then legato

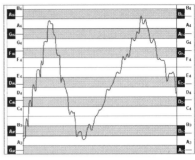

AIM	To sing an ascending and descending natural minor scale, staccato, and then legato, on a specified vowel, with pitch accuracy, consistent resonance and consistent volume.
OBJECTIVES	▶ To develop management of pitch, vowel articulation and volume, when singing an ascending and descending natural minor scale with both staccato and legato techniques. While the pentachord is the same as for the other minor scales, care needs to be taken to ensure the accuracy of the upper tetrachord, particularly the tone between the leading note and upper tonic. ▶ To enhance staccato and legato capability. ▶ To build the aural and kinaesthetic memory necessary for this task.
PHYSICAL INVOLVEMENT	▶ Abdominal and thoracic muscle groups to achieve breath management ▶ Larynx height and posture ▶ Articulators, including pharynx, velum (soft palate), tongue, lips and jaw, for appropriate vowel formation and vocal resonance

INSTRUCTIONS	1 Play the scale 2 Mentally hear the scale sung on the chosen vowel 3 Breathe the correct vowel shape 4 Position the larynx 5 Activate breath support 6 Start to sing 7 For the staccato, pay attention to precise	onset and offset while increasing breath pressure for each ascending pitch and maintaining appropriate breath pressure for each descending pitch 8 For the legato, keep connected tone and vowel shape while gradually increasing breath pressure for ascending pitch and maintaining appropriate breath pressure for descending pitch

PITCH DISPLAY	Sing the scale by directing the blue pitch line from the centre of the first note to the centre of each following note, with minimal deviation. For both staccato and legato, the optimal display will show minimal, clean horizontal lines in an upward, then equally downward, diagonal.
SPECTROGRAM	The Spectrogram should exhibit the same pattern of resonances throughout the exercise.
LEVEL METER	The volume should remain consistent throughout the exercise. *Note: Where intervals traverse register changes, this is an especially useful skill to encourage.*

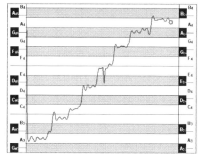

AIM	To sing an ascending melodic minor scale on a specified vowel, with accurate pitch.
OBJECTIVES	▶ To develop management of pitch when singing an ascending melodic minor scale. While the pentachord is the same as for the other minor scales, in the upper tetrachord care needs to be taken in defining the raised 6th and 7th degrees of the ascending scale in contrast with the natural form of the descending scale. ▶ To build the aural and kinaesthetic memory necessary for this task.
PHYSICAL INVOLVEMENT	▶ Abdominal and thoracic muscle groups to achieve breath management ▶ Larynx height and posture ▶ Articulators, including pharynx, velum (soft palate), tongue, lips and jaw, for appropriate vowel formation and vocal resonance
INSTRUCTIONS	1 Play the scale 2 Mentally hear the scale sung on the chosen vowel 3 Breathe the correct vowel shape 4 Position the larynx 5 Activate breath support 6 Start to sing 7 Increase breath pressure in order to increase pitch, while keeping the vowel shape
PITCH DISPLAY	Sing the scale by directing the blue pitch line from the centre of the lowest note to the centre of each following note. The optimal display will show minimal, clean horizontal lines in an upward diagonal.
SPECTROGRAM	
LEVEL METER	

Exercise S-53: Ascending melodic minor scale, legato

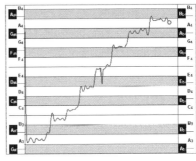

AIM 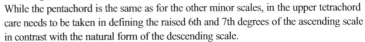	To sing an ascending melodic minor scale, legato, on a specified vowel, with pitch accuracy, consistent resonance and consistent volume.
OBJECTIVES	▶ To develop management of pitch, vowel articulation and volume, when singing an ascending melodic minor scale. While the pentachord is the same as for the other minor scales, in the upper tetrachord care needs to be taken in defining the raised 6th and 7th degrees of the ascending scale in contrast with the natural form of the descending scale. ▶ To enhance legato capability. ▶ To build the aural and kinaesthetic memory necessary for this task.
PHYSICAL INVOLVEMENT	▶ Abdominal and thoracic muscle groups to achieve breath management ▶ Larynx height and posture ▶ Articulators, including pharynx, velum (soft palate), tongue, lips and jaw, for appropriate vowel formation and vocal resonance
INSTRUCTIONS	1 Play the scale 2 Mentally hear the scale sung on the chosen vowel 3 Breathe the correct vowel shape 4 Position the larynx 5 Activate breath support 6 Start to sing 7 Gradually increase breath pressure in order to increase pitch while keeping connected tone and vowel shape
PITCH DISPLAY	Sing the scale by directing the blue pitch line from the centre of the lowest note to the centre of each following note, with minimal deviation. The optimal display will show minimal, clean horizontal lines in an upward diagonal.
SPECTROGRAM	The Spectrogram should exhibit the same pattern of resonances throughout the exercise.
LEVEL METER	The volume should remain consistent throughout the exercise. *Note: Where intervals traverse register changes, this is an especially useful skill to encourage.*

/a/

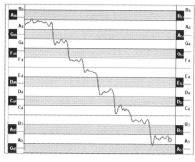

AIM	To sing a descending melodic minor scale on a specified vowel with accurate pitch.
OBJECTIVES	▶ To develop management of pitch when singing a descending melodic minor scale. While the pentachord is the same as for the other minor scales, in the upper tetrachord care needs to be taken in defining the raised 6th and 7th degrees of the ascending scale in contrast with the natural form of the descending scale. ▶ To build the aural and kinaesthetic memory necessary for this task.
PHYSICAL INVOLVEMENT	▶ Abdominal and thoracic muscle groups to achieve breath management ▶ Larynx height and posture ▶ Articulators, including pharynx, velum (soft palate), tongue, lips and jaw, for appropriate vowel formation and vocal resonance
INSTRUCTIONS	1 Play the scale 2 Mentally hear the scale sung on the chosen vowel 3 Breathe the correct vowel shape 4 Position the larynx 5 Activate breath support 6 Start to sing 7 Maintain appropriate breath pressure for the descending pitch, while keeping the vowel shape
PITCH DISPLAY	Sing the scale by directing the blue pitch line from the centre of the highest note to the centre of each following note. The optimal display will show minimal, clean horizontal lines in a downward diagonal.
SPECTROGRAM	
LEVEL METER	

Exercise S-55: Descending melodic minor scale, legato

/a/

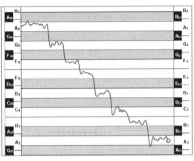

AIM	To sing a descending melodic minor scale, legato, on a specified vowel, with pitch accuracy, consistent resonance and consistent volume.
OBJECTIVES 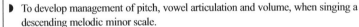	▶ To develop management of pitch, vowel articulation and volume, when singing a descending melodic minor scale. While the pentachord is the same as for the other minor scales, in the upper tetrachord care needs to be taken in defining the raised 6th and 7th degrees of the ascending scale in contrast with the natural form of the descending scale. ▶ To enhance legato capability. ▶ To build the aural and kinaesthetic memory necessary for this task.
PHYSICAL INVOLVEMENT	▶ Abdominal and thoracic muscle groups to achieve breath management ▶ Larynx height and posture ▶ Articulators, including pharynx, velum (soft palate), tongue, lips and jaw, for appropriate vowel formation and vocal resonance

INSTRUCTIONS	1 Play the scale 2 Mentally hear the scale sung on the chosen vowel 3 Breathe the correct vowel shape 4 Position the larynx 5 Activate breath support 6 Start to sing	7 Maintain appropriate breath pressure for the descending pitch, while keeping the vowel shape

PITCH DISPLAY	Sing the scale by directing the blue pitch line from the centre of the highest note to the centre of each following note, with minimal deviation. The optimal display will show minimal, clean horizontal lines in a downward diagonal.
SPECTROGRAM	The Spectrogram should exhibit the same pattern of resonances throughout the exercise.
LEVEL METER	The volume should remain consistent throughout the exercise. *Note: Where intervals traverse register changes, this is an especially useful skill to encourage.*

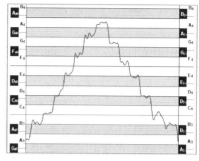

AIM	To sing an ascending and descending melodic minor scale on a specified vowel with accurate pitch.
OBJECTIVES	▶ To develop management of pitch when singing an ascending and descending melodic minor scale. While the pentachord is the same as for the other minor scales, in the upper tetrachord care needs to be taken in defining the raised 6th and 7th degrees of the ascending scale in contrast with the natural form of the descending scale. ▶ To build the aural and kinaesthetic memory necessary for this task.
PHYSICAL INVOLVEMENT	▶ Abdominal and thoracic muscle groups to achieve breath management ▶ Larynx height and posture ▶ Articulators, including pharynx, velum (soft palate), tongue, lips and jaw, for appropriate vowel formation and vocal resonance
INSTRUCTIONS	1 Play the scale 2 Mentally hear the scale sung on the chosen vowel 3 Breathe the correct vowel shape 4 Position the larynx 5 Activate breath support 6 Start to sing 7 Increase breath pressure in order to increase pitch, while keeping the vowel shape 8 Maintain appropriate pressure for the descending pitch, while keeping the vowel shape
PITCH DISPLAY	Sing the scale by directing the blue pitch line from the centre of the first note to the centre of each following note. The optimal display will show minimal, clean horizontal lines in an upward, then equally downward, diagonal.
SPECTROGRAM	
LEVEL METER	

Exercise S-57: Ascending and descending melodic minor scale, staccato

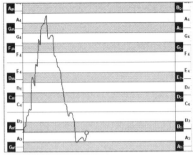

/á/

AIM	To sing an ascending and descending melodic minor scale, staccato, on a specified vowel with accurate pitch.
OBJECTIVES	▶ To develop management of pitch when singing an ascending and descending melodic minor scale, staccato. While the pentachord is the same as for the other minor scales, in the upper tetrachord care needs to be taken in defining the raised 6th and 7th degrees of the ascending scale in contrast with the natural form of the descending scale. ▶ To build the aural and kinaesthetic memory necessary for this task.
PHYSICAL INVOLVEMENT	▶ Abdominal and thoracic muscle groups to achieve breath management ▶ Larynx height and posture ▶ Articulators, including pharynx, velum (soft palate), tongue, lips and jaw, for appropriate vowel formation and vocal resonance

INSTRUCTIONS	1 Play the scale 2 Mentally hear the scale sung on the chosen vowel 3 Breathe the correct vowel shape 4 Position the larynx 5 Activate breath support 6 Start to sing	7 Pay attention to precise onset and offset while increasing breath pressure for each ascending pitch and keeping vowel shape 8 Pay attention to precise onset and offset while maintaining appropriate breath pressure for each descending pitch and keeping vowel shape

PITCH DISPLAY	Sing the scale by directing the blue pitch line from the centre of the first note to the centre of each following note, with minimal deviation. The optimal display will show minimal, clean horizontal lines in an upward, then equally downward, diagonal.

SPECTROGRAM	

LEVEL METER	

Exercise S-58: Ascending and descending melodic minor scale, legato

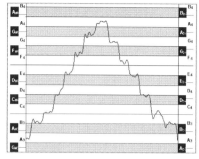

AIM	To sing an ascending and descending melodic minor scale, legato, on a specified vowel, with pitch accuracy, consistent resonance and consistent volume
OBJECTIVES	▶ To develop management of pitch, vowel articulation and volume, when singing an ascending and descending melodic minor scale. While the pentachord is the same as for the other minor scales, in the upper tetrachord care needs to be taken in defining the raised 6th and 7th degrees of the ascending scale in contrast with the natural form of the descending scale. ▶ To enhance legato capability. ▶ To build the aural and kinaesthetic memory necessary for this task.
PHYSICAL INVOLVEMENT	▶ Abdominal and thoracic muscle groups to achieve breath management ▶ Larynx height and posture ▶ Articulators, including pharynx, velum (soft palate), tongue, lips and jaw, for appropriate vowel formation and vocal resonance
INSTRUCTIONS	1 Play the scale 2 Mentally hear the scale sung on the chosen vowel 3 Breathe the correct vowel shape 4 Position the larynx 5 Activate breath support 6 Start to sing 7 Gradually increase breath pressure in order to increase pitch, while keeping connected tone and vowel shape 8 Maintain appropriate breath pressure for the descending pitch, while keeping connected tone and vowel shape
PITCH DISPLAY	Sing the scale by directing the blue pitch line from the centre of the first note to the centre of each following note, with minimal deviation. The optimal display will show minimal, clean horizontal lines in an upward, then equally downward, diagonal.
SPECTROGRAM	The Spectrogram should exhibit the same pattern of resonances throughout the exercise.
LEVEL METER	The volume should remain consistent throughout the exercise. *Note: Where intervals traverse register changes, this is an especially useful skill to encourage.*

Exercise S-59: Ascending and descending melodic minor scale, staccato, and then legato

S-59

/å/

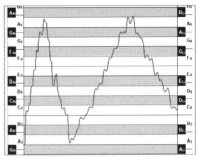

AIM	To sing an ascending and descending melodic minor scale, staccato, and then legato, on a specified vowel, with pitch accuracy, consistent resonance and consistent volume.
OBJECTIVES 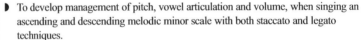	▶ To develop management of pitch, vowel articulation and volume, when singing an ascending and descending melodic minor scale with both staccato and legato techniques. While the pentachord is the same as for the other minor scales, in the upper tetrachord care needs to be taken in defining the raised 6th and 7th degrees of the ascending scale in contrast with the natural form of the descending scale. ▶ To enhance staccato and legato capability. ▶ To build the aural and kinaesthetic memory necessary for this task.
PHYSICAL INVOLVEMENT	▶ Abdominal and thoracic muscle groups to achieve breath management ▶ Larynx height and posture ▶ Articulators, including pharynx, velum (soft palate), tongue, lips and jaw, for appropriate vowel formation and vocal resonance
INSTRUCTIONS	1 Play the scale 2 Mentally hear the scale sung on the chosen vowel 3 Breathe the correct vowel shape 4 Position the larynx 5 Activate breath support 6 Start to sing 7 For the staccato, pay attention to precise	onset and offset while increasing breath pressure for each ascending pitch and maintaining appropriate breath pressure for each descending pitch 8 For the legato, keep connected tone and vowel shape while gradually increasing breath pressure for ascending pitch and maintaining appropriate breath pressure for descending pitch
PITCH DISPLAY	Sing the scale by directing the blue pitch line from the centre of the first note to the centre of each following note, with minimal deviation. The optimal display will show minimal, clean horizontal lines in an upward, then equally downward, diagonal.
SPECTROGRAM	The Spectrogram should exhibit the same pattern of resonances throughout the exercise.
LEVEL METER	The volume should remain consistent throughout the exercise. *Note: Where intervals traverse register changes, this is an especially useful skill to encourage.*

/a/

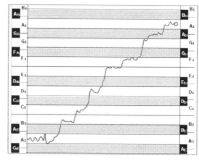

AIM	To sing an ascending harmonic minor scale on a specified vowel with accurate pitch.
OBJECTIVES	▶ To develop management of pitch when singing an ascending harmonic minor scale. In distinguishing the harmonic form from the other minor scales, the accuracy of the upper tetrachord - particularly the augmented 2nd between the 6th and 7th degrees of the scale - is important. ▶ To build the aural and kinaesthetic memory necessary for this task.
PHYSICAL INVOLVEMENT	▶ Abdominal and thoracic muscle groups to achieve breath management ▶ Larynx height and posture ▶ Articulators, including pharynx, velum (soft palate), tongue, lips and jaw, for appropriate vowel formation and vocal resonance
INSTRUCTIONS	1 Play the scale 2 Mentally hear the scale sung on the chosen vowel 3 Breathe the correct vowel shape 4 Position the larynx 5 Activate breath support 6 Start to sing 7 Increase breath pressure in order to increase pitch, while keeping the vowel shape
PITCH DISPLAY	Sing the scale by directing the blue pitch line from the centre of the lowest note to the centre of each following note. The optimal display will show minimal, clean horizontal lines in an upward diagonal.
SPECTROGRAM	
LEVEL METER	

Exercise S-61: Ascending harmonic minor scale, legato

/a/

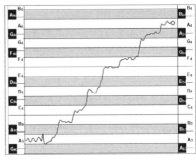

AIM	To sing an ascending major scale on a specified vowel, while maintaining consistent pitch through breath management.
OBJECTIVES 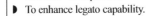	▶ To develop management of pitch, vowel articulation and volume, when singing a harmonic minor scale. In distinguishing the harmonic form from the other minor scales, the accuracy of the upper tetrachord - particularly the augmented 2nd between the 6th and 7th degrees of the scale - is important. ▶ To enhance legato capability. ▶ To build the aural and kinaesthetic memory necessary for this task.
PHYSICAL INVOLVEMENT	▶ Abdominal and thoracic muscle groups to achieve breath management ▶ Larynx height and posture ▶ Articulators, including pharynx, velum (soft palate), tongue, lips and jaw, for appropriate vowel formation and vocal resonance

INSTRUCTIONS	1 Play the scale 2 Mentally hear the scale sung on the chosen vowel 3 Breathe the correct vowel shape 4 Position the larynx 5 Activate breath support 6 Start to sing	7 Gradually increase breath pressure in order to increase pitch, while keeping connected tone and vowel shape

PITCH DISPLAY	Sing the scale by directing the blue pitch line from the centre of the lowest note to the centre of each following note, with minimal deviation. The optimal display will show minimal, clean horizontal lines in an upward diagonal.
SPECTROGRAM	The Spectrogram should exhibit the same pattern of resonances throughout the exercise.
LEVEL METER	The volume should remain consistent throughout the exercise. *Note: Where intervals traverse register changes, this is an especially useful skill to encourage.*

/a/

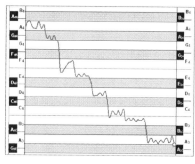

AIM	To sing a descending harmonic minor scale on a specified vowel with accurate pitch.
OBJECTIVES	❱ To develop management of pitch when singing a descending harmonic minor scale. In distinguishing the harmonic form from the other minor scales, the accuracy of the upper tetrachord - particularly the augmented 2nd between the 6th and 7th degrees of the scale - is important. ❱ To build the aural and kinaesthetic memory necessary for this task.
PHYSICAL INVOLVEMENT	❱ Abdominal and thoracic muscle groups to achieve breath management ❱ Larynx height and posture ❱ Articulators, including pharynx, velum (soft palate), tongue, lips and jaw, for appropriate vowel formation and vocal resonance
INSTRUCTIONS	1 Play the scale 2 Mentally hear the scale sung on the chosen vowel 3 Breathe the correct vowel shape 4 Position the larynx 5 Activate breath support 6 Start to sing 7 Maintain appropriate breath pressure for the descending pitch, while keeping the vowel shape
PITCH DISPLAY	Sing the scale by directing the blue pitch line from the centre of the highest note to the centre of each following note. The optimal display will show minimal, clean horizontal lines in a downward diagonal.
SPECTROGRAM	
LEVEL METER	

Exercise S-63: Descending harmonic minor scale, legato

/a/

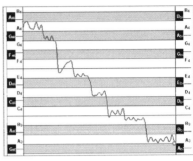

AIM	To sing a descending harmonic minor scale, legato, on a specified vowel, with pitch accuracy, consistent resonance and consistent volume.
OBJECTIVES	▶ To develop management of pitch, vowel articulation and volume, when singing a descending harmonic minor scale. In distinguishing the harmonic form from the other minor scales, the accuracy of the upper tetrachord - particularly the augmented 2nd between the 6th and 7th degrees of the scale - is important. ▶ To enhance legato capability. ▶ To build the aural and kinaesthetic memory necessary for this task.
PHYSICAL INVOLVEMENT	▶ Abdominal and thoracic muscle groups to achieve breath management ▶ Larynx height and posture ▶ Articulators, including pharynx, velum (soft palate), tongue, lips and jaw, for appropriate vowel formation and vocal resonance

INSTRUCTIONS	1 Play the scale 2 Mentally hear the scale sung on the chosen vowel 3 Breathe the correct vowel shape 4 Position the larynx 5 Activate breath support 6 Start to sing	7 Maintain appropriate breath pressure for the descending pitch, while keeping connected tone and vowel shape

PITCH DISPLAY	Sing the scale by directing the blue pitch line from the centre of the highest note to the centre of each following note, with minimal deviation. The optimal display will show minimal, clean horizontal lines in a downward diagonal.
SPECTROGRAM	The Spectrogram should exhibit the same pattern of resonances throughout the exercise.
LEVEL METER	The volume should remain consistent throughout the exercise. *Note: Where intervals traverse register changes, this is an especially useful skill to encourage.*

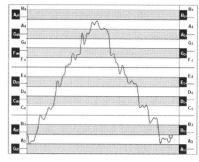

AIM	To sing an ascending and descending harmonic minor scale on a specified vowel with accurate pitch.
OBJECTIVES	▶ To develop management of pitch when singing an ascending and descending harmonic minor scale. In distinguishing the harmonic form from the other minor scales, the accuracy of the upper tetrachord - particularly the augmented 2nd between the 6th and 7th degrees of the scale - is important. ▶ To build the aural and kinaesthetic memory necessary for this task.
PHYSICAL INVOLVEMENT	▶ Abdominal and thoracic muscle groups to achieve breath management ▶ Larynx height and posture ▶ Articulators, including pharynx, velum (soft palate), tongue, lips and jaw, for appropriate vowel formation and vocal resonance
INSTRUCTIONS	1 Play the scale 2 Mentally hear the scale sung on the chosen vowel 3 Breathe the correct vowel shape 4 Position the larynx 5 Activate breath support 6 Start to sing 7 Increase breath pressure in order to increase pitch, while keeping the vowel shape 8 Maintain appropriate pressure for the descending pitch, while keeping the vowel shape
PITCH DISPLAY	Sing the scale by directing the blue pitch line from the centre of the first note to the centre of each following note. The optimal display will show minimal, clean horizontal lines in an upward, then equally downward, diagonal.
SPECTROGRAM	
LEVEL METER	

Exercise S-65: Ascending and descending harmonic minor scale, staccato

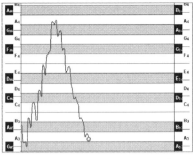

AIM	To sing an ascending and descending harmonic minor scale, staccato, on a specified vowel with accurate pitch.
OBJECTIVES	▶ To develop management of pitch when singing an ascending and descending harmonic minor scale, staccato. In distinguishing the harmonic form from the other minor scales, the accuracy of the upper tetrachord—particularly the augmented 2nd between the 6th and 7th degrees of the scale—is important. ▶ To build the aural and kinaesthetic memory necessary for this task.
PHYSICAL INVOLVEMENT	▶ Abdominal and thoracic muscle groups to achieve breath management ▶ Larynx height and posture ▶ Articulators, including pharynx, velum (soft palate), tongue, lips and jaw, for appropriate vowel formation and vocal resonance

INSTRUCTIONS	1 Play the scale 2 Mentally hear the scale sung on the chosen vowel 3 Breathe the correct vowel shape 4 Position the larynx 5 Activate breath support 6 Start to sing 7 Pay attention to precise onset and offset while increasing breath pressure for each ascending pitch and keeping vowel shape 8 Pay attention to precise onset and offset while maintaining appropriate breath pressure for each descending pitch and keeping the vowel shape
PITCH DISPLAY	Sing the scale clearly and accurately by directing the blue pitch line from the centre of the first note to the centre of each following note. The optimal display will show minimal, clean horizontal lines in an upward, then equally downward, diagonal.
SPECTROGRAM	
LEVEL METER	

190 Sing & See

Exercise S-66: Ascending and descending harmonic minor scale, legato

/a/

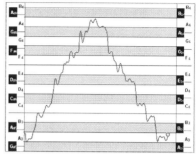

AIM	To sing an ascending and descending harmonic minor scale, legato, on a specified vowel, with pitch accuracy, consistent resonance and consistent volume.
OBJECTIVES	▶ To develop management of pitch, vowel articulation and volume, when singing an ascending and descending harmonic minor scale. In distinguishing the harmonic form from the other minor scales, the accuracy of the upper tetrachord - particularly the augmented 2nd between the 6th and 7th degrees of the scale - is important. ▶ To enhance legato capability. ▶ To build the aural and kinaesthetic memory necessary for this task.
PHYSICAL INVOLVEMENT	▶ Abdominal and thoracic muscle groups to achieve breath management ▶ Larynx height and posture ▶ Articulators, including pharynx, velum (soft palate), tongue, lips and jaw, for appropriate vowel formation and vocal resonance
INSTRUCTIONS	1 Play the scale 2 Mentally hear the scale sung on the chosen vowel 3 Breathe the correct vowel shape 4 Position the larynx 5 Activate breath support 6 Start to sing 7 Gradually increase breath pressure in order to increase pitch, while keeping connected tone and vowel shape 8 Maintain appropriate breath pressure for the descending pitch, while keeping connected tone and vowel shape
PITCH DISPLAY	Sing the scale by directing the blue pitch line from the centre of the first note to the centre of each following note, with minimal deviation. The optimal display will show minimal, clean horizontal lines in an upward, then equally downward, diagonal.
SPECTROGRAM	The Spectrogram should exhibit the same pattern of resonances throughout the exercise.
LEVEL METER	The volume should remain consistent throughout the exercise. *Note: Where intervals traverse register changes, this is an especially useful skill to encourage.*

Exercise S-67: Ascending and descending harmonic minor scale, staccato, and then legato

/a/

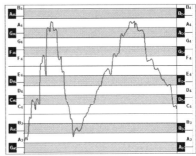

AIM	To sing an ascending and descending harmonic minor scale, first staccato and then legato, on a specified vowel, with pitch accuracy, consistent resonance and consistent volume.
OBJECTIVES	▶ To develop management of pitch, vowel articulation and volume, when singing an ascending and descending harmonic minor scale. In distinguishing the harmonic form from the other minor scales, the accuracy of the upper tetrachord - particularly the augmented 2nd between the 6th and 7th degrees of the scale - is important. ▶ To enhance staccato and legato capability. ▶ To build the aural and kinaesthetic memory necessary for this task.
PHYSICAL INVOLVEMENT	▶ Abdominal and thoracic muscle groups to achieve breath management ▶ Larynx height and posture ▶ Articulators, including pharynx, velum (soft palate), tongue, lips and jaw, for appropriate vowel formation and vocal resonance
INSTRUCTIONS	1 Play the scale 2 Mentally hear the scale sung on the chosen vowel 3 Breathe the correct vowel shape 4 Position the larynx 5 Activate breath support 6 Start to sing 7 For the staccato, pay attention to precise onset and offset while increasing breath pressure for each ascending pitch and maintaining appropriate breath pressure for each descending pitch 8 For the legato, keep connected tone and vowel shape while gradually increasing breath pressure for ascending pitch and maintaining appropriate breath pressure for descending pitch
PITCH DISPLAY	Sing the scale by directing the blue pitch line from the centre of the first note to the centre of each following note, with minimal deviation. The optimal display will show minimal, clean horizontal lines in upward, then equally downward, diagonals.
SPECTROGRAM	The Spectrogram should exhibit the same pattern of resonances throughout the exercise.
LEVEL METER	The volume should remain consistent throughout the exercise. *Note: Where intervals traverse register changes, this is an especially useful skill to encourage.*

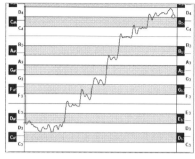

AIM	To sing an ascending Dorian mode, legato, on a specified vowel with accurate pitch.
OBJECTIVES	▶ To develop management of pitch when singing an ascending Dorian mode. While the pentachord is the same as for the minor scales, the accuracy of the upper tetrachord will define this mode. Of particular importance is the tone between the 7th degree and the final. ▶ To build the aural and kinaesthetic memory necessary for this task.
PHYSICAL INVOLVEMENT	▶ Abdominal and thoracic muscle groups to achieve breath management ▶ Larynx height and posture ▶ Articulators, including pharynx, velum (soft palate), tongue, lips and jaw, for appropriate vowel formation and vocal resonance
INSTRUCTIONS	1 Play the mode 2 Mentally hear the mode sung on the chosen vowel 3 Breathe the correct vowel shape 4 Position the larynx 5 Activate breath support 6 Start to sing 7 Increase breath pressure in order to increase pitch, while keeping the vowel shape
PITCH DISPLAY	Sing the mode by directing the blue pitch line from the centre of the lowest note to the centre of each following note. The optimal display will show minimal, clean horizontal lines in an upward diagonal.
SPECTROGRAM	
LEVEL METER	

Exercise S-69: Ascending Dorian mode, legato

/a/

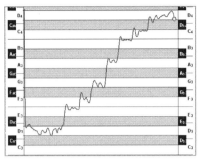

AIM	To sing an ascending Dorian mode, legato, on a specified vowel, with pitch accuracy, consistent resonance and consistent volume.
OBJECTIVES	▶ To develop management of pitch, vowel articulation and volume, when singing a Dorian mode. While the pentachord is the same as for the minor scales, the accuracy of the upper tetrachord will define this mode. Of particular importance is the tone between the 7th degree and the final. ▶ To enhance legato capability. ▶ To build the aural and kinaesthetic memory necessary for this task.
PHYSICAL INVOLVEMENT	▶ Abdominal and thoracic muscle groups to achieve breath management ▶ Larynx height and posture ▶ Articulators, including pharynx, velum (soft palate), tongue, lips and jaw, for appropriate vowel formation and vocal resonance
INSTRUCTIONS	1 Play the mode 2 Mentally hear the mode sung on the chosen vowel 3 Breathe the correct vowel shape 4 Position the larynx 5 Activate breath support 6 Start to sing	7 Gradually increase breath pressure in order to increase pitch, while keeping connected tone and vowel shape
PITCH DISPLAY	Sing the mode by directing the blue pitch line from the centre of the lowest note to the centre of each following note, with minimal deviation. The optimal display will show minimal, clean horizontal lines in an upward diagonal.
SPECTROGRAM	The Spectrogram should exhibit the same pattern of resonances throughout the exercise.
LEVEL METER	The volume should remain consistent throughout the exercise. *Note: Where intervals traverse register changes, this is an especially useful skill to encourage.*

/a/

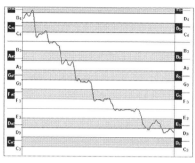

AIM	To sing a descending Dorian mode on a specified vowel with accurate pitch.
OBJECTIVES	▶ To develop management of pitch when singing a descending Dorian mode. While the pentachord is the same as for the minor scales, the accuracy of the upper tetrachord will define this mode. Of particular importance is the tone between the 7th degree and the final. ▶ To build the aural and kinaesthetic memory necessary for this task.
PHYSICAL INVOLVEMENT	▶ Abdominal and thoracic muscle groups to achieve breath management ▶ Larynx height and posture ▶ Articulators, including pharynx, velum (soft palate), tongue, lips and jaw, for appropriate vowel formation and vocal resonance
INSTRUCTIONS	1 Play the mode 2 Mentally hear the mode sung on the chosen vowel 3 Breathe the correct vowel shape 4 Position the larynx 5 Activate breath support 6 Start to sing 7 Maintain appropriate breath pressure for the descending pitch, while keeping the vowel shape
PITCH DISPLAY	Sing the mode by directing the blue pitch line from the centre of the highest note to the centre of each following note. The optimal display will show minimal, clean horizontal lines in a downward diagonal.
SPECTROGRAM	
LEVEL METER	

Exercise S-71: Descending Dorian mode, legato

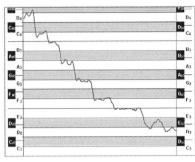

/a/

AIM	To sing a descending Dorian mode, legato, on a specified vowel, with pitch accuracy, consistent resonance and consistent volume.
OBJECTIVES 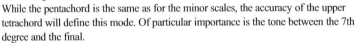 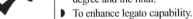	▶ To develop management of pitch, vowel articulation and volume, when singing a descending Dorian mode. While the pentachord is the same as for the minor scales, the accuracy of the upper tetrachord will define this mode. Of particular importance is the tone between the 7th degree and the final. ▶ To enhance legato capability. ▶ To build the aural and kinaesthetic memory necessary for this task.
PHYSICAL INVOLVEMENT	▶ Abdominal and thoracic muscle groups to achieve breath management ▶ Larynx height and posture ▶ Articulators, including pharynx, velum (soft palate), tongue, lips and jaw, for appropriate vowel formation and vocal resonance
INSTRUCTIONS	1 Play the mode 2 Mentally hear the mode sung on the chosen vowel 3 Breathe the correct vowel shape 4 Position the larynx 5 Activate breath support 6 Start to sing 7 Maintain appropriate breath pressure for the descending pitch, while keeping the vowel shape
PITCH DISPLAY	Sing the mode by directing the blue pitch line from the centre of the highest note to the centre of each following note, with minimal deviation. The optimal display will show minimal, clean horizontal lines in a downward diagonal.
SPECTROGRAM	The Spectrogram should exhibit the same pattern of resonances throughout the exercise.
LEVEL METER	The volume should remain consistent throughout the exercise. *Note: Where intervals traverse register changes, this is an especially useful skill to encourage.*

/a/

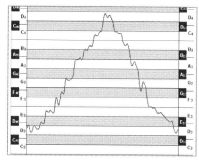

AIM	To sing an ascending and descending Dorian mode on a specified vowel with accurate pitch.
OBJECTIVES	▶ To develop management of pitch when singing an ascending and descending Dorian mode. While the pentachord is the same as for the minor scales, the accuracy of the upper tetrachord will define this mode. Of particular importance is the tone between the 7th degree and the final. ▶ To build the aural and kinaesthetic memory necessary for this task.
PHYSICAL INVOLVEMENT	▶ Abdominal and thoracic muscle groups to achieve breath management ▶ Larynx height and posture ▶ Articulators, including pharynx, velum (soft palate), tongue, lips and jaw, for appropriate vowel formation and vocal resonance
INSTRUCTIONS	1 Play the mode 2 Mentally hear the mode sung on the chosen vowel 3 Breathe the correct vowel shape 4 Position the larynx 5 Activate breath support 6 Start to sing 7 Increase breath pressure in order to increase pitch, while keeping the vowel shape 8 Maintain appropriate pressure for the descending pitch, while keeping the vowel shape
PITCH DISPLAY	Sing the mode by directing the blue pitch line from the centre of the first note to the centre of each following note. The optimal display will show minimal, clean horizontal lines in an upward, then equally downward, diagonal.
SPECTROGRAM	
LEVEL METER	

Exercise S-7 3: Ascending and descending Dorian mode, staccato

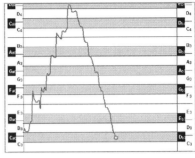

/a/

AIM	To sing an ascending and descending Dorian mode, staccato, on a specified vowel with accurate pitch.
OBJECTIVES 	▶ To develop management of pitch when singing an ascending and descending Dorian mode, staccato. While the pentachord is the same as for the minor scales, the accuracy of the upper tetrachord will define this mode. Of particular importance is the tone between the 7th degree and the final. ▶ To build the aural and kinaesthetic memory necessary for this task.
PHYSICAL INVOLVEMENT	▶ Abdominal and thoracic muscle groups to achieve breath management ▶ Larynx height and posture ▶ Articulators, including pharynx, velum (soft palate), tongue, lips and jaw, for appropriate vowel formation and vocal resonance

INSTRUCTIONS	1 Play the mode 2 Mentally hear the mode sung on the chosen vowel 3 Breathe the correct vowel shape 4 Position the larynx 5 Activate breath support 6 Start to sing	7 Pay attention to precise onset and offset while increasing breath pressure for each ascending pitch and keeping the vowel shape 8 Pay attention to precise onset and offset while maintaining appropriate breath pressure for each descending pitch and keeping the vowel shape

PITCH DISPLAY	Sing the mode by directing the blue pitch line from the centre of the first note to the centre of each following note, with minimal deviation. The optimal display will show minimal, clean horizontal lines in an upward, then equally downward, diagonal.
SPECTROGRAM	
LEVEL METER	

/a/

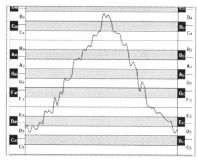

AIM	To sing an ascending and descending Dorian mode, legato, on a specified vowel, with pitch accuracy, consistent resonance and consistent volume.
OBJECTIVES	▶ To develop management of pitch, vowel articulation and volume, when singing an ascending and descending Dorian mode.. While the pentachord is the same as for the minor scales, the accuracy of the upper tetrachord will define this mode. Of particular importance is the tone between the 7th degree and the final. ▶ To enhance legato capability. ▶ To build the aural and kinaesthetic memory necessary for this task.
PHYSICAL INVOLVEMENT	▶ Abdominal and thoracic muscle groups to achieve breath management ▶ Larynx height and posture ▶ Articulators, including pharynx, velum (soft palate), tongue, lips and jaw, for appropriate vowel formation and vocal resonance
INSTRUCTIONS	1 Play the mode 2 Mentally hear the mode sung on the chosen vowel 3 Breathe the correct vowel shape 4 Position the larynx 5 Activate breath support 6 Start to sing 7 Gradually increase breath pressure in order to increase pitch, while keeping connected tone and vowel shape 8 Maintain appropriate breath pressure for the descending pitch, while keeping connected tone and vowel shape
PITCH DISPLAY	Sing the mode by directing the blue pitch line from the centre of the first note to the centre of each following note, with minimal deviation. The optimal display will show minimal, clean horizontal lines in an upward, then equally downward, diagonal.
SPECTROGRAM	The Spectrogram should exhibit the same pattern of resonances throughout the exercise.
LEVEL METER	The volume should remain consistent throughout the exercise. *Note: Where intervals traverse register changes, this is an especially useful skill to encourage.*

Exercise S-75: Ascending and descending Dorian mode, staccato, and then legato

/a/

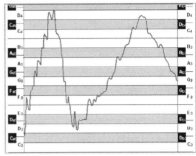

AIM	To sing an ascending and descending Dorian mode, first staccato and then legato, on a specified vowel, with pitch accuracy, consistent resonance and consistent volume.
OBJECTIVES	▶ To develop management of pitch, vowel articulation and volume, when singing an ascending and descending Dorian mode. While the pentachord is the same as for the minor scales, the accuracy of the upper tetrachord will define this mode. Of particular importance is the tone between the 7th degree and the final. ▶ To enhance staccato and legato capability. ▶ To build the aural and kinaesthetic memory necessary for this task.
PHYSICAL INVOLVEMENT	▶ Abdominal and thoracic muscle groups to achieve breath management ▶ Larynx height and posture ▶ Articulators, including pharynx, velum (soft palate), tongue, lips and jaw, for appropriate vowel formation and vocal resonance
INSTRUCTIONS	1 Play the mode 2 Mentally hear the mode sung on the chosen vowel 3 Breathe the correct vowel shape 4 Position the larynx 5 Activate breath support 6 Start to sing 7 For the staccato, pay attention to precise	onset and offset while increasing breath pressure for each ascending pitch and maintaining appropriate breath pressure for each descending pitch 8 For the legato, keep connected tone and vowel shape while gradually increasing breath pressure for ascending pitch and maintaining appropriate breath pressure for descending pitch
PITCH DISPLAY	Sing the mode by directing the blue pitch line from the centre of the first note to the centre of each following note, with minimal deviation. For both staccato and legato, the optimal display will show minimal, clean horizontal lines in upward, then equally downward, diagonals.
SPECTROGRAM	The Spectrogram should exhibit the same pattern of resonances throughout the exercise.
LEVEL METER	The volume should remain consistent throughout the exercise. *Note: Where intervals traverse register changes, this is an especially useful skill to encourage.*

/a/

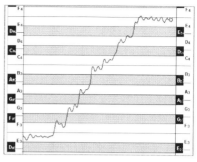

AIM	To sing an ascending Phrygian mode on a specified vowel with accurate pitch.
OBJECTIVES	▶ To develop management of pitch when singing an ascending Phrygian mode. The semitone at the beginning is particularly important in defining this mode. ▶ To build the aural and kinaesthetic memory necessary for this task.
PHYSICAL INVOLVEMENT	▶ Abdominal and thoracic muscle groups to achieve breath management ▶ Larynx height and posture ▶ Articulators, including pharynx, velum (soft palate), tongue, lips and jaw, for appropriate vowel formation and vocal resonance
INSTRUCTIONS	1 Play the mode 2 Mentally hear the mode sung on the chosen vowel 3 Breathe the correct vowel shape 4 Position the larynx 5 Activate breath support 6 Start to sing 7 Increase breath pressure in order to increase pitch, while keeping the vowel shape
PITCH DISPLAY	Sing the mode by directing the blue pitch line from the centre of the lowest note to the centre of each following note. The optimal display will show minimal, clean horizontal lines in an upward diagonal.
SPECTROGRAM	
LEVEL METER 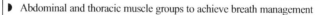	

Exercise S-77: Ascending Phrygian mode, legato

/a/

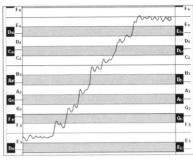

AIM	To sing an ascending Phrygian mode, legato, on a specified vowel, with pitch accuracy, consistent resonance and consistent volume.
OBJECTIVES 	▶ To develop management of pitch, vowel articulation and volume, when singing a Phrygian mode. The semitone at the beginning is particularly important in defining this mode. ▶ To enhance legato capability. ▶ To build the aural and kinaesthetic memory necessary for this task.
PHYSICAL INVOLVEMENT	▶ Abdominal and thoracic muscle groups to achieve breath management ▶ Larynx height and posture ▶ Articulators, including pharynx, velum (soft palate), tongue, lips and jaw, for appropriate vowel formation and vocal resonance

INSTRUCTIONS

1	Play the mode	7	Gradually increase breath pressure in order to increase pitch while keeping connected tone and vowel shape
2	Mentally hear the mode sung on the chosen vowel		
3	Breathe the correct vowel shape		
4	Position the larynx		
5	Activate breath support		
6	Start to sing		

PITCH DISPLAY	Sing the mode by directing the blue pitch line from the centre of the lowest note to the centre of each following note, with minimal deviation. The optimal display will show minimal, clean horizontal lines in an upward diagonal.
SPECTROGRAM	The Spectrogram should exhibit the same pattern of resonances throughout the exercise.
LEVEL METER	The volume should remain consistent throughout the exercise. *Note: Where intervals traverse register changes, this is an especially useful skill to encourage.*

/a/

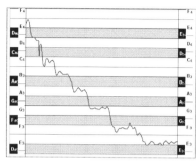

AIM 	To sing a descending Phrygian mode on a specified vowel with accurate pitch.
OBJECTIVES 	▶ To develop management of pitch when singing a descending Phrygian mode. The semitone at the beginning is particularly important in defining this mode. ▶ To build the aural and kinaesthetic memory necessary for this task.
PHYSICAL INVOLVEMENT 	▶ Abdominal and thoracic muscle groups to achieve breath management ▶ Larynx height and posture ▶ Articulators, including pharynx, velum (soft palate), tongue, lips and jaw, for appropriate vowel formation and vocal resonance
INSTRUCTIONS 	1 Play the mode 2 Mentally hear the mode sung on the chosen vowel 3 Breathe the correct vowel shape 4 Position the larynx 5 Activate breath support 6 Start to sing 7 Maintain appropriate breath pressure for the descending pitch, while keeping the vowel shape
PITCH DISPLAY	Sing the mode by directing the blue pitch line from the centre of the highest note to the centre of each following note. The optimal display will show minimal, clean horizontal lines in a downward diagonal.
SPECTROGRAM	
LEVEL METER	

Exercise S-79: Descending Phrygian mode, legato

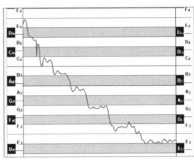

/a/

AIM	To sing a descending Phrygian mode, legato, on a specified vowel, with pitch accuracy, consistent resonance and consistent volume.
OBJECTIVES	▶ To develop management of pitch, vowel articulation and volume, when singing a descending Phrygian mode. The semitone at the beginning is particularly important in defining this mode. ▶ To enhance legato capability. ▶ To build the aural and kinaesthetic memory necessary for this task.
PHYSICAL INVOLVEMENT	▶ Abdominal and thoracic muscle groups to achieve breath management ▶ Larynx height and posture ▶ Articulators, including pharynx, velum (soft palate), tongue, lips and jaw, for appropriate vowel formation and vocal resonance

INSTRUCTIONS	1 Play the mode 2 Mentally hear the mode sung on the chosen vowel 3 Breathe the correct vowel shape 4 Position the larynx 5 Activate breath support 6 Start to sing	7 Maintain appropriate breath pressure for the descending pitch, while keeping connected tone and vowel shape

PITCH DISPLAY	Sing the mode by directing the blue pitch line from the centre of the highest note to the centre of each following note, with minimal deviation. The optimal display will show minimal, clean horizontal lines in a downward diagonal.
SPECTROGRAM	The Spectrogram should exhibit the same pattern of resonances throughout the exercise.
LEVEL METER	The volume should remain consistent throughout the exercise. *Note: Where intervals traverse register changes, this is an especially useful skill to encourage.*

/a/

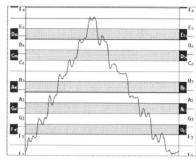

AIM	To sing an ascending and descending Phrygian mode on a specified vowel with accurate pitch.
OBJECTIVES	▶ To develop management of pitch when singing an ascending and descending Phrygian mode. The semitone at the beginning is particularly important in defining this mode. ▶ To build the aural and kinaesthetic memory necessary for this task.
PHYSICAL INVOLVEMENT	▶ Abdominal and thoracic muscle groups to achieve breath management ▶ Larynx height and posture ▶ Articulators, including pharynx, velum (soft palate), tongue, lips and jaw, for appropriate vowel formation and vocal resonance
INSTRUCTIONS	1 Play the mode 2 Mentally hear the mode sung on the chosen vowel 3 Breathe the correct vowel shape 4 Position the larynx 5 Activate breath support 6 Start to sing 7 Increase breath pressure in order to increase pitch, while keeping the vowel shape 8 Maintain appropriate pressure for the descending pitch, while keeping the vowel shape
PITCH DISPLAY	Sing the mode by directing the blue pitch line from the centre of the first note to the centre of each following note. The optimal display will show minimal, clean horizontal lines in an upward, then equally downward, diagonal.
SPECTROGRAM	
LEVEL METER	

Exercise S-81: Ascending and descending Phrygian mode, staccato

/a/

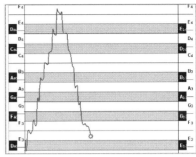

AIM	To sing an ascending and descending Phrygian mode, staccato, on a specified vowel with accurate pitch.

OBJECTIVES	▶ To develop management of pitch when singing an ascending and descending Phrygian mode, staccato. The semitone at the beginning is particularly important in defining this mode. ▶ To build the aural and kinaesthetic memory necessary for this task.

PHYSICAL INVOLVEMENT	▶ Abdominal and thoracic muscle groups to achieve breath management ▶ Larynx height and posture ▶ Articulators, including pharynx, velum (soft palate), tongue, lips and jaw, for appropriate vowel formation and vocal resonance

INSTRUCTIONS	1 Play the mode 2 Mentally hear the mode sung on the chosen vowel 3 Breathe the correct vowel shape 4 Position the larynx 5 Activate breath support 6 Start to sing	7 Pay attention to precise onset and offset while increasing breath pressure for each ascending pitch and keeping vowel shape 8 Pay attention to precise onset and offset while maintaining appropriate breath pressure for each descending pitch and keeping vowel shape

PITCH DISPLAY	Sing the mode by directing the blue pitch line from the centre of the first note to the centre of each following note, with minimal deviation. The optimal display will show minimal, clean horizontal lines in an upward, then equally downward, diagonal.

SPECTROGRAM	

LEVEL METER	

/a/

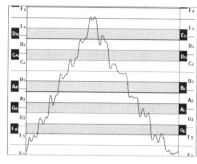

AIM	To sing an ascending and descending Phrygian mode, legato, on a specified vowel, with pitch accuracy, consistent resonance and consistent volume.
OBJECTIVES 	▶ To develop management of pitch, vowel articulation and volume, when singing an ascending and descending Phrygian mode. The semitone at the beginning is particularly important in defining this mode. ▶ To enhance legato capability. ▶ To build the aural and kinaesthetic memory necessary for this task.
PHYSICAL INVOLVEMENT	▶ Abdominal and thoracic muscle groups to achieve breath management ▶ Larynx height and posture ▶ Articulators, including pharynx, velum (soft palate), tongue, lips and jaw, for appropriate vowel formation and vocal resonance
INSTRUCTIONS	1 Play the mode 2 Mentally hear the mode sung on the chosen vowel 3 Breathe the correct vowel shape 4 Position the larynx 5 Activate breath support 6 Start to sing 7 Gradually increase breath pressure in order to increase pitch, while keeping connected tone and vowel shape 8 Maintain appropriate breath pressure for the descending pitch, while keeping connected tone and vowel shape
PITCH DISPLAY	Sing the mode by directing the blue pitch line from the centre of the first note to the centre of each following note, with minimal deviation and no breaks in the line. The optimal display will show minimal, clean horizontal lines in an upward, then equally downward, diagonal.
SPECTROGRAM	The Spectrogram should exhibit the same pattern of resonances throughout the exercise.
LEVEL METER	The volume should remain consistent throughout the exercise. *Note: Where intervals traverse register changes, this is an especially useful skill to encourage.*

Exercise S-83: Ascending and descending Phrygian mode, staccato and then legato

/a/

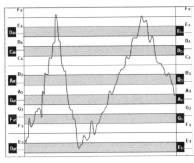

AIM	To sing an ascending and descending Phrygian mode, first staccato and then legato, on a specified vowel, with pitch accuracy, consistent resonance and consistent volume.
OBJECTIVES	▶ To develop management of pitch, vowel articulation and volume, when singing an ascending and descending Phrygian mode. The semitone at the beginning is particularly important in defining this mode. ▶ To enhance staccato and legato capability. ▶ To build the aural and kinaesthetic memory necessary for this task.
PHYSICAL INVOLVEMENT	▶ Abdominal and thoracic muscle groups to achieve breath management ▶ Larynx height and posture ▶ Articulators, including pharynx, velum (soft palate), tongue, lips and jaw, for appropriate vowel formation and vocal resonance
INSTRUCTIONS	1 Play the mode 2 Mentally hear the mode sung on the chosen vowel 3 Breathe the correct vowel shape 4 Position the larynx 5 Activate breath support 6 Start to sing 7 For the staccato, pay attention to precise	onset and offset while increasing breath pressure for each ascending pitch and maintaining appropriate breath pressure for each descending pitch 8 For the legato, keep connected tone and vowel shape while gradually increasing breath pressure for ascending pitch and maintaining appropriate breath pressure for descending pitch
PITCH DISPLAY	Sing the mode by directing the blue pitch line from the centre of the first note to the centre of each following note, with minimal deviation. The optimal display will show minimal, clean horizontal lines in upward, then equally downward, diagonals.
SPECTROGRAM	The Spectrogram should exhibit the same pattern of resonances throughout the exercise.
LEVEL METER	The volume should remain consistent throughout the exercise. *Note: Where intervals traverse register changes, this is an especially useful skill to encourage.*

/a/

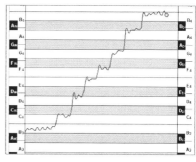

AIM	To sing an ascending Locrian mode on a specified vowel with accurate pitch.
OBJECTIVES	▶ To develop management of pitch when singing an ascending Locrian mode. The semitone at the beginning, and the tone between the 7th degree and the final, are particularly important in defining this mode. ▶ To build the aural and kinaesthetic memory necessary for this task.
PHYSICAL INVOLVEMENT	▶ Abdominal and thoracic muscle groups to achieve breath management ▶ Larynx height and posture ▶ Articulators, including pharynx, velum (soft palate), tongue, lips and jaw, for appropriate vowel formation and vocal resonance
INSTRUCTIONS	1 Play the mode 2 Mentally hear the mode sung on the chosen vowel 3 Breathe the correct vowel shape 4 Position the larynx 5 Activate breath support 6 Start to sing 7 Increase breath pressure in order to increase pitch, while keeping the vowel shape
PITCH DISPLAY	Sing the mode by directing the blue pitch line from the centre of the lowest note to the centre of each following note. The optimal display will show minimal, clean horizontal lines in an upward diagonal.
SPECTROGRAM	
LEVEL METER	

Exercise S-85: Ascending Locrian mode, legato

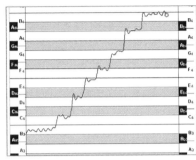

/a/

AIM	To sing an ascending Locrian mode, legato, on a specified vowel, with pitch accuracy, consistent resonance and consistent volume.
OBJECTIVES	▶ To develop management of pitch, vowel articulation and volume, when singing a Locrian mode. The semitone at the beginning, and the tone between the 7th degree and the final, are particularly important in defining this mode. ▶ To enhance legato capability. ▶ To build the aural and kinaesthetic memory necessary for this task.
PHYSICAL INVOLVEMENT	▶ Abdominal and thoracic muscle groups to achieve breath management ▶ Larynx height and posture ▶ Articulators, including pharynx, velum (soft palate), tongue, lips and jaw, for appropriate vowel formation and vocal resonance
INSTRUCTIONS	1 Play the mode 2 Mentally hear the mode sung on the chosen vowel 3 Breathe the correct vowel shape 4 Position the larynx 5 Activate breath support 6 Start to sing	7 Gradually increase breath pressure in order to increase pitch, while keeping connected tone and vowel shape.
PITCH DISPLAY	Sing the mode by directing the blue pitch line from the centre of the lowest note to the centre of each following note, with minimal deviation. The optimal display will show minimal, clean horizontal lines in an upward diagonal.
SPECTROGRAM	The Spectrogram should exhibit the same pattern of resonances throughout the exercise.
LEVEL METER	The volume should remain consistent throughout the exercise. *Note: Where intervals traverse register changes, this is an especially useful skill to encourage.*

/a/

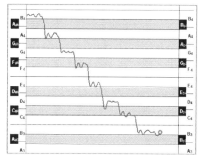

AIM	To sing a descending Locrian mode on a specified vowel with accurate pitch.
OBJECTIVES	▶ To develop management of pitch when singing a descending Locrian mode. The semitone at the beginning, and the tone between the 7th degree and the final, are particularly important in defining this mode. ▶ To build the aural and kinaesthetic memory necessary for this task.
PHYSICAL INVOLVEMENT	▶ Abdominal and thoracic muscle groups to achieve breath management ▶ Larynx height and posture ▶ Articulators, including pharynx, velum (soft palate), tongue, lips and jaw, for appropriate vowel formation and vocal resonance

INSTRUCTIONS	1 Play the mode 2 Mentally hear the mode sung on the chosen vowel 3 Breathe the correct vowel shape 4 Position the larynx 5 Activate breath support 6 Start to sing	7 Maintain appropriate breath pressure for the descending pitch, while keeping connected tone and vowel shape

PITCH DISPLAY	Sing the mode by directing the blue pitch line from the centre of the highest note to the centre of each following note. The optimal display will show minimal, clean horizontal lines in a downward diagonal.
SPECTROGRAM	
LEVEL METER	

Exercise S-87: Descending Locrian mode, legato

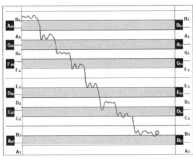

/a/

AIM	To sing a descending Locrian mode, legato, on a specified vowel, with pitch accuracy, consistent resonance and consistent volume.
OBJECTIVES	▶ To develop management of pitch, vowel articulation and volume, when singing a descending Locrian mode. The semitone at the beginning, and the tone between the 7th degree and the final, are particularly important in defining this mode. ▶ To enhance legato capability. ▶ To build the aural and kinaesthetic memory necessary for this task.
PHYSICAL INVOLVEMENT	▶ Abdominal and thoracic muscle groups to achieve breath management ▶ Larynx height and posture ▶ Articulators, including pharynx, velum (soft palate), tongue, lips and jaw, for appropriate vowel formation and vocal resonance
INSTRUCTIONS	1 Play the mode 2 Mentally hear the mode sung on the chosen vowel 3 Breathe the correct vowel shape 4 Position the larynx 5 Activate breath support 6 Start to sing 7 Maintain appropriate breath pressure for the descending pitch, while keeping connected tone and vowel shape
PITCH DISPLAY	Sing the mode by directing the blue pitch line from the centre of the highest note to the centre of each following note, with minimal deviation. The optimal display will show minimal, clean horizontal lines in a downward diagonal.
SPECTROGRAM	The Spectrogram should exhibit the same pattern of resonances throughout the exercise.
LEVEL METER	The volume should remain consistent throughout the exercise. *Note: Where intervals traverse register changes, this is an especially useful skill to encourage.*

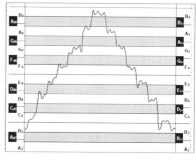

AIM	To sing an ascending and descending Locrian mode on a specified vowel with accurate pitch.
OBJECTIVES 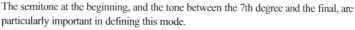	▶ To develop management of pitch when singing an ascending and descending Locrian mode. The semitone at the beginning, and the tone between the 7th degree and the final, are particularly important in defining this mode. ▶ To build the aural and kinaesthetic memory necessary for this task.
PHYSICAL INVOLVEMENT 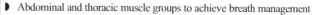	▶ Abdominal and thoracic muscle groups to achieve breath management ▶ Larynx height and posture ▶ Articulators, including pharynx, velum (soft palate), tongue, lips and jaw, for appropriate vowel formation and vocal resonance
INSTRUCTIONS	1 Play the mode 2 Mentally hear the mode sung on the chosen vowel 3 Breathe the correct vowel shape 4 Position the larynx 5 Activate breath support 6 Start to sing 7 Increase breath pressure in order to increase pitch, while keeping the vowel shape 8 Maintain appropriate breath pressure for the descending pitch, while keeping the vowel shape
PITCH DISPLAY	Sing the mode by directing the blue pitch line from the centre of the first note to the centre of each following note. The optimal display will show minimal, clean horizontal lines in an upward, then equally downward, diagonal.
SPECTROGRAM	
LEVEL METER	

Exercise S-89: Ascending and descending Locrian mode, staccato

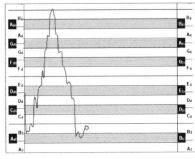

AIM	To sing an ascending and descending Locrian mode, staccato, on a specified vowel with accurate pitch.
OBJECTIVES	▶ To develop management of pitch when singing an ascending and descending Locrian mode, staccato. The semitone at the beginning, and the tone between the 7th degree and the final, are particularly important in defining this mode. ▶ To build the aural and kinaesthetic memory necessary for this task.
PHYSICAL INVOLVEMENT	▶ Abdominal and thoracic muscle groups to achieve breath management ▶ Larynx height and posture ▶ Articulators, including pharynx, velum (soft palate), tongue, lips and jaw, for appropriate vowel formation and vocal resonance

INSTRUCTIONS

1 Play the mode 2 Mentally hear the mode sung on the chosen vowel 3 Breathe the correct vowel shape 4 Position the larynx 5 Activate breath support 6 Start to sing	7 Pay attention to precise onset and offset, while increasing breath pressure for each ascending pitch and keeping the vowel shape 8 Pay attention to precise onset and offset while maintaining appropriate breath pressure for each descending pitch and keeping the vowel shape

PITCH DISPLAY	Sing the mode by directing the blue pitch line from the centre of the first note to the centre of each following note, with minimal deviation. The optimal display will show minimal, clean horizontal lines in an upward, then equally downward, diagonal.
SPECTROGRAM	
LEVEL METER	

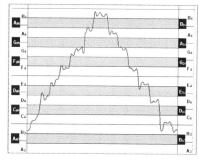

AIM	To sing an ascending and descending Locrian mode, legato, on a specified vowel, with pitch accuracy, consistent resonance and consistent volume.
OBJECTIVES 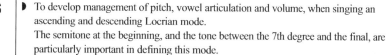	▶ To develop management of pitch, vowel articulation and volume, when singing an ascending and descending Locrian mode. The semitone at the beginning, and the tone between the 7th degree and the final, are particularly important in defining this mode. ▶ To enhance legato capability. ▶ To build the aural and kinaesthetic memory necessary for this task.
PHYSICAL INVOLVEMENT	▶ Abdominal and thoracic muscle groups to achieve breath management ▶ Larynx height and posture ▶ Articulators, including pharynx, velum (soft palate), tongue, lips and jaw, for appropriate vowel formation and vocal resonance
INSTRUCTIONS 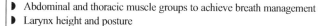	1 Play the mode 2 Mentally hear the mode sung on the chosen vowel 3 Breathe the correct vowel shape 4 Position the larynx 5 Activate breath support 6 Start to sing 7 Gradually increase breath pressure in order to increase pitch, while keeping connected tone and vowel shape 8 Maintain appropriate breath pressure for the descending pitch, while keeping connected tone and vowel shape
PITCH DISPLAY	Sing the mode by directing the blue pitch line from the centre of the first note to the centre of each following note, with minimal deviation. The optimal display will show minimal, clean horizontal lines in an upward, then equally downward, diagonal.
SPECTROGRAM	The Spectrogram should exhibit the same pattern of resonances throughout the exercise.
LEVEL METER	The volume should remain consistent throughout the exercise. *Note: Where intervals traverse register changes, this is an especially useful skill to encourage.*

Exercise S-91: Ascending and descending Locrian mode, staccato and then legato

/a/

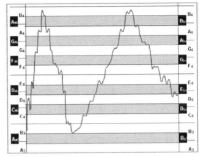

AIM	To sing an ascending and descending Locrian mode, first staccato and then legato, on a specified vowel, with pitch accuracy, consistent resonance and consistent volume.
OBJECTIVES	▶ To develop management of pitch, vowel articulation and volume, when singing an ascending and descending Locrian mode. The semitone at the beginning, and the tone between the 7th degree and the final, are particularly important in defining this mode. ▶ To enhance staccato and legato capability. ▶ To build the aural and kinaesthetic memory necessary for this task.
PHYSICAL INVOLVEMENT	▶ Abdominal and thoracic muscle groups to achieve breath management ▶ Larynx height and posture ▶ Articulators, including pharynx, velum (soft palate), tongue, lips and jaw, for appropriate vowel formation and vocal resonance
INSTRUCTIONS	1 Play the mode 2 Mentally hear the mode sung on the chosen vowel 3 Breathe the correct vowel shape 4 Position the larynx 5 Activate breath support 6 Start to sing 7 For the staccato, pay attention to precise onset and offset while increasing breath pressure for each ascending pitch and maintaining appropriate breath pressure for each descending pitch 8 For the legato, keep connected tone and vowel shape while gradually increasing breath pressure for ascending pitch and maintaining appropriate breath pressure for descending pitch
PITCH DISPLAY	Sing the mode by directing the blue pitch line from the centre of the first note to the centre of each following note, with minimal deviation. The optimal display will show minimal, clean horizontal lines in upward, then equally downward, diagonals.
SPECTROGRAM	The Spectrogram should exhibit the same pattern of resonances throughout the exercise.
LEVEL METER	The volume should remain consistent throughout the exercise. *Note: Where intervals traverse register changes, this is an especially useful skill to encourage.*

/a/

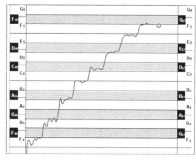

AIM 	To sing an ascending Lydian mode on a specified vowel with accurate pitch.
OBJECTIVES 	❱ To develop management of pitch when singing an ascending Lydian mode. The accuracy of the tone between the 3rd and 4th degrees, and the semitone between the 7th degree and the final, are important in establishing this mode. ❱ To build the aural and kinaesthetic memory necessary for this task.
PHYSICAL INVOLVEMENT 	❱ Abdominal and thoracic muscle groups to achieve breath management ❱ Larynx height and posture ❱ Articulators, including pharynx, velum (soft palate), tongue, lips and jaw, for appropriate vowel formation and vocal resonance
INSTRUCTIONS	1 Play the mode 2 Mentally hear the mode sung on the chosen vowel 3 Breathe the correct vowel shape 4 Position the larynx 5 Activate breath support 6 Start to sing 7 Increase breath pressure in order to increase pitch, while keeping the vowel shape
PITCH DISPLAY	Sing the mode by directing the blue pitch line from the centre of the lowest note to the centre of each following note. The optimal display will show minimal, clean horizontal lines in an upward diagonal.
SPECTROGRAM	
LEVEL METER	

Exercise S-93: Ascending Lydian mode, legato

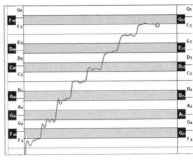

/a/

AIM	To sing an ascending Lydian mode, legato, on a specified vowel, with pitch accuracy, consistent resonance and consistent volume.
OBJECTIVES 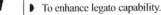	▶ To develop management of pitch, vowel articulation and volume, when singing a Lydian mode. The accuracy of the tone between the 3rd and 4th degrees, and the semitone between the 7th degree and the final, are important in establishing this mode. ▶ To enhance legato capability. ▶ To build the aural and kinaesthetic memory necessary for this task.
PHYSICAL INVOLVEMENT	▶ Abdominal and thoracic muscle groups to achieve breath management ▶ Larynx height and posture ▶ Articulators, including pharynx, velum (soft palate), tongue, lips and jaw, for appropriate vowel formation and vocal resonance
INSTRUCTIONS	1 Play the mode 2 Mentally hear the mode sung on the chosen vowel 3 Breathe the correct vowel shape 4 Position the larynx 5 Activate breath support 6 Start to sing 7 Gradually increase breath pressure in order to increase pitch, while keeping connected tone and vowel shape
PITCH DISPLAY	Sing the mode by directing the blue pitch line from the centre of the lowest note to the centre of each following note, with minimal deviation. The optimal display will show minimal, clean horizontal lines in an upward diagonal.
SPECTROGRAM	The Spectrogram should exhibit the same pattern of resonances throughout the exercise.
LEVEL METER	The volume should remain consistent throughout the exercise. *Note: Where intervals traverse register changes, this is an especially useful skill to encourage.*

/a/

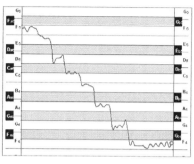

AIM	To sing a descending Lydian mode on a specified vowel with accurate pitch.
OBJECTIVES	▸ To develop management of pitch when singing a descending Lydian mode. The accuracy of the tone between the 3rd and 4th degrees, and the semitone between the 7th degree and the final, are important in establishing this mode. ▸ To build the aural and kinaesthetic memory necessary for this task.
PHYSICAL INVOLVEMENT	▸ Abdominal and thoracic muscle groups to achieve breath management ▸ Larynx height and posture ▸ Articulators, including pharynx, velum (soft palate), tongue, lips and jaw, for appropriate vowel formation and vocal resonance
INSTRUCTIONS	1 Play the mode 2 Mentally hear the mode sung on the chosen vowel 3 Breathe the correct vowel shape 4 Position the larynx 5 Activate breath support 6 Start to sing 7 Maintain appropriate breath pressure for the descending pitch, while keeping the vowel shape
PITCH DISPLAY	Sing the mode by directing the blue pitch line from the centre of the highest note to the centre of each following note. The optimal display will show minimal, clean horizontal lines in a downward diagonal.
SPECTROGRAM	
LEVEL METER	

Exercise S-95: Descending Lydian mode, legato

/a/

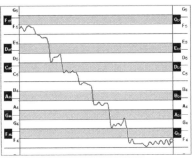

AIM	To sing a descending Lydian mode, legato, on a specified vowel, with pitch accuracy, consistent resonance and consistent volume.
OBJECTIVES	▶ To develop management of pitch, vowel articulation and volume, when singing a descending Lydian mode. The accuracy of the tone between the 3rd and 4th degrees, and the semitone between the 7th degree and the final, are important in establishing this mode. ▶ To enhance legato capability. ▶ To build the aural and kinaesthetic memory necessary for this task.
PHYSICAL INVOLVEMENT	▶ Abdominal and thoracic muscle groups to achieve breath management ▶ Larynx height and posture ▶ Articulators, including pharynx, velum (soft palate), tongue, lips and jaw, for appropriate vowel formation and vocal resonance
INSTRUCTIONS	1 Play the mode 2 Mentally hear the mode sung on the chosen vowel 3 Breathe the correct vowel shape 4 Position the larynx 5 Activate breath support 6 Start to sing 7 Maintain appropriate breath pressure for the descending pitch, while keeping connected tone and vowel shape
PITCH DISPLAY	Sing the mode by directing the blue pitch line from the centre of the highest note to the centre of each following note, with minimal deviation. The optimal display will show minimal, clean horizontal lines in a downward diagonal.
SPECTROGRAM	The Spectrogram should exhibit the same pattern of resonances throughout the exercise.
LEVEL METER	The volume should remain consistent throughout the exercise. *Note: Where intervals traverse register changes, this is an especially useful skill to encourage.*

/a/

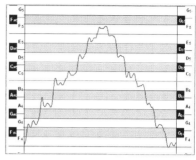

AIM	To sing an ascending and descending Lydian mode on a specified vowel with accurate pitch.
OBJECTIVES 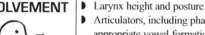	▶ To develop management of pitch when singing an ascending and descending Lydian mode. The accuracy of the tone between the 3rd and 4th degrees, and the semitone between the 7th degree and the final, are important in establishing this mode. ▶ To build the aural and kinaesthetic memory necessary for this task.
PHYSICAL INVOLVEMENT	▶ Abdominal and thoracic muscle groups to achieve breath management ▶ Larynx height and posture ▶ Articulators, including pharynx, velum (soft palate), tongue, lips and jaw, for appropriate vowel formation and vocal resonance

INSTRUCTIONS	1 Play the mode 2 Mentally hear the mode sung on the chosen vowel 3 Breathe the correct vowel shape 4 Position the larynx 5 Activate breath support 6 Start to sing	7 Increase breath pressure in order to increase pitch, while keeping the vowel shape 8 Maintain appropriate breath pressure for the descending pitch, while keeping connected tone and vowel shape

PITCH DISPLAY	Sing the mode by directing the blue pitch line from the centre of the first note to the centre of each following note. The optimal display will show minimal, clean horizontal lines in an upward, then equally downward, diagonal.
SPECTROGRAM	
LEVEL METER	

Exercise S-97: Ascending and descending Lydian mode, staccato

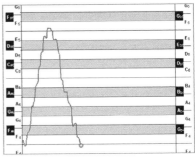

/a/

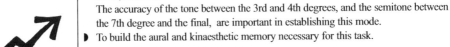

AIM	To sing an ascending and descending Lydian mode, staccato, on a specified vowel with accurate pitch.
OBJECTIVES	▶ To develop management of pitch when singing an ascending and descending Lydian mode, staccato. The accuracy of the tone between the 3rd and 4th degrees, and the semitone between the 7th degree and the final, are important in establishing this mode. ▶ To build the aural and kinaesthetic memory necessary for this task.
PHYSICAL INVOLVEMENT	▶ Abdominal and thoracic muscle groups to achieve breath management ▶ Larynx height and posture ▶ Articulators, including pharynx, velum (soft palate), tongue, lips and jaw, for appropriate vowel formation and vocal resonance
INSTRUCTIONS	1 Play the mode 2 Mentally hear the mode sung on the chosen vowel 3 Breathe the correct vowel shape 4 Position the larynx 5 Activate breath support 6 Start to sing 7 Pay attention to precise onset and offset while increasing breath pressure for each ascending pitch and keeping the vowel shape 8 Pay attention to precise onset and offset while maintaining appropriate breath pressure for each descending pitch and keeping the vowel shape
PITCH DISPLAY	Sing the mode by directing the blue pitch line from the centre of the first note to the centre of each following note, with minimal deviation. The optimal display will show minimal, clean horizontal lines in an upward, then equally downward, diagonal.
SPECTROGRAM	
LEVEL METER	

/a/

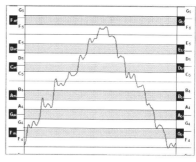

AIM	To sing an ascending and descending Lydian mode, legato, on a specified vowel, with pitch accuracy, consistent resonance and consistent volume.
OBJECTIVES	▶ To develop management of pitch, vowel articulation and volume, when singing an ascending and descending Lydian mode. The accuracy of the tone between the 3rd and 4th degrees, and the semitone between the 7th degree and the final, are important in establishing this mode. ▶ To enhance legato capability. ▶ To build the aural and kinaesthetic memory necessary for this task.
PHYSICAL INVOLVEMENT	▶ Abdominal and thoracic muscle groups to achieve breath management ▶ Larynx height and posture ▶ Articulators, including pharynx, velum (soft palate), tongue, lips and jaw, for appropriate vowel formation and vocal resonance
INSTRUCTIONS	1 Play the mode 2 Mentally hear the mode sung on the chosen vowel 3 Breathe the correct vowel shape 4 Position the larynx 5 Activate breath support 6 Start to sing 7 Gradually increase breath pressure in order to increase pitch, while keeping connected tone and vowel shape 8 Maintain appropriate breath pressure for the descending pitch, while keeping connected tone and vowel shape
PITCH DISPLAY	Sing the mode by directing the blue pitch line from the centre of the first note to the centre of each following note, with minimal deviation. The optimal display will show minimal, clean horizontal lines in an upward, then equally downward, diagonal.
SPECTROGRAM	The Spectrogram should exhibit the same pattern of resonances throughout the exercise.
LEVEL METER	The volume should remain consistent throughout the exercise. *Note: Where intervals traverse register changes, this is an especially useful skill to encourage.*

Exercise S-99: Ascending and descending Lydian mode, staccato and then legato

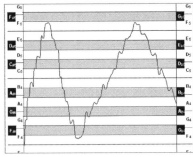

/a/

AIM	To sing an ascending and descending Lydian mode, first staccato and then legato, on a specified vowel, with pitch accuracy, consistent resonance and consistent volume.
OBJECTIVES	▶ To develop management of pitch, vowel articulation and volume, when singing an ascending and descending Lydian mode. The accuracy of the tone between the 3rd and 4th degrees, and the semitone between the 7th degree and the final, are important in establishing this mode. ▶ To enhance staccato and legato capability. ▶ To build the aural and kinaesthetic memory necessary for this task.
PHYSICAL INVOLVEMENT	▶ Abdominal and thoracic muscle groups to achieve breath management ▶ Larynx height and posture ▶ Articulators, including pharynx, velum (soft palate), tongue, lips and jaw, for appropriate vowel formation and vocal resonance
INSTRUCTIONS	1 Play the mode 2 Mentally hear the mode sung on the chosen vowel 3 Breathe the correct vowel shape 4 Position the larynx 5 Activate breath support 6 Start to sing 7 For the staccato, pay attention to precise onset and offset while increasing breath pressure for each ascending pitch and maintaining appropriate breath pressure for each descending pitch 8 For the legato, keep connected tone and vowel shape while gradually increasing breath pressure for ascending pitch and maintaining appropriate breath pressure for descending pitch
PITCH DISPLAY	Sing the mode by directing the blue pitch line from the centre of the first note to the centre of each following note, with minimal deviation. For both staccato and legato, the optimal display will show minimal, clean horizontal lines in upward, then equally downward, diagonals.
SPECTROGRAM	The Spectrogram should exhibit the same pattern of resonances throughout the exercise.
LEVEL METER	The volume should remain consistent throughout the exercise. *Note: Where intervals traverse register changes, this is an especially useful skill to encourage.*

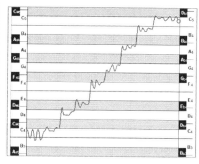

/a/

AIM	To sing an ascending major scale with lowered 3rd on a specified vowel with accurate pitch.
OBJECTIVES	▶ To develop management of pitch when singing an ascending major scale with lowered 3rd. The semitone between the 2nd and 3rd degrees of the scale is important. The pentachord is the same as for minor scales, while the upper tetrachord is the same as for a major scale. ▶ To build the aural and kinaesthetic memory necessary for this task.
PHYSICAL INVOLVEMENT	▶ Abdominal and thoracic muscle groups to achieve breath management ▶ Larynx height and posture ▶ Articulators, including pharynx, velum (soft palate), tongue, lips and jaw, for appropriate vowel formation and vocal resonance
INSTRUCTIONS	1 Play the scale 2 Mentally hear the scale sung on the chosen vowel 3 Breathe the correct vowel shape 4 Position the larynx 5 Activate breath support 6 Start to sing 7 Increase breath pressure in order to increase pitch, while keeping the vowel shape
PITCH DISPLAY	Sing the scale by directing the blue pitch line from the centre of the lowest note to the centre of each following note. The optimal display will show minimal, clean horizontal lines in an upward diagonal.
SPECTROGRAM	
LEVEL METER	

Exercise S-101: Ascending blues scale - Major scale with lowered 3rd, legato

/a/

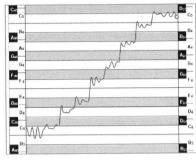

AIM	To sing an ascending major scale with lowered 3rd, legato, on a specified vowel, with pitch accuracy, consistent resonance and consistent volume.
OBJECTIVES	▶ To develop management of pitch, vowel articulation and volume, when singing a major blues scale with lowered 3rd. The semitone between the 2nd and 3rd degrees of the scale is important. The pentachord is the same as for minor scales, while the upper tetrachord is the same as for a major scale. ▶ To enhance legato capability. ▶ To build the aural and kinaesthetic memory necessary for this task.
PHYSICAL INVOLVEMENT	▶ Abdominal and thoracic muscle groups to achieve breath management ▶ Larynx height and posture ▶ Articulators, including pharynx, velum (soft palate), tongue, lips and jaw, for appropriate vowel formation and vocal resonance

INSTRUCTIONS	1 Play the scale 2 Mentally hear the scale sung on the chosen vowel 3 Breathe the correct vowel shape 4 Position the larynx 5 Activate breath support 6 Start to sing	7 Gradually increase breath pressure in order to increase pitch, while keeping connected tone and vowel shape.

PITCH DISPLAY	Sing the scale by directing the blue pitch line from the centre of the lowest note to the centre of each following note, with minimal deviation. The optimal display will show minimal, clean horizontal lines in an upward diagonal.
SPECTROGRAM	The Spectrogram should exhibit the same pattern of resonances throughout the exercise.
LEVEL METER	The volume should remain consistent throughout the exercise. *Note: Where intervals traverse register changes, this is an especially useful skill to encourage.*

/a/

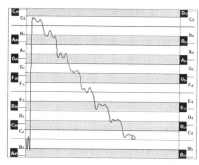

AIM	To sing a descending major scale with lowered 3rd on a specified vowel with accurate pitch.
OBJECTIVES 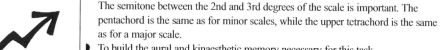	▶ To develop management of pitch when singing a descending major blues scale with lowered 3rd. The semitone between the 2nd and 3rd degrees of the scale is important. The pentachord is the same as for minor scales, while the upper tetrachord is the same as for a major scale. ▶ To build the aural and kinaesthetic memory necessary for this task.
PHYSICAL INVOLVEMENT 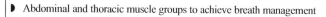	▶ Abdominal and thoracic muscle groups to achieve breath management ▶ Larynx height and posture ▶ Articulators, including pharynx, velum (soft palate), tongue, lips and jaw, for appropriate vowel formation and vocal resonance
INSTRUCTIONS	1 Play the scale 2 Mentally hear the scale sung on the chosen vowel 3 Breathe the correct vowel shape 4 Position the larynx 5 Activate breath support 6 Start to sing 7 Maintain appropriate breath pressure foe the descending pitch, while keeping the vowel shape
PITCH DISPLAY	Sing the scale by directing the blue pitch line from the centre of the highest note to the centre of each following note. The optimal display will show minimal, clean horizontal lines in a downward diagonal.
SPECTROGRAM	
LEVEL METER	

Exercise S-103: Descending blues scale - Major scale with lowered 3rd, legato

 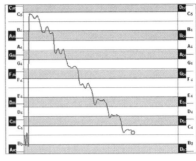

/a/

AIM	To sing a descending major scale with lowered 3rd, legato, on a specified vowel, with pitch accuracy, consistent resonance and consistent volume.
OBJECTIVES	▶ To develop management of pitch, vowel articulation and volume, when singing a descending major blues scale with lowered 3rd. The semitone between the 2nd and 3rd degrees of the scale is important. The pentachord is the same as for minor scales, while the upper tetrachord is the same as for a major scale. ▶ To enhance legato capability. ▶ To build the aural and kinaesthetic memory necessary for this task.
PHYSICAL INVOLVEMENT	▶ Abdominal and thoracic muscle groups to achieve breath management ▶ Larynx height and posture ▶ Articulators, including pharynx, velum (soft palate), tongue, lips and jaw, for appropriate vowel formation and vocal resonance
INSTRUCTIONS	1 Play the scale 2 Mentally hear the scale sung on the chosen vowel 3 Breathe the correct vowel shape 4 Position the larynx 5 Activate breath support 6 Start to sing 7 Maintain appropriate breath pressure for the descending pitch, while keeping connected tone and vowel shape
PITCH DISPLAY	Sing the scale by directing the blue pitch line from the centre of the highest note to the centre of each following note, with minimal deviation. The optimal display will show minimal horizontal lines in a downward diagonal.
SPECTROGRAM	The Spectrogram should exhibit the same pattern of resonances throughout the exercise.
LEVEL METER	The volume should remain consistent throughout the exercise. *Note: Where intervals traverse register changes, this is an especially useful skill to encourage.*

/a/

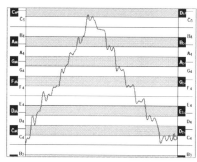

AIM	To sing an ascending and descending major scale with lowered 3rd on a specified vowel with accurate pitch.
OBJECTIVES	▶ To develop management of pitch when singing an ascending and descending major blues scale with lowered 3rd. The semitone between the 2nd and 3rd degrees of the scale is important. The pentachord is the same as for minor scales, while the upper tetrachord is the same as for a major scale. ▶ To build the aural and kinaesthetic memory necessary for this task.
PHYSICAL INVOLVEMENT	▶ Abdominal and thoracic muscle groups to achieve breath management ▶ Larynx height and posture ▶ Articulators, including pharynx, velum (soft palate), tongue, lips and jaw, for appropriate vowel formation and vocal resonance
INSTRUCTIONS	1 Play the scale 2 Mentally hear the scale sung on the chosen vowel 3 Breathe the correct vowel shape 4 Position the larynx 5 Activate breath support 6 Start to sing 7 Increase breath pressure in order to increase pitch, while keeping the vowel shape 8 Maintain appropriate pressure for the descending pitch, while keeping the vowel shape
PITCH DISPLAY	Sing the scale by directing the blue pitch line from the centre of the first note to the centre of each following note. The optimal display will show minimal, clean horizontal lines in an upward, then equally downward, diagonal.
SPECTROGRAM	
LEVEL METER	

Exercise S-105: Ascending and descending blues scale - Major scale with lowered 3rd, staccato

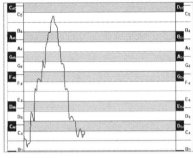

/a/

AIM	To sing an ascending and descending major scale with lowered 3rd, staccato, on a given vowel, with accurate pitch.
OBJECTIVES	▶ To develop management of pitch when singing an ascending and descending major blues scale with lowered 3rd, staccato. The semitone between the 2nd and 3rd degrees of the scale is important. The pentachord is the same as for minor scales, while the upper tetrachord is the same as for a major scale. ▶ To build the aural and kinaesthetic memory necessary for this task.
PHYSICAL INVOLVEMENT	▶ Abdominal and thoracic muscle groups to achieve breath management ▶ Larynx height and posture ▶ Articulators, including pharynx, velum (soft palate), tongue, lips and jaw, for appropriate vowel formation and vocal resonance
INSTRUCTIONS	1 Play the scale 2 Mentally hear the scale sung on the chosen vowel 3 Breathe the correct vowel shape 4 Position the larynx 5 Activate breath support 6 Start to sing 7 Pay attention to precise onset and offset while increasing breath pressure for each ascending pitch and keeping the vowel shape 8 Pay attention to precise onset and offset while maintaining appropriate breath pressure for each descending pitch and keeping the vowel shape
PITCH DISPLAY	Sing the scale by directing the blue pitch line from the centre of the first note to the centre of each following note, with minimal deviation The optimal display will show minimal, clean horizontal lines in an upward, then equally downward, diagonal.
SPECTROGRAM	
LEVEL METER	

/a/

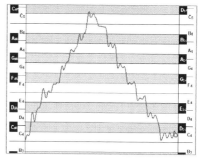

AIM	To sing an ascending and descending major scale with lowered 3rd, legato, on a specified vowel, with pitch accuracy, consistent resonance and consistent volume.
OBJECTIVES	▶ To develop management of pitch, vowel articulation and volume, when singing an ascending and descending major blues scale with lowered 3rd. The semitone between the 2nd and 3rd degrees of the scale is important. The pentachord is the same as for minor scales, while the upper tetrachord is the same as for a major scale. ▶ To enhance legato capability. ▶ To build the aural and kinaesthetic memory necessary for this task.
PHYSICAL INVOLVEMENT	▶ Abdominal and thoracic muscle groups to achieve breath management ▶ Larynx height and posture ▶ Articulators, including pharynx, velum (soft palate), tongue, lips and jaw, for appropriate vowel formation and vocal resonance
INSTRUCTIONS	1 Play the scale 2 Mentally hear the scale sung on the chosen vowel 3 Breathe the correct vowel shape 4 Position the larynx 5 Activate breath support 6 Start to sing 7 Gradually increase breath pressure in order to increase pitch, while keeping connected tone and vowel shape 8 Maintain appropriate breath pressure for the descending pitch, while keeping connected tone and vowel shape
PITCH DISPLAY	Sing the scale by directing the blue pitch line from the centre of the first note to the centre of each following note, with minimal deviation. The optimal display will show minima, clean horizontal lines in an upward, then equally downward, diagonal.
SPECTROGRAM	The Spectrogram should exhibit the same pattern of resonances throughout the exercise.
LEVEL METER	The volume should remain consistent throughout the exercise. *Note: Where intervals traverse register changes, this is an especially useful skill to encourage.*

Exercise S-107: Ascending and descending blues scale - Major scale with lowered 3rd, staccato, and then legato

/a/

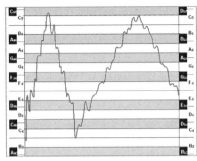

AIM	To sing an ascending and descending major scale with lowered 3rd, first staccato and then legato, on a specified vowel, with pitch accuracy, consistent resonance and consistent volume.
OBJECTIVES	▶ To develop management of pitch, vowel articulation and volume, when singing an ascending and descending major blues scale with lowered 3rd. The semitone between the 2nd and 3rd degrees of the scale is important. The pentachord is the same as for minor scales, while the upper tetrachord is the same as for a major scale. ▶ To enhance staccato and legato capability. ▶ To build the aural and kinaesthetic memory necessary for this task.
PHYSICAL INVOLVEMENT	▶ Abdominal and thoracic muscle groups to achieve breath management ▶ Larynx height and posture ▶ Articulators, including pharynx, velum (soft palate), tongue, lips and jaw, for appropriate vowel formation and vocal resonance
INSTRUCTIONS	1 Play the scale 2 Mentally hear the scale sung on the chosen vowel 3 Breathe the correct vowel shape 4 Position the larynx 5 Activate breath support 6 Start to sing 7 For the staccato, pay attention to precise	onset and offset while increasing breath pressure for each ascending pitch and maintaining appropriate breath pressure for each descending pitch 8 For the legato, keep connected tone and vowel shape while gradually increasing breath pressure for ascending pitch and maintaining appropriate breath pressure for descending pitch
PITCH DISPLAY	Sing the scale by directing the blue pitch line from the centre of the first note to the centre of each following note, with minimal deviation. For both staccato and legato the optimal display will show minimal, clean horizontal lines in upward, then equally downward, diagonals.
SPECTROGRAM	The Spectrogram should exhibit the same pattern of resonances throughout the exercise.
LEVEL METER	The volume should remain consistent throughout the exercise. *Note: Where intervals traverse register changes, this is an especially useful skill to encourage.*

/a/

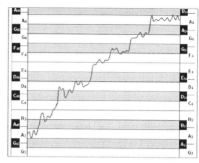

AIM	To sing an ascending natural minor scale with raised 3rd on a specified vowel with accurate pitch.
OBJECTIVES 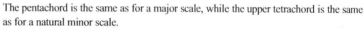	▶ To develop management of pitch when singing an ascending natural minor scale with raised 3rd. The pentachord is the same as for a major scale, while the upper tetrachord is the same as for a natural minor scale. ▶ To build the aural and kinaesthetic memory necessary for this task.
PHYSICAL INVOLVEMENT 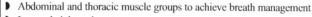	▶ Abdominal and thoracic muscle groups to achieve breath management ▶ Larynx height and posture ▶ Articulators, including pharynx, velum (soft palate), tongue, lips and jaw, for appropriate vowel formation and vocal resonance
INSTRUCTIONS	1 Play the scale 2 Mentally hear the scale sung on the chosen vowel 3 Breathe the correct vowel shape 4 Position the larynx 5 Activate breath support 6 Start to sing 7 Increase breath pressure in order to increase pitch, while keeping the vowel shape
PITCH DISPLAY	Sing the scale by directing the blue pitch line from the centre of the lowest note to the centre of each following note. The optimal display will show minimal, clean horizontal lines in an upward diagonal.
SPECTROGRAM	
LEVEL METER	

Exercise S-109: Ascending blues scale - Natural minor with raised 3rd, legato

/a/

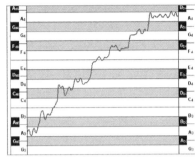

AIM	To sing an ascending natural minor scale with raised 3rd, legato, on a specified vowel, with pitch accuracy, consistent resonance and consistent volume.
OBJECTIVES	▶ To develop management of pitch, vowel articulation and volume, when singing a natural minor blues scale with raised 3rd. The pentachord is the same as for a major scale, while the upper tetrachord is the same as for a natural minor scale. ▶ To enhance legato capability. ▶ To build the aural and kinaesthetic memory necessary for this task.
PHYSICAL INVOLVEMENT	▶ Abdominal and thoracic muscle groups to achieve breath management ▶ Larynx height and posture ▶ Articulators, including pharynx, velum (soft palate), tongue, lips and jaw, for appropriate vowel formation and vocal resonance
INSTRUCTIONS	1 Play the scale 2 Mentally hear the scale sung on the chosen vowel 3 Breathe the correct vowel shape 4 Position the larynx 5 Activate breath support 6 Start to sing 7 Gradually increase breath pressure in order to increase pitch, while maintaining the vowel shape
PITCH DISPLAY	Sing the scale by directing the blue pitch line from the centre of the lowest note to the centre of each following note, with minimal deviation. The optimal display will show minimal, clean horizontal lines in an upward diagonal.
SPECTROGRAM	The Spectrogram should exhibit the same pattern of resonances throughout the exercise.
LEVEL METER	The volume should remain consistent throughout the exercise. *Note: Where intervals traverse register changes, this is an especially useful skill to encourage.*

Sing&See

/a/

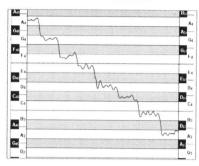

AIM	To sing a descending natural minor scale with raised 3rd on a specified vowel with accurate pitch.
OBJECTIVES	▶ To develop management of pitch when singing a descending natural minor blues scale with raised 3rd. The pentachord is the same as for a major scale, while the upper tetrachord is the same as for a natural minor scale. ▶ To build the aural and kinaesthetic memory necessary for this task.
PHYSICAL INVOLVEMENT	▶ Abdominal and thoracic muscle groups to achieve breath management ▶ Larynx height and posture ▶ Articulators, including pharynx, velum (soft palate), tongue, lips and jaw, for appropriate vowel formation and vocal resonance
INSTRUCTIONS	1 Play the scale 2 Mentally hear the scale sung on the chosen vowel 3 Breathe the correct vowel shape 4 Position the larynx 5 Activate breath support 6 Start to sing	7 Maintain appropriate breath pressure for the descending pitch, while keeping the vowel shape
PITCH DISPLAY	Sing the scale by directing the blue pitch line from the centre of the highest note to the centre of each following note. The optimal display will show minimal, clean horizontal lines in a downward diagonal.
SPECTROGRAM	
LEVEL METER	

Exercise S-111: Descending blues scale - Natural minor with raised 3rd, legato

/a/

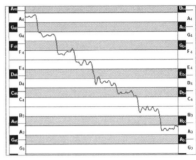

AIM	To sing a descending natural minor scale with raised 3rd, legato, on a specified vowel, with pitch accuracy, consistent resonance and consistent volume.
OBJECTIVES	▶ To develop management of pitch, vowel articulation and volume, when singing a descending natural minor blues scale with raised 3rd. The pentachord is the same as for a major scale, while the upper tetrachord is the same as for a natural minor scale. ▶ To enhance legato capability. ▶ To build the aural and kinaesthetic memory necessary for this task.
PHYSICAL INVOLVEMENT	▶ Abdominal and thoracic muscle groups to achieve breath management ▶ Larynx height and posture ▶ Articulators, including pharynx, velum (soft palate), tongue, lips and jaw, for appropriate vowel formation and vocal resonance

INSTRUCTIONS	
1 Play the scale 2 Mentally hear the scale sung on the chosen vowel 3 Breathe the correct vowel shape 4 Position the larynx 5 Activate breath support 6 Start to sing	7 Maintain appropriate breath pressure for the descending pitch, while keeping the vowel shape

PITCH DISPLAY	Sing the scale by directing the blue pitch line from the centre of the highest note to the centre of each following note, with minimal deviation. The optimal display will show minimal, clean horizontal lines in a downward diagonal.
SPECTROGRAM	The Spectrogram should exhibit the same pattern of resonances throughout the exercise.
LEVEL METER	The volume should remain consistent throughout the exercise. *Note: Where intervals traverse register changes, this is an especially useful skill to encourage.*

Exercise S-112: Ascending and descending blues scale - Natural minor with raised 3rd

/a/

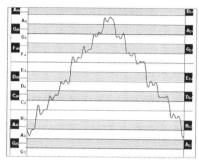

AIM	To sing an ascending and descending natural minor scale with raised 3rd on a specified vowel with accurate pitch.
OBJECTIVES 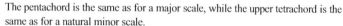	▶ To develop management of pitch when singing an ascending and descending natural minor blues scale with raised 3rd. The pentachord is the same as for a major scale, while the upper tetrachord is the same as for a natural minor scale. ▶ To build the aural and kinaesthetic memory necessary for this task.
PHYSICAL INVOLVEMENT	▶ Abdominal and thoracic muscle groups to achieve breath management ▶ Larynx height and posture ▶ Articulators, including pharynx, velum (soft palate), tongue, lips and jaw, for appropriate vowel formation and vocal resonance
INSTRUCTIONS	1 Play the scale 2 Mentally hear the scale sung on the chosen vowel 3 Breathe the correct vowel shape 4 Position the larynx 5 Activate breath support 6 Start to sing 7 Increase breath pressure in order to increase pitch, while keeping the vowel shape 8 Maintain appropriate breath pressure for the descending pitch, while keeping the vowel shape
PITCH DISPLAY	Sing the scale by directing the blue pitch line from the centre of the first note to the centre of each following note. The optimal display will show minimal, clean horizontal lines in an upward, then equally downward, diagonal.
SPECTROGRAM	
LEVEL METER	

Exercise S-113: Ascending and descending blues scale - Natural minor scale with raised 3rd, staccato

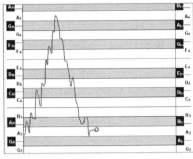

/a/

AIM	To sing an ascending and descending natural minor scale with raised 3rd, staccato, on a specified vowel with accurate pitch.
OBJECTIVES	▸ To develop management of pitch when singing an ascending and descending natural minor blues scale with raised 3rd, staccato. The pentachord is the same as for a major scale, while the upper tetrachord is the same as for a natural minor scale. ▸ To build the aural and kinaesthetic memory necessary for this task.
PHYSICAL INVOLVEMENT	▸ Abdominal and thoracic muscle groups to achieve breath management ▸ Larynx height and posture ▸ Articulators, including pharynx, velum (soft palate), tongue, lips and jaw, for appropriate vowel formation and vocal resonance

INSTRUCTIONS

1. Play the scale
2. Mentally hear the scale sung on the chosen vowel
3. Breathe the correct vowel shape
4. Position the larynx
5. Activate breath support
6. Start to sing

7. Pay attention to precise onset and offset while increasing breath pressure for each ascending pitch and keeping the vowel shape
8. Pay attention to precise onset and offset while maintaining appropriate breath pressure for each descending pitch and keeping the vowel shape

PITCH DISPLAY

Sing the scale by directing the blue pitch line from the centre of the first note to the centre of each following note, with minimal deviation. The optimal display will show minimal, clean horizontal lines in an upward, then equally downward, diagonal.

SPECTROGRAM

LEVEL METER

/a/

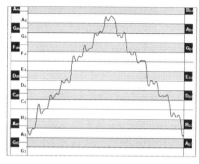

AIM	To sing an ascending and descending natural minor scale with raised 3rd, legato, on a specified vowel, with pitch accuracy, consistent resonance and consistent volume.
OBJECTIVES	▶ To develop management of pitch, vowel articulation and volume, when singing an ascending and descending natural minor blues scale with raised 3rd. The pentachord is the same as for a major scale, while the upper tetrachord is the same as for a natural minor scale. ▶ To enhance legato capability. ▶ To build the aural and kinaesthetic memory necessary for this task.
PHYSICAL INVOLVEMENT	▶ Abdominal and thoracic muscle groups to achieve breath management ▶ Larynx height and posture ▶ Articulators, including pharynx, velum (soft palate), tongue, lips and jaw, for appropriate vowel formation and vocal resonance
INSTRUCTIONS	1 Play the scale 2 Mentally hear the scale sung on the chosen vowel 3 Breathe the correct vowel shape 4 Position the larynx 5 Activate breath support 6 Start to sing 7 Gradually increase breath pressure in order to increase pitch, while keeping connected tone and vowel shape 8 Maintain appropriate breath pressure for the descending pitch, while keeping connected tone and vowel shape
PITCH DISPLAY	Sing the scale by directing the blue pitch line from the centre of the first note to the centre of each following note, with minimal deviation. The optimal display will show minimal, clean horizontal lines in an upward, then equally downward, diagonal.
SPECTROGRAM	The Spectrogram should exhibit the same pattern of resonances throughout the exercise.
LEVEL METER	The volume should remain consistent throughout the exercise. *Note: Where intervals traverse register changes, this is an especially useful skill to encourage.*

Exercise S-115: Ascending and descending blues scale - Natural minor with raised 3rd, staccato, and then legato

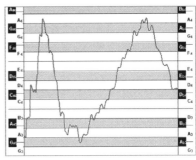

/a/

AIM	To sing an ascending and descending natural minor scale with raised 3rd, first staccato and then legato, on a specified vowel, with pitch accuracy, consistent resonance and consistent volume.
OBJECTIVES	▶ To develop management of pitch, vowel articulation and volume, when singing an ascending and descending natural minor blues scale with raised 3rd. The pentachord is the same as for a major scale, while the upper tetrachord is the same as for a natural minor scale. ▶ To enhance staccato and legato capability. ▶ To build the aural and kinaesthetic memory necessary for this task.
PHYSICAL INVOLVEMENT	▶ Abdominal and thoracic muscle groups to achieve breath management ▶ Larynx height and posture ▶ Articulators, including pharynx, velum (soft palate), tongue, lips and jaw, for appropriate vowel formation and vocal resonance
INSTRUCTIONS	1 Play the scale 2 Mentally hear the scale sung on the chosen vowel 3 Breathe the correct vowel shape 4 Position the larynx 5 Activate breath support 6 Start to sing 7 For the staccato, pay attention to precise	onset and offset while increasing breath pressure for each ascending pitch and maintaining appropriate breath pressure for each descending pitch 8 For the legato, keep connected tone and vowel shape while gradually increasing breath pressure for ascending pitch and maintaining appropriate breath pressure for descending pitch
PITCH DISPLAY	Sing the scale by directing the blue pitch line from the centre of the first note to the centre of each following note, with minimal deviation. For both staccato and legato, the optimal display will show minimal, clean horizontal lines in upward, then equally downward, diagonals.
SPECTROGRAM	The Spectrogram should exhibit the same pattern of resonances throughout the exercise.
LEVEL METER	The volume should remain consistent throughout the exercise. *Note: Where intervals traverse register changes, this is an especially useful skill to encourage.*

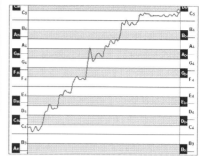

AIM	To sing an ascending major scale with raised 5th on a specified vowel with accurate pitch.
OBJECTIVES	▶ To develop management of pitch when singing an ascending major scale with raised 5th. The augmented second between the 4th and the 5th degrees of the scale is of particular importance. ▶ To build the aural and kinaesthetic memory necessary for this task.
PHYSICAL INVOLVEMENT	▶ Abdominal and thoracic muscle groups to achieve breath management ▶ Larynx height and posture ▶ Articulators, including pharynx, velum (soft palate), tongue, lips and jaw, for appropriate vowel formation and vocal resonance
INSTRUCTIONS	1 Play the scale 2 Mentally hear the scale sung on the chosen vowel 3 Breathe the correct vowel shape 4 Position the larynx 5 Activate breath support 6 Start to sing 7 Increase breath pressure in order to increase pitch, while keeping the vowel shape
PITCH DISPLAY	Sing the scale by directing the blue pitch line from the centre of the lowest note to the centre of each following note. The optimal display will show minimal, clean horizontal lines in an upward diagonal.
SPECTROGRAM	
LEVEL METER	

Exercise S-117: Ascending blues scale - Major scale with raised 5th, legato

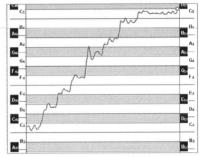

/a/

AIM	To sing an ascending major scale with raised 5th, legato, on a specified vowel, with pitch accuracy, consistent resonance and consistent volume.
OBJECTIVES 	▶ To develop management of pitch, vowel articulation and volume, when singing a major blues scale with raised 5th. The augmented second between the 4th and the 5th degrees of the scale is of particular importance. ▶ To enhance legato capability. ▶ To build the aural and kinaesthetic memory necessary for this task.
PHYSICAL INVOLVEMENT	▶ Abdominal and thoracic muscle groups to achieve breath management ▶ Larynx height and posture ▶ Articulators, including pharynx, velum (soft palate), tongue, lips and jaw, for appropriate vowel formation and vocal resonance
INSTRUCTIONS	1 Play the scale 2 Mentally hear the scale sung on the chosen vowel 3 Breathe the correct vowel shape 4 Position the larynx 5 Activate breath support 6 Start to sing 7 Gradually increase breath pressure in order to increase pitch, while keeping connected tone and vowel shape.
PITCH DISPLAY	Sing the scale by directing the blue pitch line from the centre of the lowest note to the centre of each following note, with minimal deviation. The optimal display will show minimal, clean horizontal lines in an upward diagonal.
SPECTROGRAM	The Spectrogram should exhibit the same pattern of resonances throughout the exercise.
LEVEL METER	The volume should remain consistent throughout the exercise. *Note: Where intervals traverse register changes, this is an especially useful skill to encourage.*

Sing&See

/a/

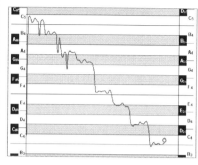

AIM	To sing a descending major scale with raised 5th on a specified vowel with accurate pitch.
OBJECTIVES	▶ To develop management of pitch when singing a descending major blues scale with raised 5th. The augmented second between the 4th and the 5th degrees of the scale is of particular importance. ▶ To build the aural and kinaesthetic memory necessary for this task.
PHYSICAL INVOLVEMENT	▶ Abdominal and thoracic muscle groups to achieve breath management ▶ Larynx height and posture ▶ Articulators, including pharynx, velum (soft palate), tongue, lips and jaw, for appropriate vowel formation and vocal resonance

INSTRUCTIONS	1 Play the scale 2 Mentally hear the scale sung on the chosen vowel 3 Breathe the correct vowel shape 4 Position the larynx 5 Activate breath support 6 Start to sing	7 Maintain appropriate breath pressure for the descending pitch, while keeping the vowel shape

PITCH DISPLAY	Sing the scale by directing the blue pitch line from the centre of the highest note to the centre of each following note. The optimal display will show minimal, clean horizontal lines in a downward diagonal.
SPECTROGRAM	
LEVEL METER	

Exercise S-119: Descending blues scale - Major scale with raised 5th, legato

/a/

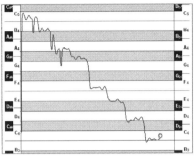

AIM	To sing a descending major scale with raised 5th, legato, on a specified vowel, with pitch accuracy, consistent resonance and consistent volume.
OBJECTIVES	▶ To develop management of pitch, vowel articulation and volume, when singing a descending major blues scale with raised 5th. The augmented second between the 4th and the 5th degrees of the scale is of particular importance. ▶ To enhance legato capability. ▶ To build the aural and kinaesthetic memory necessary for this task.
PHYSICAL INVOLVEMENT	▶ Abdominal and thoracic muscle groups to achieve breath management ▶ Larynx height and posture ▶ Articulators, including pharynx, velum (soft palate), tongue, lips and jaw, for appropriate vowel formation and vocal resonance

INSTRUCTIONS	1 Play the scale 2 Mentally hear the scale sung on the chosen vowel 3 Breathe the correct vowel shape 4 Position the larynx 5 Activate breath support 6 Start to sing	7 Maintain appropriate breath pressure for the descending pitch, while keeping connected tone and vowel shape

PITCH DISPLAY	Sing the scale by directing the blue pitch line from the centre of the highest note to the centre of each following note, with minimal deviation. The optimal display will show minimal, clean horizontal lines in a downward diagonal.
SPECTROGRAM	The Spectrogram should exhibit the same pattern of resonances throughout the exercise.
LEVEL METER	The volume should remain consistent throughout the exercise. *Note: Where intervals traverse register changes, this is an especially useful skill to encourage.*

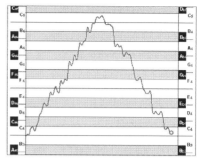

/a/

AIM	To sing an ascending and descending major scale with raised 5th on a specified vowel with accurate pitch.

OBJECTIVES	▶ To develop management of pitch when singing an ascending and descending major blues scale with raised 5th. The augmented second between the 4th and the 5th degrees of the scale is of particular importance. ▶ To build the aural and kinaesthetic memory necessary for this task.

PHYSICAL INVOLVEMENT	▶ Abdominal and thoracic muscle groups to achieve breath management ▶ Larynx height and posture ▶ Articulators, including pharynx, velum (soft palate), tongue, lips and jaw, for appropriate vowel formation and vocal resonance

INSTRUCTIONS	1 Play the scale 2 Mentally hear the scale sung on the chosen vowel 3 Breathe the correct vowel shape 4 Position the larynx 5 Activate breath support 6 Start to sing	7 Increase breath pressure in order to increase pitch, while keeping the vowel shape 8 Maintain appropriate breath pressure for the descending pitch, while keeping the vowel shape

PITCH DISPLAY 	Sing the scale by directing the blue pitch line from the centre of the first note to the centre of each following note. The optimal display will show minimal, clean horizontal lines in an upward, then equally downward, diagonal.

SPECTROGRAM 	

LEVEL METER 	

Exercise S-121: Ascending and descending blues scale - Major scale with raised 5th, staccato

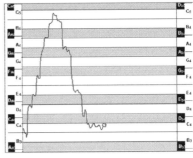

AIM	To sing an ascending and descending major scale with raised 5th, staccato, on a specified vowel with accurate pitch.
OBJECTIVES	▶ To develop management of pitch when singing an ascending and descending major blues scale with raised 5th, staccato. The augmented second between the 4th and the 5th degrees of the scale is of particular importance. ▶ To build the aural and kinaesthetic memory necessary for this task.
PHYSICAL INVOLVEMENT	▶ Abdominal and thoracic muscle groups to achieve breath management ▶ Larynx height and posture ▶ Articulators, including pharynx, velum (soft palate), tongue, lips and jaw, for appropriate vowel formation and vocal resonance
INSTRUCTIONS	1 Play the scale 2 Mentally hear the scale sung on the chosen vowel 3 Breathe the correct vowel shape 4 Position the larynx 5 Activate breath support 6 Start to sing 7 Pay attention to precise onset and offset while increasing breath pressure for each ascending pitch and keeping vowel the shape 8 Pay attention to precise onset and offset while maintaining appropriate breath pressure for each descending pitch and keeping the vowel shape
PITCH DISPLAY	Sing the scale by directing the blue pitch line from the centre of the first note to the centre of each following note, with minimal deviation. The optimal display will show minimal, clean horizontal lines in an upward, then equally downward, diagonal.
SPECTROGRAM	
LEVEL METER	

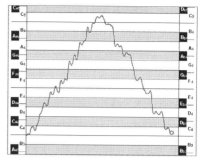

AIM	To sing an ascending and descending major scale with raised 5th, legato, on a specified vowel, with pitch accuracy, consistent resonance and consistent volume.
OBJECTIVES	▶ To develop management of pitch, vowel articulation and volume, when singing an ascending and descending major blues scale with raised 5th. The augmented second between the 4th and the 5th degrees of the scale is of particular importance. ▶ To enhance legato capability. ▶ To build the aural and kinaesthetic memory necessary for this task.
PHYSICAL INVOLVEMENT	▶ Abdominal and thoracic muscle groups to achieve breath management ▶ Larynx height and posture ▶ Articulators, including pharynx, velum (soft palate), tongue, lips and jaw, for appropriate vowel formation and vocal resonance
INSTRUCTIONS	1 Play the scale 2 Mentally hear the scale sung on the chosen vowel 3 Breathe the correct vowel shape 4 Position the larynx 5 Activate breath support 6 Start to sing 7 Gradually increase breath pressure in order to increase pitch, while keeping connected tone and vowel shape 8 Maintain appropriate breath pressure for the descending pitch, while keeping connected tone and vowel shape
PITCH DISPLAY	Sing the scale by directing the blue pitch line from the centre of the first note to the centre of each following note, with minimal deviation. The optimal display will show minimal, clean horizontal lines in an upward, then equally downward, diagonal.
SPECTROGRAM	The Spectrogram should exhibit the same pattern of resonances throughout the exercise.
LEVEL METER	The volume should remain consistent throughout the exercise. *Note: Where intervals traverse register changes, this is an especially useful skill to encourage.*

Exercise S-123: Ascending and descending blues scale - Major scale with raised 5th, staccato, and then legato

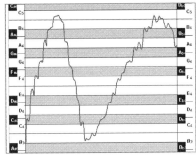

AIM	To sing an ascending and descending major scale with raised 5th, first staccato and then legato, on a specified vowel, with pitch accuracy, consistent resonance and consistent volume.
OBJECTIVES	▶ To develop management of pitch, vowel articulation and volume, when singing an ascending and descending major blues scale with raised 5th. The augmented second between the 4th and the 5th degrees of the scale is of particular importance. ▶ To enhance staccato and legato capability. ▶ To build the aural and kinaesthetic memory necessary for this task.
PHYSICAL INVOLVEMENT	▶ Abdominal and thoracic muscle groups to achieve breath management ▶ Larynx height and posture ▶ Articulators, including pharynx, velum (soft palate), tongue, lips and jaw, for appropriate vowel formation and vocal resonance
INSTRUCTIONS	1 Play the scale 2 Mentally hear the scale sung on the chosen vowel 3 Breathe the correct vowel shape 4 Position the larynx 5 Activate breath support 6 Start to sing 7 For the staccato, pay attention to precise	onset and offset while increasing breath pressure for each ascending pitch and maintaining appropriate breath pressure for each descending pitch 8 For the legato, keep connected tone and vowel shape while gradually increasing breath pressure for ascending pitch and maintaining appropriate breath pressure for descending pitch

PITCH DISPLAY	Sing the scale by directing the blue pitch line from the centre of the first note to the centre of each following note, with minimal deviation. The optimal display will show minimal, clean horizontal lines in upward, then equally downward, diagonals.
SPECTROGRAM	The Spectrogram should exhibit the same pattern of resonances throughout the exercise.
LEVEL METER	The volume should remain consistent throughout the exercise. *Note: Where intervals traverse register changes, this is an especially useful skill to encourage.*

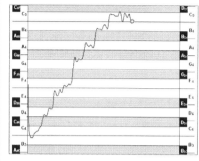

/a/

AIM	To sing an ascending major scale with lowered 5th on a specified vowel with accurate pitch.
OBJECTIVES	▶ To develop management of pitch when singing an ascending major scale with lowered 5th. The semitone between the 4th and 5th degrees of the scale, and the augmented second between the 5th and 6th degrees, are of particular importance. ▶ To build the aural and kinaesthetic memory necessary for this task.
PHYSICAL INVOLVEMENT	▶ Abdominal and thoracic muscle groups to achieve breath management ▶ Larynx height and posture ▶ Articulators, including pharynx, velum (soft palate), tongue, lips and jaw, for appropriate vowel formation and vocal resonance
INSTRUCTIONS	1 Play the scale 2 Mentally hear the scale sung on the chosen vowel 3 Breathe the correct vowel shape 4 Position the larynx 5 Activate breath support 6 Start to sing 7 Increase breath pressure in order to increase pitch, while keeping the vowel shape
PITCH DISPLAY	Sing the scale by directing the blue pitch line from the centre of the lowest note to the centre of each following note. The optimal display will show minimal, clean horizontal lines in an upward diagonal.
SPECTROGRAM	
LEVEL METER	

Exercise S-125: Ascending blues scale - Major scale with lowered 5th, legato

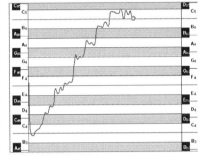

/a/

AIM	To sing an ascending major scale with lowered 5th, legato, on a specified vowel, with pitch accuracy, consistent resonance and consistent volume.
OBJECTIVES	▶ To develop management of pitch, vowel articulation and volume, when singing a major blues scale with lowered 5th. The semitone between the 4th and 5th degrees of the scale, and the augmented second between the 5th and 6th degrees, are of particular importance. ▶ To enhance legato capability. ▶ To build the aural and kinaesthetic memory necessary for this task.
PHYSICAL INVOLVEMENT	▶ Abdominal and thoracic muscle groups to achieve breath management ▶ Larynx height and posture ▶ Articulators, including pharynx, velum (soft palate), tongue, lips and jaw, for appropriate vowel formation and vocal resonance
INSTRUCTIONS	1 Play the scale 2 Mentally hear the scale sung on the chosen vowel 3 Breathe the correct vowel shape 4 Position the larynx 5 Activate breath support 6 Start to sing 7 Gradually increase breath pressure in order to increase pitch, while keeping connected tone and vowel shape
PITCH DISPLAY	Sing the scale by directing the blue pitch line from the centre of the lowest note to the centre of each following note, with minimal deviation. The optimal display will show minimal, clean horizontal lines in an upward diagonal.
SPECTROGRAM	The Spectrogram should exhibit the same pattern of resonances throughout the exercise.
LEVEL METER	The volume should remain consistent throughout the exercise. *Note: Where intervals traverse register changes, this is an especially useful skill to encourage.*

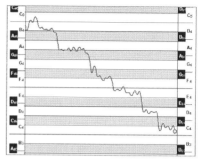

AIM	To sing a descending major scale with lowered 5th on a specified vowel with accurate pitch.
OBJECTIVES 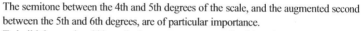	▶ To develop management of pitch when singing a descending major blues scale with lowered 5th. The semitone between the 4th and 5th degrees of the scale, and the augmented second between the 5th and 6th degrees, are of particular importance. ▶ To build the aural and kinaesthetic memory necessary for this task.
PHYSICAL INVOLVEMENT 	▶ Abdominal and thoracic muscle groups to achieve breath management ▶ Larynx height and posture ▶ Articulators, including pharynx, velum (soft palate), tongue, lips and jaw, for appropriate vowel formation and vocal resonance
INSTRUCTIONS 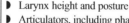	1 Play the scale 2 Mentally hear the scale sung on the chosen vowel 3 Breathe the correct vowel shape 4 Position the larynx 5 Activate breath support 6 Start to sing 7 Maintain appropriate breath pressure for the descending pitch, while keeping the vowel shape
PITCH DISPLAY	Sing the scale by directing the blue pitch line from the centre of the highest note to the centre of each following note. The optimal display will show minimal, clean horizontal lines in a downward diagonal.
SPECTROGRAM	
LEVEL METER	

Exercise S-127: Descending blues scale - Major scale with lowered 5th, legato

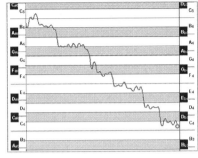

/a/

AIM	To sing a descending major scale with lowered 5th, legato, on a specified vowel, with pitch accuracy, consistent resonance and consistent volume.
OBJECTIVES	▶ To develop management of pitch, vowel articulation and volume, when singing a descending major blues scale with lowered 5th. The semitone between the 4th and 5th degrees of the scale, and the augmented second between the 5th and 6th degrees, are of particular importance. ▶ To enhance legato capability. ▶ To build the aural and kinaesthetic memory necessary for this task.
PHYSICAL INVOLVEMENT	▶ Abdominal and thoracic muscle groups to achieve breath management ▶ Larynx height and posture ▶ Articulators, including pharynx, velum (soft palate), tongue, lips and jaw, for appropriate vowel formation and vocal resonance
INSTRUCTIONS	1 Play the scale 2 Mentally hear the scale sung on the chosen vowel 3 Breathe the correct vowel shape 4 Position the larynx 5 Activate breath support 6 Start to sing 7 Maintain appropriate breath pressure for the descending pitch, while keeping the vowel shape
PITCH DISPLAY	Sing the scale by directing the blue pitch line from the centre of the highest note to the centre of each following note, with minimal deviation. The optimal display will show minimal, clean horizontal lines in a downward diagonal.
SPECTROGRAM	The Spectrogram should exhibit the same pattern of resonances throughout the exercise.
LEVEL METER	The volume should remain consistent throughout the exercise. *Note: Where intervals traverse register changes, this is an especially useful skill to encourage.*

/a/

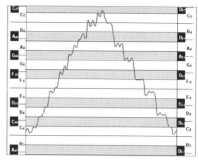

AIM	To sing an ascending and descending major scale with lowered 5th on a specified vowel with accurate pitch.
OBJECTIVES 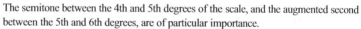	▸ To develop management of pitch when singing an ascending and descending major blues scale with lowered 5th. The semitone between the 4th and 5th degrees of the scale, and the augmented second between the 5th and 6th degrees, are of particular importance. ▸ To build the aural and kinaesthetic memory necessary for this task.
PHYSICAL INVOLVEMENT 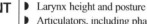	▸ Abdominal and thoracic muscle groups to achieve breath management ▸ Larynx height and posture ▸ Articulators, including pharynx, velum (soft palate), tongue, lips and jaw, for appropriate vowel formation and vocal resonance
INSTRUCTIONS	1 Play the scale 2 Mentally hear the scale sung on the chosen vowel 3 Breathe the correct vowel shape 4 Position the larynx 5 Activate breath support 6 Start to sing 7 Increase breath pressure in order to increase pitch, while keeping the vowel shape 8 Maintain appropriate breath pressure for the descending pitch, while keeping the vowel shape
PITCH DISPLAY	Sing the scale by directing the blue pitch line from the centre of the first note to the centre of each following note. The optimal display will show minimal, clean horizontal lines in an upward, then equally downward, diagonal.
SPECTROGRAM	
LEVEL METER	

Exercise S-129: Ascending and descending blues scale - Major scale with lowered 5th, staccato

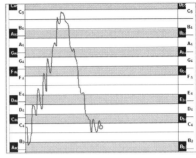

AIM	To sing an ascending and descending major scale with lowered 5th, staccato, on a specified vowel with accurate pitch.
OBJECTIVES 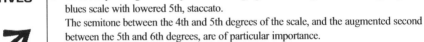	▶ To develop management of pitch when singing an ascending and descending major blues scale with lowered 5th, staccato. The semitone between the 4th and 5th degrees of the scale, and the augmented second between the 5th and 6th degrees, are of particular importance. ▶ To build the aural and kinaesthetic memory necessary for this task.
PHYSICAL INVOLVEMENT	▶ Abdominal and thoracic muscle groups to achieve breath management ▶ Larynx height and posture ▶ Articulators, including pharynx, velum (soft palate), tongue, lips and jaw, for appropriate vowel formation and vocal resonance
INSTRUCTIONS	1 Play the scale 2 Mentally hear the scale sung on the chosen vowel 3 Breathe the correct vowel shape 4 Position the larynx 5 Activate breath support 6 Start to sing 7 Pay attention to precise onset and offset while increasing breath pressure for each ascending pitch and keeping the vowel shape 8 Pay attention to precise onset and offset while maintaining appropriate breath pressure for each descending pitch and keeping the vowel shape
PITCH DISPLAY	Sing the scale by directing the blue pitch line from the centre of the first note to the centre of each following note, with minimal deviation. The optimal display will show minimal, clean horizontal lines in an upward, then equally downward, diagonal.
SPECTROGRAM	
LEVEL METER	

/a/

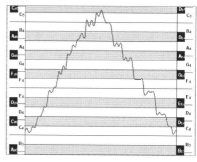

AIM	To sing an ascending and descending major scale with lowered 5th, legato, on a specified vowel, with pitch accuracy, consistent resonance and consistent volume.
OBJECTIVES	▶ To develop management of pitch, vowel articulation and volume, when singing an ascending and descending major blues scale with lowered 5th. The semitone between the 4th and 5th degrees of the scale, and the augmented second between the 5th and 6th degrees, are of particular importance. ▶ To enhance legato capability. ▶ To build the aural and kinaesthetic memory necessary for this task.
PHYSICAL INVOLVEMENT	▶ Abdominal and thoracic muscle groups to achieve breath management ▶ Larynx height and posture ▶ Articulators, including pharynx, velum (soft palate), tongue, lips and jaw, for appropriate vowel formation and vocal resonance
INSTRUCTIONS	1 Play the scale 2 Mentally hear the scale sung on the chosen vowel 3 Breathe the correct vowel shape 4 Position the larynx 5 Activate breath support 6 Start to sing 7 Gradually increase breath pressure in order to increase pitch, while keeping connected tone and vowel shape 8 Maintain appropriate breath pressure for the descending pitch, while keeping connected tone and vowel shape
PITCH DISPLAY	Sing the scale by directing the blue pitch line from the centre of the first note to the centre of each following note, with minimal deviation. The optimal display will show minimal, clean horizontal lines in an upward, then equally downward, diagonal.
SPECTROGRAM	The Spectrogram should exhibit the same pattern of resonances throughout the exercise.
LEVEL METER	The volume should remain consistent throughout the exercise. *Note: Where intervals traverse register changes, this is an especially useful skill to encourage.*

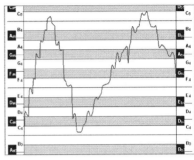

AIM	To sing an ascending and descending major scale with lowered 5th, first staccato and then legato, on a specified vowel, with pitch accuracy, consistent resonance and consistent volume.
OBJECTIVES	▶ To develop management of pitch, vowel articulation and volume, when singing an ascending and descending major blues scale with lowered 5th. The semitone between the 4th and 5th degrees of the scale, and the augmented second between the 5th and 6th degrees, are of particular importance. ▶ To enhance staccato and legato capability. ▶ To build the aural and kinaesthetic memory necessary for this task.
PHYSICAL INVOLVEMENT	▶ Abdominal and thoracic muscle groups to achieve breath management ▶ Larynx height and posture ▶ Articulators, including pharynx, velum (soft palate), tongue, lips and jaw, for appropriate vowel formation and vocal resonance
INSTRUCTIONS	1 Play the scale 2 Mentally hear the scale sung on the chosen vowel 3 Breathe the correct vowel shape 4 Position the larynx 5 Activate breath support 6 Start to sing 7 For the staccato, pay attention to precise	onset and offset while increasing breath pressure for each ascending pitch and maintaining appropriate breath pressure for each descending pitch 8 For the legato, keep connected tone and vowel shape while gradually increasing breath pressure for ascending pitch and maintaining appropriate breath pressure for descending pitch
PITCH DISPLAY	Sing the scale by directing the blue pitch line from the centre of the first note to the centre of each following note, with minimal deviation. For both staccato and legato, the optimal display will show minimal, clean horizontal lines in upward, then equally downward, diagonals.
SPECTROGRAM	The Spectrogram should exhibit the same pattern of resonances throughout the exercise.
LEVEL METER	The volume should remain consistent throughout the exercise. *Note: Where intervals traverse register changes, this is an especially useful skill to encourage.*

Exercise S-132 : Ascending blues scale - Locrian mode with raised 5th (STTT STT)

/a/

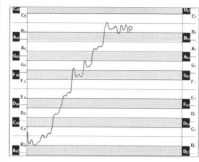

AIM	To sing an ascending Locrian mode with raised 5th, on a specified vowel with accurate pitch.
OBJECTIVES 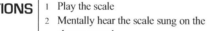	▶ To develop management of pitch when singing an ascending Locrian mode with raised 5th. The semitone at the beginning, and the augmented 2nd between the 4th and 5th degrees, need particular attention. ▶ To build the aural and kinaesthetic memory necessary for this task.
PHYSICAL INVOLVEMENT	▶ Abdominal and thoracic muscle groups to achieve breath management ▶ Larynx height and posture ▶ Articulators, including pharynx, velum (soft palate), tongue, lips and jaw, for appropriate vowel formation and vocal resonance
INSTRUCTIONS	1 Play the scale 2 Mentally hear the scale sung on the chosen vowel 3 Breathe the correct vowel shape 4 Position the larynx 5 Activate breath support 6 Start to sing 7 Increase breath pressure in order to increase pitch, while keeping the vowel shape
PITCH DISPLAY	Sing the scale by directing the blue pitch line from the centre of the lowest note to the centre of each following note. The optimal display will show minimal, clean horizontal lines in an upward diagonal.
SPECTROGRAM	
LEVEL METER	

Exercise S-133: Ascending blues scale - Locrian mode with raised 5th, legato

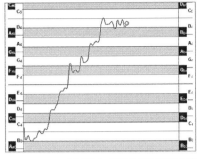

AIM	To sing an ascending Locrian mode with raised 5th, legato, on a specified vowel, with pitch accuracy, consistent resonance and consistent volume.
OBJECTIVES 	▶ To develop management of pitch, vowel articulation and volume, when singing a Locrian mode with raised 5th. The semitone at the beginning, and the augmented 2nd between the 4th and 5th degrees, need particular attention. ▶ To enhance legato capability. ▶ To build the aural and kinaesthetic memory necessary for this task.
PHYSICAL INVOLVEMENT 	▶ Abdominal and thoracic muscle groups to achieve breath management ▶ Larynx height and posture ▶ Articulators, including pharynx, velum (soft palate), tongue, lips and jaw, for appropriate vowel formation and vocal resonance
INSTRUCTIONS 	1 Play the scale 2 Mentally hear the scale sung on the chosen vowel 3 Breathe the correct vowel shape 4 Position the larynx 5 Activate breath support 6 Start to sing 7 Increase breath pressure in order to increase pitch, while keeping the vowel shape
PITCH DISPLAY	Sing the scale by directing the blue pitch line from the centre of the lowest note to the centre of each following note, with minimal deviation. The optimal display will show minimal, clean horizontal lines in an upward diagonal.
SPECTROGRAM	The Spectrogram should exhibit the same pattern of resonances throughout the exercise.
LEVEL METER	The volume should remain consistent throughout the exercise. *Note: Where intervals traverse register changes, this is an especially useful skill to encourage.*

Exercise S-134: Descending blues scale - Locrian mode with raised 5th

/a/

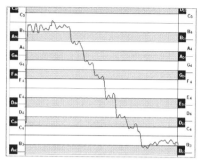

AIM	To sing a descending Locrian mode with raised 5th on a specified vowel with accurate pitch.
OBJECTIVES	▶ To develop management of pitch when singing a descending Locrian mode with raised 5th. The semitone at the beginning, and the augmented 2nd between the 4th and 5th degrees, need particular attention. ▶ To build the aural and kinaesthetic memory necessary for this task.
PHYSICAL INVOLVEMENT	▶ Abdominal and thoracic muscle groups to achieve breath management ▶ Larynx height and posture ▶ Articulators, including pharynx, velum (soft palate), tongue, lips and jaw, for appropriate vowel formation and vocal resonance
INSTRUCTIONS	1 Play the scale 2 Mentally hear the scale sung on the chosen vowel 3 Breathe the correct vowel shape 4 Position the larynx 5 Activate breath support 6 Start to sing	7 Maintain appropriate breath pressure for the descending pitch, while keeping the vowel shape
PITCH DISPLAY	Sing the scale by directing the blue pitch line from the centre of the highest note to the centre of each following note. The optimal display will show minimal, clean horizontal lines in a downward diagonal.
SPECTROGRAM	
LEVEL METER	

Sing&See • 259

Exercise S-135: Descending blues scale - Locrian mode with raised 5th, legato

/a/

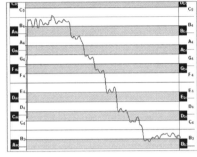

AIM	To sing a descending Locrian mode with raised 5th, legato, on a specified vowel, with pitch accuracy, consistent resonance and consistent volume.
OBJECTIVES 	▶ To develop management of pitch, vowel articulation and volume, when singing a descending Locrian mode with raised 5th. The semitone at the beginning, and the augmented 2nd between the 4th and 5th degrees, need particular attention. ▶ To enhance legato capability. ▶ To build the aural and kinaesthetic memory necessary for this task.
PHYSICAL INVOLVEMENT	▶ Abdominal and thoracic muscle groups to achieve breath management ▶ Larynx height and posture ▶ Articulators, including pharynx, velum (soft palate), tongue, lips and jaw, for appropriate vowel formation and vocal resonance
INSTRUCTIONS	1 Play the scale 2 Mentally hear the scale sung on the chosen vowel 3 Breathe the correct vowel shape 4 Position the larynx 5 Activate breath support 6 Start to sing	7 Maintain appropriate breath pressure for the descending pitch, while keeping the vowel shape
PITCH DISPLAY	Sing the scale by directing the blue pitch line from the centre of the highest note to the centre of each following note, with minimal deviation. The optimal display will show minimal, clean horizontal lines in a downward diagonal.
SPECTROGRAM	The Spectrogram should exhibit the same pattern of resonances throughout the exercise.
LEVEL METER	The volume should remain consistent throughout the exercise. *Note: Where intervals traverse register changes, this is an especially useful skill to encourage.*

Exercise S-136: Ascending and descending blues scale - Locrian mode with raised 5th

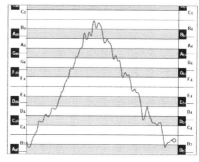

AIM	To sing an ascending and descending Locrian mode with raised 5th on a specified vowel with accurate pitch.
OBJECTIVES 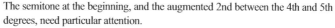	▶ To develop management of pitch when singing an ascending and descending Locrian mode with raised 5th. The semitone at the beginning, and the augmented 2nd between the 4th and 5th degrees, need particular attention. ▶ To build the aural and kinaesthetic memory necessary for this task.
PHYSICAL INVOLVEMENT	▶ Abdominal and thoracic muscle groups to achieve breath management ▶ Larynx height and posture ▶ Articulators, including pharynx, velum (soft palate), tongue, lips and jaw, for appropriate vowel formation and vocal resonance
INSTRUCTIONS	1 Play the scale 2 Mentally hear the scale sung on the chosen vowel 3 Breathe the correct vowel shape 4 Position the larynx 5 Activate breath support 6 Start to sing 7 Increase breath pressure in order to increase pitch, while keeping the vowel shape 8 Maintain appropriate breath pressure for the descending pitch, while keeping the vowel shape
PITCH DISPLAY	Sing the scale by directing the blue pitch line from the centre of the first note to the centre of each following note. The optimal display will show minimal, clean horizontal lines in an upward, then equally downward, diagonal.
SPECTROGRAM	
LEVEL METER	

Exercise S-137: Ascending and descending blues scale - Locrian mode with raised 5th, staccato

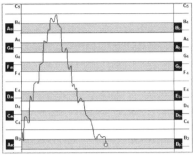

/à/

AIM 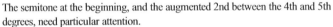	To sing an ascending and descending Locrian mode with raised 5th, staccato, on a specified vowel with accurate pitch.
OBJECTIVES 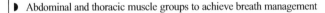	▶ To develop management of pitch when singing an ascending and descending Locrian mode with raised 5th, staccato. The semitone at the beginning, and the augmented 2nd between the 4th and 5th degrees, need particular attention. ▶ To build the aural and kinaesthetic memory necessary for this task.
PHYSICAL INVOLVEMENT	▶ Abdominal and thoracic muscle groups to achieve breath management ▶ Larynx height and posture ▶ Articulators, including pharynx, velum (soft palate), tongue, lips and jaw, for appropriate vowel formation and vocal resonance
INSTRUCTIONS	1 Play the scale 2 Mentally hear the scale sung on the chosen vowel 3 Breathe the correct vowel shape 4 Position the larynx 5 Activate breath support 6 Start to sing	7 Pay attention to precise onset and offset while increasing breath pressure for each ascending pitch and keeping the vowel shape 8 Pay attention to precise onset and offset while maintaining appropriate breath pressure for each descending pitch and keeping the vowel shape
PITCH DISPLAY	Sing the scale by directing the blue pitch line from the centre of the first note to the centre of each following note, with minimal deviation. The optimal display will show minimal, clean horizontal lines in an upward, then equally downward, diagonal.
SPECTROGRAM	
LEVEL METER	

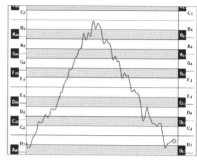

AIM	To sing an ascending and descending Locrian mode with raised 5th, legato, on a specified vowel, with pitch accuracy, consistent resonance and consistent volume.
OBJECTIVES	▶ To develop management of pitch, vowel articulation and volume, when singing an ascending and descending Locrian mode with raised 5th. The semitone at the beginning, and the augmented 2nd between the 4th and 5th degrees, need particular attention. ▶ To enhance legato capability. ▶ To build the aural and kinaesthetic memory necessary for this task.
PHYSICAL INVOLVEMENT	▶ Abdominal and thoracic muscle groups to achieve breath management ▶ Larynx height and posture ▶ Articulators, including pharynx, velum (soft palate), tongue, lips and jaw, for appropriate vowel formation and vocal resonance
INSTRUCTIONS	1 Play the scale 2 Mentally hear the scale sung on the chosen vowel 3 Breathe the correct vowel shape 4 Position the larynx 5 Activate breath support 6 Start to sing — 7 Gradually increase breath pressure in order to increase pitch, while keeping connected tone and vowel shape 8 Maintain appropriate breath pressure for the descending pitch, while keeping connected tone and vowel shape
PITCH DISPLAY	Sing the scale by directing the blue pitch line from the centre of the first note to the centre of each following note, with minimal deviation. The optimal display will show minimal, clean horizontal lines in an upward, then equally downward, diagonal.
SPECTROGRAM	The Spectrogram should exhibit the same pattern of resonances throughout the exercise.
LEVEL METER	The volume should remain consistent throughout the exercise. *Note: Where intervals traverse register changes, this is an especially useful skill to encourage.*

Exercise S-139: Ascending and descending blues scale - Locrian mode with raised 5th, staccato and then legato

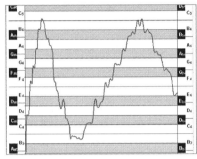

AIM	To sing an ascending and descending Locrian mode with raised 5th, first staccato and then legato, on a specified vowel, with pitch accuracy, consistent resonance and consistent volume.
OBJECTIVES	▶ To develop management of pitch, vowel articulation and volume, when singing an ascending and descending Locrian mode with raised 5th. The semitone at the beginning, and the augmented 2nd between the 4th and 5th degrees, need particular attention. ▶ To enhance staccato and legato capability. ▶ To build the aural and kinaesthetic memory necessary for this task.
PHYSICAL INVOLVEMENT	▶ Abdominal and thoracic muscle groups to achieve breath management ▶ Larynx height and posture ▶ Articulators, including pharynx, velum (soft palate), tongue, lips and jaw, for appropriate vowel formation and vocal resonance
INSTRUCTIONS	1 Play the scale 2 Mentally hear the scale sung on the chosen vowel 3 Breathe the correct vowel shape 4 Position the larynx 5 Activate breath support 6 Start to sing 7 For the staccato, pay attention to precise	onset and offset while increasing breath pressure for each ascending pitch and maintaining appropriate breath pressure for each descending pitch 8 For the legato, keep connected tone and vowel shape while gradually increasing breath pressure for ascending pitch and maintaining appropriate breath pressure for descending pitch
PITCH DISPLAY	Sing the scale by directing the blue pitch line from the centre of the first note to the centre of each following note, with minimal deviation. The optimal display will show minimal, clean horizontal lines in upward, then equally downward, diagonals.
SPECTROGRAM	The Spectrogram should exhibit the same pattern of resonances throughout the exercise.
LEVEL METER	The volume should remain consistent throughout the exercise. *Note: Where intervals traverse register changes, this is an especially useful skill to encourage.*

/a/

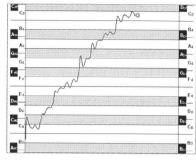

AIM	To sing an ascending major scale with lowered 7th on a specified vowel with accurate pitch.
OBJECTIVES	▶ To develop management of pitch when singing an ascending major scale with lowered 7th. The tone between the 7th degree and the tonic is of particular importance. ▶ To build the aural and kinaesthetic memory necessary for this task.
PHYSICAL INVOLVEMENT	▶ Abdominal and thoracic muscle groups to achieve breath management ▶ Larynx height and posture ▶ Articulators, including pharynx, velum (soft palate), tongue, lips and jaw, for appropriate vowel formation and vocal resonance
INSTRUCTIONS	1 Play the scale 2 Mentally hear the scale sung on the chosen vowel 3 Breathe the correct vowel shape 4 Position the larynx 5 Activate breath support 6 Start to sing	7 Increase breath pressure in order to increase pitch, while keeping the vowel shape
PITCH DISPLAY	Sing the scale by directing the blue pitch line from the centre of the lowest note to the centre of each following note. The optimal display will show minimal, clean horizontal lines in an upward diagonal.
SPECTROGRAM	
LEVEL METER	

Exercise S-141: Ascending blues scale - Major scale with lowered 7th, legato

/a/

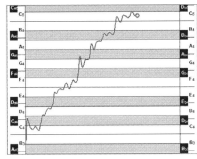

AIM	To sing an ascending major scale with lowered 7th, legato, on a specified vowel, with pitch accuracy, consistent resonance and consistent volume.
OBJECTIVES	▶ To develop management of pitch, vowel articulation and volume, when singing a major blues scale with lowered 7th. The tone between the 7th degree and the tonic is of particular importance. ▶ To enhance legato capability. ▶ To build the aural and kinaesthetic memory necessary for this task.
PHYSICAL INVOLVEMENT	▶ Abdominal and thoracic muscle groups to achieve breath management ▶ Larynx height and posture ▶ Articulators, including pharynx, velum (soft palate), tongue, lips and jaw, for appropriate vowel formation and vocal resonance
INSTRUCTIONS	1 Play the scale 2 Mentally hear the scale sung on the chosen vowel 3 Breathe the correct vowel shape 4 Position the larynx 5 Activate breath support 6 Start to sing	7 Gradually increase breath pressure in order to increase pitch, while keeping connected tone and vowel shape

PITCH DISPLAY	Sing the scale by directing the blue pitch line from the centre of the lowest note to the centre of each following note, with minimal deviation. The optimal display will show minimal, clean horizontal lines in an upward diagonal.
SPECTROGRAM	The Spectrogram should exhibit the same pattern of resonances throughout the exercise.
LEVEL METER	The volume should remain consistent throughout the exercise. *Note: Where intervals traverse register changes, this is an especially useful skill to encourage.*

/a/

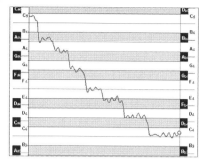

AIM	To sing a descending major scale with lowered 7th on a specified vowel with accurate pitch.
OBJECTIVES	▶ To develop management of pitch when singing a descending major blues scale with lowered 7th. The tone between the 7th degree and the tonic is of particular importance. ▶ To build the aural and kinaesthetic memory necessary for this task.
PHYSICAL INVOLVEMENT	▶ Abdominal and thoracic muscle groups to achieve breath management ▶ Larynx height and posture ▶ Articulators, including pharynx, velum (soft palate), tongue, lips and jaw, for appropriate vowel formation and vocal resonance
INSTRUCTIONS	1 Play the scale 2 Mentally hear the scale sung on the chosen vowel 3 Breathe the correct vowel shape 4 Position the larynx 5 Activate breath support 6 Start to sing 7 Maintain appropriate breath pressure for the descending pitch, while keeping the vowel shape
PITCH DISPLAY	Sing the scale by directing the blue pitch line from the centre of the highest note to the centre of each following note. The optimal display will show minimal, clean horizontal lines in a downward diagonal.
SPECTROGRAM	
LEVEL METER	

Exercise S-143: Descending blues scale - Major scale with lowered 7th, legato

/a/

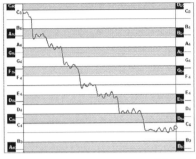

AIM	To sing a descending major scale with lowered 7th, legato, on a specified vowel, with pitch accuracy, consistent resonance and consistent volume.
OBJECTIVES	▶ To develop management of pitch, vowel articulation and volume, when singing a descending major blues scale with lowered 7th. The tone between the 7th degree and the tonic is of particular importance. ▶ To enhance legato capability. ▶ To build the aural and kinaesthetic memory necessary for this task.
PHYSICAL INVOLVEMENT	▶ Abdominal and thoracic muscle groups to achieve breath management ▶ Larynx height and posture ▶ Articulators, including pharynx, velum (soft palate), tongue, lips and jaw, for appropriate vowel formation and vocal resonance
INSTRUCTIONS	1 Play the scale 2 Mentally hear the scale sung on the chosen vowel 3 Breathe the correct vowel shape 4 Position the larynx 5 Activate breath support 6 Start to sing 7 Maintain appropriate breath pressure for the descending pitch, while keeping connected tone and vowel shape
PITCH DISPLAY	Sing the scale by directing the blue pitch line from the centre of the highest note to the centre of each following note, with minimal deviation. The optimal display will show minimal, clean horizontal lines in a downward diagonal.
SPECTROGRAM	The Spectrogram should exhibit the same pattern of resonances throughout the exercise.
LEVEL METER	The volume should remain consistent throughout the exercise. *Note: Where intervals traverse register changes, this is an especially useful skill to encourage.*

Exercise S-144: Ascending and descending blues scale - Major scale with lowered 7th

/a/

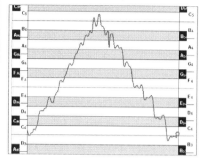

AIM	To sing an ascending and descending major scale with lowered 7th on a specified vowel with accurate pitch.
OBJECTIVES	▸ To develop management of pitch when singing an ascending and descending major blues scale with lowered 7th. The tone between the 7th degree and the tonic is of particular importance. ▸ To build the aural and kinaesthetic memory necessary for this task.
PHYSICAL INVOLVEMENT	▸ Abdominal and thoracic muscle groups to achieve breath management ▸ Larynx height and posture ▸ Articulators, including pharynx, velum (soft palate), tongue, lips and jaw, for appropriate vowel formation and vocal resonance

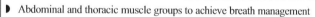

INSTRUCTIONS	1 Play the scale 2 Mentally hear the scale sung on the chosen vowel 3 Breathe the correct vowel shape 4 Position the larynx 5 Activate breath support 6 Start to sing 7 Increase breath pressure in order to increase pitch, while keeping the vowel shape 8 Maintain appropriate breath pressure for the descending pitch, while keeping the vowel shape
PITCH DISPLAY	Sing the scale by directing the blue pitch line from the centre of the first note to the centre of each following note. The optimal display will show minimal, clean horizontal lines in an upward, then equally downward, diagonal.
SPECTROGRAM	
LEVEL METER	

Exercise S-145: Ascending and descending blues scale - Major scale with lowered 7th, staccato

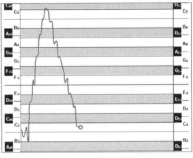

AIM	To sing an ascending and descending major scale with lowered 7th, staccato, on a specified vowel with accurate pitch.
OBJECTIVES	▶ To develop management of pitch when singing an ascending and descending major blues scale with lowered 7th, staccato. The tone between the 7th degree and the tonic is of particular importance. ▶ To build the aural and kinaesthetic memory necessary for this task.
PHYSICAL INVOLVEMENT	▶ Abdominal and thoracic muscle groups to achieve breath management ▶ Larynx height and posture ▶ Articulators, including pharynx, velum (soft palate), tongue, lips and jaw, for appropriate vowel formation and vocal resonance

INSTRUCTIONS	1 Play the scale 2 Mentally hear the scale sung on the chosen vowel 3 Breathe the correct vowel shape 4 Position the larynx 5 Activate breath support 6 Start to sing	7 Pay attention to precise onset and offset while increasing breath pressure for each ascending pitch and keeping the vowel shape 8 Pay attention to precise onset and offset while maintaining appropriate breath pressure for each descending pitch and keeping the vowel shape

PITCH DISPLAY	Sing the scale by directing the blue pitch line from the centre of the first note to the centre of each following note, with minimal deviation. The optimal display will show minimal, clean horizontal lines in an upward, then equally downward, diagonal.
SPECTROGRAM	
LEVEL METER	

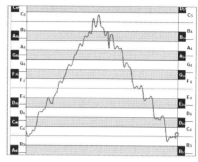

AIM	To sing an ascending and descending major scale with lowered 7th, legato, on a specified vowel, with pitch accuracy, consistent resonance and consistent volume.
OBJECTIVES	▶ To develop management of pitch, vowel articulation and volume, when singing an ascending and descending major blues scale with lowered 7th. The tone between the 7th degree and the tonic is of particular importance.. ▶ To enhance legato capability. ▶ To build the aural and kinaesthetic memory necessary for this task.
PHYSICAL INVOLVEMENT	▶ Abdominal and thoracic muscle groups to achieve breath management ▶ Larynx height and posture ▶ Articulators, including pharynx, velum (soft palate), tongue, lips and jaw, for appropriate vowel formation and vocal resonance
INSTRUCTIONS	1 Play the scale 2 Mentally hear the scale sung on the chosen vowel 3 Breathe the correct vowel shape 4 Position the larynx 5 Activate breath support 6 Start to sing	7 Gradually increase breath pressure in order to increase pitch, while keeping connected tone and vowel shape 8 Maintain appropriate breath pressure for the descending pitch, while keeping connected tone and vowel shape

PITCH DISPLAY	Sing the scale by directing the blue pitch line from the centre of the first note to the centre of each following note, with minimal deviation. The optimal display will show minimal, clean horizontal lines in an upward, then equally downward, diagonal.
SPECTROGRAM	The Spectrogram should exhibit the same pattern of resonances throughout the exercise.
LEVEL METER	The volume should remain consistent throughout the exercise. *Note: Where intervals traverse register changes, this is an especially useful skill to encourage.*

Exercise S-147: Ascending and descending blues scale - Major scale with lowered 7th, staccato, and then legato

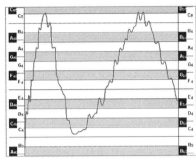

AIM	To sing an ascending and descending major scale with lowered 7th, first staccato and then legato, on a specified vowel, with pitch accuracy, consistent resonance and consistent volume.
OBJECTIVES	▶ To develop management of pitch, vowel articulation and volume, when singing an ascending and descending major blues scale with lowered 7th. The tone between the 7th degree and the tonic is of particular importance. ▶ To enhance staccato and legato capability. ▶ To build the aural and kinaesthetic memory necessary for this task.
PHYSICAL INVOLVEMENT	▶ Abdominal and thoracic muscle groups to achieve breath management ▶ Larynx height and posture ▶ Articulators, including pharynx, velum (soft palate), tongue, lips and jaw, for appropriate vowel formation and vocal resonance
INSTRUCTIONS	1 Play the scale 2 Mentally hear the scale sung on the chosen vowel 3 Breathe the correct vowel shape 4 Position the larynx 5 Activate breath support 6 Start to sing 7 For the staccato, pay attention to precise onset and offset while increasing breath pressure for each ascending pitch and maintaining appropriate breath pressure for each descending pitch 8 For the legato, keep connected tone and vowel shape while gradually increasing breath pressure for ascending pitch and maintaining appropriate breath pressure for descending pitch
PITCH DISPLAY	Sing the scale by directing the blue pitch line from the centre of the first note to the centre of each following note, with minimal deviation. For both staccato and legato, the optimal display will show minimal, clean horizontal lines in upward, then equally downward, diagonals.
SPECTROGRAM	The Spectrogram should exhibit the same pattern of resonances throughout the exercise.
LEVEL METER	The volume should remain consistent throughout the exercise. *Note: Where intervals traverse register changes, this is an especially useful skill to encourage.*

APPENDIX 1

Vowels from the International Phonetic Alphabet

/ i /   beat, Liebe (German), prima (Italian), lit (French)

/ ɪ /   bit, ich (German)

/ e /   chaos, pena (Italian), arriver (French)

/ ɛ /   bet, Bett (German), tempo (Italian)

/æ/   bat

/ ɑ /   father, Stadt (German), facile (French)

/ ɒ /   hot, Sommer (German),

/ ɔ /   thaw

/ o /   boat, Not (German), voce (Italian)

/ ʊ /   full

/ u /   fool, nous (French), luce (Italian)

/ ʌ /   up

/ ə /   ago, demain (French)

/ y /   müde (German), une (French)

/Y/   Glück (German)

/ ø /   schön (German), peu (French)

/œ/   Köpfe (German), heure (French)

APPENDIX 2

International Pitch Labelling

Frequency (Hz)	Note name	Pitch label
783.9	G	G_5
740.0	$F^\#$	$F^\#_5$
698.4	F	F_5
659.3	E	E_5
622.3	$D^\#$	$D^\#_5$
587.3	D	D_5
554.4	$C^\#$	$C^\#_5$
523.2	C	C_5
493.9	B	B_4
466.2	$A^\#$	$A^\#_4$
440.0	A	A_4
415.3	$G^\#$	$G^\#_4$
392.0	G	G_4
370.0	$F^\#$	$F^\#_4$
349.2	F	F_4
329.6	E	E_4
311.1	$D^\#$	$D^\#_4$
293.7	D	$D4$
277.2	$C^\#$	$C^\#_4$
261.6	Middle C	C_4
246.9	B	B_3
233.1	$A^\#$	$A^\#_3$
220.0	A	A_3
207.7	$G^\#$	$G^\#_3$
196.0	G	G_3
185.0	$F^\#$	$F^\#_3$
174.6	F	F^3
164.8	E	E_3
155.6	$D^\#$	$D^\#_3$
146.8	D	D_3
138.6	$C^\#$	$C^\#_3$
130.8	C	C_3
123.4	B	B_2

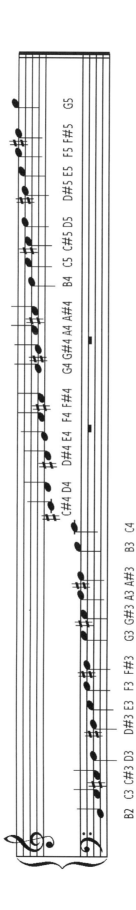

GLOSSARY

Abdomen

That part of the torso (except the back) lying between the pelvis and the thorax; the cavity of this part of the torso, lined by the peritoneum, enclosed by the walls of the body, the diaphragm, and containing the viscera.

Acoustic features of the voice

Fundamental frequency (perceptual correlate pitch); sound pressure level (perceptual correlate loudness); harmonic pattern (perceptual correlate timbre).

Aeolian mode

The mode built on the white keys of the keyboard, beginning on A (the same as a natural minor scale). [See p. 13.]

Algorithm

See Pitch Algorithm.

Arpeggio

A chord whose pitches are sounded successively, rather than simultaneously.

Articulation

Musical - the characteristics of attack and decay of single notes or groups of notes and the means by which these characteristics are produced. For example, staccato and legato are types of articulation.

Vocal - adjustment of the shape, and therefore the acoustical properties, of the vocal tract, affecting both speech production and vocal resonance.

Articulators

The movable structures responsible for modification of the acoustic properties of the vocal tract, i.e. velum (soft palate), mandible (jaw), cheeks, tongue and lips.

Audiation

Mental hearing, the ability to hear and comprehend musical sound that is no longer present, or that may never have been present.

Blues scales

Scales used in blues and jazz in which the 3rd, 5th and 7th degrees may be raised or lowered. [See p. 14.]

Chromatic scale

The scale that includes all of the 12 semitones contained in the octave.

Dorian mode

The mode built on the white keys of the keyboard, beginning on D. [See p. 13.]

Dynamics

Degrees of loudness.

Feedback

The returning of a part of the output of any system - mechanical, electronic, or biological - as input, especially for correction or control purposes. May be internal (visual, tactile, auditory, kinaesthetic, proprioceptive) or external (audience, teacher, colleagues, recording, etc.).

Frequency
    The number of vibrations or cycles per second, measured in Hertz (Hz). The greater the number of vibrations per second, the higher the pitch.

Fundamental frequency (Fo)
    The lowest repetition frequency in a periodic waveform. In musical terms, the pitch of a note.

Formant
    A resonance of the vocal tract.

Harmonics
    The partials or overtones of a fundamental, integer multiples of the fundamental.

International Phonetic Alphabet (IPA)
    An alphabet in which single language sounds are represented by single symbols. [See Appendix 1.]

Interval
    The distance in pitch between two notes.

Ionian mode
    The mode built on the white keys of the keyboard, beginning on C, the same as a major scale. [See p. 13.]

Larynx
    The organ of the body, situated at the superior terminal of the trachea, that houses the vocal folds. The principal structure for producing a vibrating air stream.

Legato
    Sung smoothly with no separation between successive notes; the opposite of staccato.

Locrian mode
    The mode built on the white keys of the keyboard, beginning on B. [See p. 13.]

Lydian mode
    The mode built on the white keys of the keyboard, beginning on F. [See p. 13.]

***Messa di voce* (Italian)**
    A controlled crescendo and decrescendo on a sustained note, maintaining consistent tone.

Mixolydian mode
    The mode built on the white keys of the keyboard, beginning on G. [See p. 13.]

Mode
    A collection of pitches, usually with some internal hierarchy, but not implying diatonic harmony. Commonly used in Western music of the Middle Ages and Renaissance and in folk and non-Western musics. [See p. 13.]

Modelling
    Providing a standard or example for imitation or comparison (as, for example, in the teacher singing, or playing a recording).

Neuromuscular
> Concerning both nerves and muscles.

***Passaggio* (Italian)**
> A vocal register transition.

Pentachord
> A collection of five pitches; the arrangement of intervals that defines the structure of a collection of five pitches.

Pentatonic scale
> A scale consisting of five pitches or pitch classes.

Pharynx
> The cavity extending from the base of the skull to the posterior surface of the base of the cricoid cartilage of the larynx. It has three parts: the nasopharynx, the oropharynx (buccopharynx) and laryngopharynx.

Pitch
> See Fundamental frequency.

Phoneme
> The minimal unit in the sound system of a language.

Phrygian mode
> The mode built on the white keys of the keyboard, beginning on E. [See p. 13.]

Pitch algorithm
> A computer program which automatically determines the pitch of vocal sound.

Portamento
> A smooth sliding from one pitch to another through all of the intervening pitches without sounding these discretely.

Psychomotor
> Related to voluntary movement.

Register
> A range of pitches having a consistent timbre. In singing, the concept of register is concerned mainly with a change in voice quality at particular pitches due to changes in the action of the interdependent cricothyroid and the lateral and vocalis muscles of the larynx.

Scale
> A collection of pitches (commonly spanning an octave) arranged in order from lowest to highest

Scale degrees
> The numbered positions of individual pitches within a major or minor scale, representing how each degree functions in relation to others melodically and harmonically. Traditionally Roman numerals are used: I tonic; II supertonic; III mediant, IV subdominant, V dominant, VI submediant, VII leading note or subtonic.

Singer's formant
A high spectrum envelope peak appearing in the vicinity of 3 kHz in all vowel spectra that gives brilliance to the voice.

Spectrograph/Spectrogram
A two-dimensional graphic representation of the distribution of acoustic energy with respect to both frequency range and time. [See p. 8.]

Spectrum (spectrum of frequencies)
A display of relative magnitudes of the component frequencies of a wave form. [See p. 9.]

Staccato
Detached.

Tessitura
The particular range of a vocal part or composition, or the range most used, as distinct from the total range.

Tetrachord
A system of four pitches contained within the limits of a perfect 4th.

Thorax
That part of the torso which houses the organs of breathing, situated between the neck and the abdomen, supported by the ribs, the costal cartilages, and the sternum

Velum
Soft palate.

Vibrato
An undulation of the fundamental frequency—in singing, produced by the phonatory mechanism. Usually described in terms of rate (number of undulations per second), extent (how far phonation frequency departs up and down from its average during a vibrato cycle), regularity (how similar the frequency excursions are to one another), and the waveform of the undulations.

Vocal tract
The structures above the vocal folds—pharyngeal, nasal, and mouth cavities.

Vowel
A voiced speech sound articulated without a complete closure in the mouth or a degree of narrowing which would produce audible friction (as distinct from consonants). Often classified by reference to the position of the main body of the tongue in the oral cavity and the position of the lips.

WAV format
A sound file in Microsoft Windows.

Whole-tone scale:
A scale consisting only of whole tones, i.e. with six pitches in each octave.

Selected Biobliography

Articles

Austin, S.F. (1995). Nasal resonance—Dispelling the myth. *Australian Voice*, 1, 18-23.

Austin, S.F. (1997). Movement of the velum during speech and singing in classically trained singers. *Journal of Voice*, 11(2), 212-221.

Baken, R.J. (1991). An overview of laryngeal function for voice production. In R.T. Sataloff (Ed.), *Professional voice: The science and art of clinical care* (pp. 19-47). New York: Raven Press.

Bloothooft, G. & Plomp, R. (1984). Spectral analysis of sung vowels. I. Variation due to differences between vowels, singers, and modes of singing. *Journal of the Acoustical Society of America*, 75(4), 1259-1264.

Bloothooft, G. & Plomp, R. (1985). Spectral analysis of sung vowels. II. The effect of fundamental frequency on vowel spectra. *Journal of the Acoustical Society of America*, 77(4), 1580-1588.

Bloothooft, G. & Plomp, R. (1986). The sound level of the singer's formant in professional singing. *Journal of the Acoustical Society of America*, 79, 2028-2033.

Callaghan, J. (2002). Learning to sing, in C. Stevens, D. Burnham, G. McPherson, E. Schubert, & J. Renwick (Eds), *Proceedings of the 7th International Conference on Music Perception and Cognition*, Sydney, 2002.

Callaghan, J., Thorpe, W. & van Doorn, J. (1999). Computer-assisted visual feedback in the teaching of singing. In M.S. Barrett, G.E. McPherson & R. Smith (Eds), *Children and Music: Developmental Perspectives* (pp. 105-111). Proceedings of the 2nd Asia-Pacific Symposium on Music Education Research and the XXI Annual Conference of the Australian Association for Research in Music Education, Launceston.

Collins, A. (1991). Cognitive apprenticeship and instructional technology. In L. Idol & B.F. Jones (Eds.), *Educational values and cognitive instruction* (pp. 121-138). Hillsdale, NJ: Lawrence Erlbaum Associates.

Cleveland, T.F. (1993). Voice pedagogy for the twenty-first century: The importance of range and timbre in the determination of voice classification. *The NATS Journal*, 49(3), 30-31.

Cleveland, T.F. (1994). A clearer view of singing voice production: 25 years of progress. *Journal of Voice*, 8(1), 18-23.

Cooksey, J.M. & Welch, G.F. (1998). Adolescence, singing development and national curricula design. *British Journal of Music Education*, 15(1), 99-119.

Emmons, S. (1988). Breathing for singing. *Journal of Voice*, 2(1), 30-35.

Griffin, B., Woo, P., Colton, R., Casper, J. & Brewer, D. (1995). Physiological characteristics of the supported singing voice. A preliminary study. *Journal of Voice*, 9(1), 45-56.

Hoit, J.D., Christie, L.J., Watson, P.J. & Cleveland, T.F. (1996). Respiratory function during speaking and singing in professional country singers. *Journal of Voice*, 10(1), 39-49.

Huff-Gackle, L. (1991). The adolescent female voice: The characteristics of change and stages of development. *The Choral Journal*, 31(8), 17-25.

Leanderson, R. & Sundberg, J. (1988). Breathing for singing. *Journal of Voice*, 2(1), 2-12.

Nisbet, A. (1995). Spectrographic analysis of the singing voice applied to the teaching of singing. *Australian Voice*, 1, 65-68.

Rossiter, D. & Howard, D.M. (1996). ALBERT: A real-time visual feedback computer tool for professional vocal development, *Journal of Voice*, 10(4), 321-336.

Sataloff, R.T. (1992). The human voice. *Scientific American*, 267(6), 108-115.

Shipp, T. & Izdebski, K. (1975). Vocal frequency and vertical larynx positioning by singers and nonsingers. *Journal of the Acoustical Society of America*, 58(5), 1104-1106.

Sundberg, J. (1974). Articulatory interpretation of the 'singing formant'. Journal of the Acoustical Society of America, 55, 838-844.

Sundberg, J. (1983). Raised and lowered larynx: The effect on vowel formant frequencies. *Journal of Research in Singing*, 6, 7-15.

Sundberg, J. (1991). Comparisons of pharynx, source, formant and pressure characteristics in operatic and musical theatre singing. *Speech Transmission Laboratory Quarterly Progress Status Report* (KTH, Stockholm), 2-3, 23-36.

Sundberg, J. (1991). Vocal tract resonance. In R.T. Sataloff (Ed.), *Professional voice. The science and art of clinical care* (pp. 49-68). New York: Raven Press.

Sundberg, J. (1993). Breathing behavior during singing. *The NATS Journal*, 49(3), 4-51.

Sundberg, J. (1995). The singer's formant revisited. *Voice*, 4, 106-109.

Thorpe, C.W., Callaghan, J., van Doorn, J. (1999). Visual feedback of acoustic voice features: New tools for the teaching of singing, *Australian Voice*, 5, 2-39.

Titze, I.R. (1988). A framework for the study of vocal registers. *Journal of Voice*, 2(3), 183-194.

Titze, I.R. (1995). Voice research: Speaking vowels versus singing vowels. *Journal of Singing*, 52(1), 41-42.

Watson, P.J., Hixon, T.J., Stathopoulos, E.T. & Sullivan, D.R. (1990). Respiratory kinematics in female classical singers. *Journal of Voice*, 4(2), 120-128.

Watson, P.J., Hoit, J.D., Lansing, R.W. & Hixon, T.J. (1989). Abdominal muscle activity during classical singing. *Journal of Voice*, 3(1), 24-31.

Welch, G.F., Howard, D.M. & Rush, C. (1989). Real-time visual feedback in the development of vocal pitch accuracy in singing. *Psychology of Music*, 17, 246-157.

Yanagisawa, E., Estill, J., Kmucha, S.T. & Leder, S.B. (1989). The contribution of aryepiglottic constriction to 'ringing' voice quality—a videolaryngoscopic study with acoustic analysis. *Journal of Voice*, 4, 342-350.

Yanagisawa, E., Kmucha, S.T. & Estill, J. (1990). Role of the soft palate in laryngeal functions and selected voice qualities. Simultaneous velolaryngeal videoendoscopy. *Annals of Otology, Rhinology and Laryngology*, 99, 18-28.

Books

Bunch, M. (1997). *Dynamics of the singing voice* (4th ed.). Wien: Springer-Verlag.

Callaghan, J. (2000). *Singing and voice science*. San Diego, CA: Singular.

Cooksey, J.M. (1992). *Working with the adolescent voice*. St Louis: Concordia.

Denes, P.B. & Pinson, E.N. (1993). *The speech chain. The physics and biology of spoken language* (2nd ed.). New York: Freeman.

Estill, J. (1995). *Voice craft. A user's guide to voice quality. Vol. 2: Some basic voice qualities*. Santa Rosa, CA: Estill Voice Training Systems.

Estill, J. (1996). *Voice craft. A user's guide to voice quality. Level One: Primer of compulsory figures*. Santa Rosa, CA: Estill Voice Training Systems.

Gordon, E.E. (1993). *Learning sequences in music. Skill, content, and patterns. A music learning theory*. Chicago: GIA Publications.

McKinney, J.C. (1982). *The diagnosis & correction of vocal faults*. Nashville, TN: Broadman Press.

Miller, R. (1986). *The structure of singing. System and art in vocal technique*. New York: Schirmer Books.

Miller, R. (1996). *On the Art of Singing*, Articles 90-94 (pp. 275-306). New York: Oxford University Press.

Nair, G (1999). *Voice tradition and technology: A state-of-the-art studio*, San Diego : Singular

Pickett, J.M. (1980). *The sounds of speech communication*. Baltimore: University Park Press.

Phillips, Kenneth (1992). *Teaching kids to sing*, New York: Schirmer Books.

Serafine, M.L. (1988). *Music as cognition. The development of thought in sound*. New York: Columbia University Press

Storr, A. (1992). *Music and the mind*. London: Harper Collins.

Sundberg, J. (1987). *The science of singing*. Dekalb, IL: Northern Illinois University Press.

Thurman, L. & Welch, G. (Eds). (2000). *Bodymind & Voice* (rev. ed.). Collegeville, MN: TheVoiceCare Network.

Titze, I.R. (1994). *Principles of voice production*. Englewood Cliffs, NJ: Prentice Hall.

Vennard, W. (1967). *Singing—the mechanism and the technic* (rev. ed.). New York: Carl Fischer.

Wilson, P. (2001). *The singing voice: An owner's manual*. Sydney: Currency Press.

Made in the USA
Lexington, KY
15 February 2011